Pascal Quignard
Towards the Vanishing Point

LEGENDA

LEGENDA is the Modern Humanities Research Association's book imprint for new research in the Humanities. Founded in 1995 by Malcolm Bowie and others within the University of Oxford, Legenda has always been a collaborative publishing enterprise, directly governed by scholars. The Modern Humanities Research Association (MHRA) joined this collaboration in 1998, became half-owner in 2004, in partnership with Maney Publishing and then Routledge, and has since 2016 been sole owner. Titles range from medieval texts to contemporary cinema and form a widely comparative view of the modern humanities, including works on Arabic, Catalan, English, French, German, Greek, Italian, Portuguese, Russian, Spanish, and Yiddish literature. Editorial boards and committees of more than 60 leading academic specialists work in collaboration with bodies such as the Society for French Studies, the British Comparative Literature Association and the Association of Hispanists of Great Britain & Ireland.

The MHRA encourages and promotes advanced study and research in the field of the modern humanities, especially modern European languages and literature, including English, and also cinema. It aims to break down the barriers between scholars working in different disciplines and to maintain the unity of humanistic scholarship. The Association fulfils this purpose through the publication of journals, bibliographies, monographs, critical editions, and the MHRA Style Guide, and by making grants in support of research. Membership is open to all who work in the Humanities, whether independent or in a University post, and the participation of younger colleagues entering the field is especially welcomed.

RESEARCH MONOGRAPHS IN FRENCH STUDIES

The *Research Monographs in French Studies* (RMFS) form a separate series within the Legenda programme and are published in association with the Society for French Studies. Individual members of the Society are entitled to purchase all RMFS titles at a discount.

The series seeks to publish the best new work in all areas of the literature, thought, theory, culture, film and language of the French-speaking world. Its distinctiveness lies in the relative brevity of its publications (50,000–60,000 words). As innovation is a priority of the series, volumes should predominantly consist of new material, although, subject to appropriate modification, previously published research may form up to one third of the whole. Proposals may include critical editions as well as critical studies. They should be sent with one or two sample chapters for consideration to Professor Diana Knight, Department of French and Francophone Studies, University of Nottingham, University Park, Nottingham NG7 2RD.

❖

PUBLISHED IN THIS SERIES

1. *Privileged Anonymity: The Writings of Madame de Lafayette* by Anne Green
2. *Stéphane Mallarmé. Correspondance: compléments et suppléments*
edited by Lloyd James Austin, Bertrand Marchal and Nicola Luckhurst
3. *Critical Fictions: Nerval's 'Les Illuminés'* by Meryl Tyers
4. *Towards a Cultural Philology* by Amy Wygant
5. *George Sand and Autobiography* by Janet Hiddleston
6. *Expressivism* by Johnnie Gratton
7. *Memory and Survival: The French Cinema of Krzysztof Kieślowski* by Emma Wilson
8. *Between Sequence and 'Sirventes'* by Catherine Léglu
9. *All Puns Intended* by Walter Redfern
10. *Saint-Evremond: A Voice From Exile* edited by Denys Potts
11. *La Cort d'Amor: A Critical Edition* edited by Matthew Bardell
12. *Race and the Unconscious* by Celia Britton
13. *Proust: La Traduction du sensible* by Nathalie Aubert
14. *Silent Witness: Racine's Non-Verbal Annotations of Euripides* by Susanna Phillippo
15. *Robert Antelme: Humanity, Community, Testimony* by Martin Crowley
16. *By the People for the People?* by Christopher Prendergast
17. *Alter Ego: The Critical Writings of Michel Leiris* by Seán Hand
18. *Two Old French Satires on the Power of the Keys* edited by Daron Burrows
19. *Oral Narration in Modern French* by Janice Carruthers
20. *Selfless Cinema? Ethics and French Documentary* by Sarah Cooper
21. *Poisoned Words: Slander and Satire in Early Modern France* by Emily Butterworth
22. *France/China: Intercultural Imaginings* by Alex Hughes
23. *Biography in Early Modern France 1540–1630* by Katherine MacDonald
24. *Balzac and the Model of Painting* by Diana Knight
25. *Exotic Subversions in Nineteenth-Century French Literature* by Jennifer Yee
26. *The Syllables of Time: Proust and the History of Reading* by Teresa Whitington
27. *Personal Effects: Reading the 'Journal' of Marie Bashkirtseff* by Sonia Wilson
28. *The Choreography of Modernism in France* by Julie Townsend
29. *Voices and Veils* by Anna Kemp
30. *Syntactic Borrowing in Contemporary French: A Linguistic Analysis of News Translation* by Mairi McLaughlin
31. *Dreams of Lovers and Lies of Poets: Poetry, Knowledge, and Desire in the 'Roman de la Rose'* by Sylvia Huot
32. *Maryse Condé and the Space of Literature* by Eva Sansavior
33. *The Livres-Souvenirs of Colette: Genre and the Telling of Time* by Anne Freadman
34. *Furetière's* Roman bourgeois *and the Problem of Exchange* by Craig Moyes
35. *The Subversive Poetics of Alfred Jarry: Ubusing Culture in the Almanachs du Père Ubu* by Marieke Dubbelboer

www.legendabooks.com

Pascal Quignard

Towards the Vanishing Point

❖

Léa Vuong

l

LEGENDA

Research Monographs in French Studies 48
Modern Humanities Research Association
2016

Published by Legenda
An imprint of the Modern Humanities Research Association
Salisbury House, Station Road, Cambridge CB1 2LA

ISBN 978-1-909662-91-9 (HB)
ISBN 978-1-78188-333-4 (PB)

First published 2016

Copy-Editor: Dr Susan Wharton

CONTENTS

❖

Acknowledgements   vii

Translations Used   viii

List of Abbreviations   xii

Introduction   I

1   A Vanishing Act   9

2   From Language to Silence   27

3   Towards the Invisible   45

4   The Lure of the *Jadis*   61

5   Incendiary Writing   77

Conclusion   97

Bibliography   101

Index   110

To T. and J.

ACKNOWLEDGEMENTS

❖

I should like to express my gratitude to Graham Nelson, Managing Editor of Legenda, and Diana Knight, General Editor of the *Research Monographs in French Studies*.

I am also very grateful to Johanna Malt for her great support and much-valued guidance. I am indebted to Dominique Rabaté, Pascal Quignard, Chantal Lapeyre-Desmaison, and Mireille Calle-Gruber for their encouragement and interest in my research.

This monograph was published during my tenure as a Leverhulme Early Career Fellow and I would like to express my utmost gratitude to the Leverhulme Trust for its support of my academic research.

Part of Chapter 5 appeared in a different form as 'L'enfant fétiche dans l'œuvre de Pascal Quignard', in the special issue 'Pascal Quignard et l'amour', *Littératures*, 69 (2013), 107–22, and I thank the editors, Christine Rodriguez and Sylvie Vignes, for their advice in the writing of that paper.

Finally, my warmest thanks go to Siobhán McIlvanney and Akane Kawakami for their precious input.

L.V., London, July 2016

TRANSLATIONS USED

❖

Translations are adapted from the following published sources. Where no published English edition is available, endnote references are to French originals, and the translation in the text is my own.

Translations of Works by Pascal Quignard

Albucius, trans. by Bruce Boone (Venice, CA: The Lapis Press, 1992)
On Wooden Tablets: Apronenia Avitia, trans. by Bruce X (Providence, RI: Burning Deck, 2001)
Sarx, trans. by Keith Waldrop (Providence, RI: Burning Deck, 1997)
Sex and Terror, trans. by Chris Turner (Calcutta: Seagull Books, 2011)
The Hatred of Music, trans. by Matthew Amos and Fredrik Rönnbäck (New Haven, CT: Yale University Press, 2016)
The Salon in Württemberg, trans. by Barbara Bray (New York: Grove Press, 1986)
The Sexual Night, trans. by Chris Turner (Calcutta: Seagull Books, 2014)
The Silent Crossing, trans. by Chris Turner (Calcutta: Seagull Books, 2013)

Other Translations

ALAIN BADIOU, *Wittgenstein's Antiphilosophy*, trans. by Bruno Bosteels (London: Verso Books, 2011)
ROLAND BARTHES, *Critical Essays*, trans. by Richard Howard (Evanston, IL: Northwestern University Press, 1972)
—— *The Pleasure of the Text*, trans. by Richard Miller (New York: Hill and Wang, 1975)
—— *The Rustle of Language*, trans. by Richard Howard (Oakland: University of California Press, 1989)
GEORGES BATAILLE, *Lascaux or the Birth of Art*, trans. by Austryn Wainhouse (Lausanne: Skira, 1955)
MAURICE BLANCHOT, *A Voice From Elsewhere*, trans. by Charlotte Mandell (Albany: State University of New York Press, 2007)
—— *Friendship*, trans. by Elizabeth Rottenberg (Stanford, CA: Stanford University Press, 1997)
—— *The Space of Literature*, trans. by Ann Smock (Lincoln: University of Nebraska Press, 1982)
—— *The Unavowable Community*, trans. by Pierre Joris (Barrytown, NY: Station Hill, 2000)
—— *The Work of Fire*, trans. by Charlotte Mandell (Stanford, CA: Stanford University Press, 1995)
LOUIS-RENÉ DES FORÊTS, *The Children's Room*, trans. by Jean Stewart (London: John Calder, 1963)
—— *Poems of Samuel Wood*, trans. by Anthony Barnett (Lewes: Allardyce Book, 2011)
JULIA KRISTEVA, *Revolution in Poetic Language*, trans. by Margaret Waller (New York: Columbia University Press, 1984)

——*Language: the Unknown*, trans. by Anne M. Menke (New York: Columbia University Press, 1989)

JACQUES LACAN, *Écrits: The First Complete Edition in English*, trans. by Bruce Fink (New York: Norton, 2006)

——*The Ethics of Psychoanalysis (1959–1960). The Seminar of Jacques Lacan edited by Jacques-Alain Miller, Book VII*, trans. by Dennis Porter (London: Routledge, 1992)

——*The Seminar of Jacques Lacan: Book 1, Freud's Papers on Technique, 1953–1954*, trans. by John Forrester (New York: Norton, 1991)

CLAUDE LÉVI-STRAUSS, *The Raw and the Cooked*, trans. by John and Doreen Weightman (Harmondsworth: Penguin, 1986)

JEAN-FRANÇOIS LYOTARD, *The Postmodern Condition: A Report on Knowledge*, trans. by Geoff Bennington and Brian Massumi (Manchester: Manchester University Press, 1984)

——'Anamnesis of the Visible 2', trans. by John Ronan, *Qui Parle*, 11 (1999), 21–36

STÉPHANE MALLARMÉ, *Selected Poetry and Prose*, ed. by Mary Ann Caws (New York: New Directions Books, 1982)

CHARLES PERRAULT, *The Complete Fairy Tales in Verse and Prose*, trans. and ed. by Stanley Appelbaum (Mineola, NY: Dover, 2002)

STENDHAL, *The Red and the Black*, trans. by Roger Gard (New York: Penguin, 2002)

LIST OF ABBREVIATIONS

❖

Works by Pascal Quignard

AL	*Albucius*
ALe	*Albucius*, trans. by Bruce Boone
BO	*Boutès*
EDE	*Écrits de l'éphémère*
EW	*Ethelrude et Wolframm*
GTF	*Une gêne technique à l'égard des fragments*
LBS	*La Barque silencieuse (Dernier royaume VI)*
LBSe	*The Silent Crossing*, trans. by Chris Turner
LEC	*Les Escaliers de Chambord*
LEVCM	*L'Enfant au visage couleur de la mort*
'LFCM'	'Les fêtes des chants du Marais'
'LFCMe'	'The Singing Festivals of the Marais', trans. by Chris Turner
LHM	*La Haine de la musique*
LHMe	*The Hatred of Music*
LL	*Le Lecteur*
'LMR'	'La Métayère de Rodez'
LNBL	*Le Nom sur le bout de la langue*
LNS	*La Nuit sexuelle*
LNSe	*The Sexual Night*, trans. by Chris Turner
LPD	*La Parole de la Délie, essai sur Maurice Scève*
LS	*Pascal Quignard le solitaire*, with Chantal Lapeyre-Desmaison
LSE	*Le Sexe et l'effroi*
LSEe	*Sex and Terror*, trans. by Chris Turner
LSM	*Les Solidarités mystérieuses*
LSW	*Le Salon du Wurtemberg*
LSWe	*The Salon in Württemberg*, trans. by Barbara Bray
LTBAA	*Les Tablettes de buis d'Apronenia Avitia*
LTBAAe	*On Wooden Tablets: Apronenia Avitia*, trans. by Bruce X
'LVP'	'La Voix perdue'
LVS	*Le Vœu de silence sur Louis-René des Forêts*
LZ	*Lycophron et Zétès*
PT	*Petits traités*
RS	*Rhétorique spéculative*
SA	*Sarx*
SAe	*Sarx*, trans. by Keith Waldrop
SLJ	*Sur le Jadis (Dernier royaume II)*
SO	*Sordidissimes (Dernier royaume V)*
TAR	*Terrasse à Rome*
VA	*Villa Amalia*
VS	*Vie secrète (Dernier royaume VIII)*
MDP	*Mourir de penser (Dernier royaume IX)*

Other Works Cited

LCE	*La Chambre des enfants*, by Louis-René des Forêts
LCEe	*The Children's Room*, trans. by Jean Stewart
LCI	*Le Langage, cet inconnu*, by Julia Kristeva
LCIe	*Language: the Unknown*, trans. by Anne M. Menke
LEL	*L'Espace littéraire*, by Maurice Blanchot
LELe	*The Space of Literature*, trans. by Ann Smock
'LNA'	'Lascaux, ou la naissance de l'art', by Georges Bataille
'LNAe'	*Lascaux or the Birth of Art*, trans. by Austryn Wainhouse
LPF	*La Part du feu*, by Maurice Blanchot
LPFe	*The Work of Fire*, trans. by Charlotte Mandell
LSIV	*Le Séminaire, livre IV, la relation d'objet, 1956–7*, by Jacques Lacan
LSVII	*Le Séminaire, livre VII, l'éthique de la psychanalyse, 1959–60*, by Jacques Lacan
LSVIIe	*The Ethics of Psychoanalysis (1959–1960). The Seminar of Jacques Lacan. Book VII*, trans. by Dennis Porter

INTRODUCTION

❖

On 3 June 1968, about sixty miles south of Naples in the Italian province of Salerno, a team of archaeologists led by Professor Mario Napoli discovered a tomb just outside the walls of Paestum, also known as the ancient Greek city Poseidonia. The tomb contained the remains of a young man, alongside an oil jar and a lyre made from a tortoise's shell. Composed of five limestone slabs arranged into a rectangular shape sealed from above, it was built in 470 BC and has been known since its discovery as 'The Tomb of the Diver'. It is, as R. Ross Holloway notes, 'the only example of Greek painting with figured scenes [...] to survive in its entirety [and] amongst the thousands of Greek tombs known from this time [...] the only one to have been decorated with frescoes of human subjects.'[1] The frescoes in question are painted on the inside of each slab; this has kept intact their original colours and shapes. The four walls depict a continuous scene, narrating the events of a symposium, a drinking party: men are lying on couches, some are singing, others are playing the lyre or engrossed in a game of skill. What Holloway describes as the 'general atmosphere of erotic relationships' and the convivial and festive air of the paintings are striking considering the funeral context in which they were created.[2] Even more surprising is the painting found on the ceiling of the tomb, which bears no obvious relation to the other four: against a bare landscape, which features a pool of water framed by an olive tree on the left and, on the right, a tower placed besides another tree that appears to grow from the face of cliff, a lone man, naked, is caught in mid-air as he dives into the water below.

In 1968, as Napoli and his team discovered the 'Tomb of the Diver' in Paestum, and in Paris students and workers mounted protests against the French government, the twenty-year-old Pascal Quignard abandoned his studies in philosophy and sent his first manuscript to the publisher Gallimard. It was rejected, but the budding author caught the attention of a member of the reading committee, the poet and novelist Louis-René des Forêts. Des Forêts became Quignard's mentor, and it was under his tutelage that he later published his first book, started a career as a reader at Gallimard, and contributed to the art and poetry magazine *L'Éphémère* founded by des Forêts, alongside intellectual and literary figures such as Paul Celan, Michel Leiris and Yves Bonnefoy. Since then, Quignard has written essays and studies on writers, musicians and painters. In 1976, he published *Le Lecteur* (*The Reader*), his first work of fiction. More than sixty novels, tales, treatises and poems have followed, as well as numerous collaborations with musicians, choreographers, dancers, visual artists and filmmakers. In 1994, Pascal Quignard decided to devote himself fully to writing and left Paris for the city of Sens in Burgundy. In 2002, he published the first of a series of books entitled *Dernier royaume* (*Last Kingdom*), of which fourteen volumes have been announced. The latest, *Mourir de penser* (*Dernier royaume IX*) (*Death in Thought*), appeared in 2014.

The enigmatic features of the 'Tomb of the Diver' — the uniqueness of its eponymous figure, forever fixed in an unfinished descent, the joint display of a solitary dive towards death and of trivial joys found in collective life, and the contemporary feel of its well-preserved paintings, resonate with some of the key questions posed by Pascal Quignard's oeuvre. The diver of Paestum is a recurring presence in Quignard's texts, and in *Vie secrète* (*Dernier royaume VIII*) (*Secret Life*), Quignard writes about 'la part damnée de l'art: se jeter à l'eau' [the curse of art: taking the plunge] and the awareness that 'tout artiste doit consentir à renoncer à la vie' [any artist must be willing to withdraw from life].[3] The ineluctability of death, or more precisely the journey towards a promised but unreachable vanishing point, is at the heart of Quignard's writing. The vanishing point in art is an imaginary point where parallel lines intersect: it is what gives an image its internal structure and its depth; it is also the point from which the image should be viewed, and the one that directs the viewer's gaze. Quignard's literary oeuvre is driven by an effort towards disappearance that affects all its aspects, from the representation of the writer to the texts he produces, including the characters they contain and the words that compose them.

Pascal Quignard is far from being the first author to face the paradox of a literary enterprise consumed by a desire to vanish. 'The death of the author' announced by Roland Barthes in his eponymous 1968 essay,[4] Jacques Lacan's definition of the speaking subject as alienated by the language it inhabits, and the critiques of discourse developed by structuralist and post-structuralist thought in France influenced him at the time he was a student. Pascal Quignard is part of what Dominique Rabaté has called — alluding to the title of John Barth's 1967 essay — 'la littérature de l'épuisement' [the literature of exhaustion].[5] 'Un espace éminemment paradoxal' [an eminently paradoxical space], it is defined as 'une voix écrite [qui] se développe dans le défaut de la parole dont elle veut, en redoublant la contradiction de cette communication retardée, "retarder" — selon la formule de Mallarmé — la cadence' [a voice that develops through writing the desire to suspend — to borrow a verb used by Stéphane Mallarmé — the rhythm of speech by replaying, in writing, the very limitations that define it].[6] In a 2011 article, and more recently in 2015, in a lecture at Oxford University, Rabaté extended his argument to include 'l'inscription d'une problématique envie de disparaître' [the mark of a problematic desire to disappear] in recent and contemporary literature produced in France.[7]

Rabaté argues that a common attraction to figures of disappearance unites the works of living French writers such as Pascal Quignard, Patrick Modiano, recipient of the 2014 Nobel Prize for Literature, Jean Echenoz, whose novel *Je m'en vais* (*I'm Off*) was awarded the Prix Goncourt in 1999, and Emmanuel Carrère, known for his 2000 text *L'Adversaire* (*The Adversary*) based on the real-life murderer Jean-Claude Romand. These authors deal with disappearance first as a narrative device, writing novels and literary accounts that deal with the vanishing of a character, protagonist or narrator. Disappearances are both celebrated, as acts of individual freedom, and feared: Rabaté mentions in particular Modiano's 'obsession de la trace' [obsession with traces] in his novel *Dora Bruder*.[8] This ambiguity is also present in each writer's relation to disappearance. The group identified by Rabaté, which could also include Michel Houellebecq and Annie Ernaux, concerns writers who share a taste for discretion, if not total solitude. Houellebecq, for instance, regularly stages his own disappearance — he did so most recently in a feature film, entitled *L'Enlèvement de Michel Houellebecq* (*The Kidnapping of Michel Houellebecq*). Quignard, like Jean Echenoz and Annie Ernaux, shies away from newspaper and television interviews. His reluctance to appear in public, except in the specific settings of academic conferences devoted to his work and performances given alongside other artists, is linked to his symbolic departure from Paris, which this time aligns him with writers of an older generation: Louis-René des Forêts and Maurice Blanchot, who left Paris for an anonymous life in the countryside. Yet what separates Quignard from these figures, and brings him closer to his contemporaries, is a personal relation to disappearance anchored in larger historical events. Quignard, Echenoz, Ernaux and Modiano were all born during or just after the Second World War. As Rabaté argues, 'le motif de la disparition est liée à cette angoisse majeure [...]: il a été possible (il est toujours possible) d'annihiler des millions de gens, d'effacer leurs vies et leurs traces' [the motif of disappearance is linked to a great source of anguish: it really was possible (it still is) to annihilate millions of people, to erase any trace of them and their lives].[9]

Disappearance functions as a unifying trend for a generation of writers who did not live through the war but are still affected by its aftermath. As a writer who pushes the motif of disappearance to its extremes, Quignard undeniably belongs to this group, yet he actively resists inclusion into a community of contemporary writers. Contemporariness takes on a very specific meaning in his work, which is organized as a quest for what the writer calls the *Jadis* [the erstwhile] — a term used to designate the unreachable site of origins towards which all of his texts are directed. It implies that present, past and future times are contemporary in relation to this all-important yet unreachable point. Quignard's oeuvre displays an evident preference for eras and figures that came before him and have now disappeared: in an interview given in 1981, he expressed the wish to 'rivaliser avec les précédents plutôt que se démarquer des amis' [compete with his elders rather than trying to distance himself from his friends].[10] His texts are populated with figures plucked from the past: from the twentieth century, the seventeenth century, the Middle Ages, Ancient Rome and Greece, to prehistory and beyond, towards the mythical and the legendary.

His career in literature is defined by an oscillation not only between past and present, but also exposure and concealment; between his characterization as 'un homme du monde' [a worldly man] and 'un homme du livre' [a bookish man].[11] Born in 1948 in Verneuil-sur-Avre in Normandy, Quignard comes from a family of prominent intellectuals and academics. His mother Anne was the daughter of the linguist and grammarian Charles Bruneau, and the sister of Jean Bruneau, a scholar renowned for his work on Gustave Flaubert, and a Resistance figure who survived Dachau.[12] His father, Jacques Quignard, was the head of the Centre International d'Études Pédagogiques de Sèvres, just outside Paris, where the writer lived from the age of eleven. In interviews, Quignard contrasts his life in Sèvres to his early years in the port of Le Havre, which had been almost entirely destroyed during the Second World War, and where he lived 'entre les ruines, les rats, et quelques immeubles qui s'élèvaient à nouveau' [amongst the ruins, the rats, and the few buildings that had been rebuilt].[13] The arrival in Sèvres marks the entry into a wondrous environment: a luxurious family apartment, furnished with delicate items made in the famed blue china of Sèvres, and enclosed in a park that contains a 'pavillon anachorétique aux proportions magnifiques' [an anchoretic lodge of magnificent proportions], originally built in the seventeenth century and named after one of its occupants, the French composer Jean-Baptiste Lully.[14]

When describing his childhood years, Quignard also mentions the rivalry between his paternal and maternal cultural heritages. On his mother's side, he comes from a family of specialists in French language and culture, whilst his father is of German descent and comes from a line of musicians. As a child, Quignard was a budding musician and composer; in his early twenties, he briefly worked as an organist in the town of Ancenis, taking over the post from one of his aunts, Marthe Quignard.[15] Alongside the practice of music, the writer's adolescent years were spent practising painting and drawing, before his sudden renunciation, in 1968, of both music and painting in favour of writing. In interviews, Quignard endows this abandonment of youthful practices with a symbolic nature, describing how he one day decided to burn his paintings in front of Lully's lodge in Sèvres.[16] Yet the musical and the visual are two themes that return relentlessly in his texts, and their haunting presence is something this study will explore.

The decision to turn to literature quickly resulted for Quignard in a successful career as a reader, editor, critic and author. The writer Alain Veinstein, whom Quignard met in the mid-1970s when they were both involved with the poet Emmanuel Hocquard's small press Orange Export Ltd, describes the young Quignard as 'un solitaire absolu qui se tenait à l'écart de tout' [an utterly solitary figure, who always kept his distance]. Veinstein also explains how, throughout the next two decades, he underwent a metamorphosis and 'un passage à vide dans les allées du pouvoir' [difficult years spent in the corridors of power].[17] This corresponds to the period when Quignard became an increasingly influential figure at Gallimard. During the twenty-four years he spent at the publishing house, he played a considerable role in shaping the French literary scene. Annie Ernaux confirms this in an interview, where she describes the backstage discussions leading to a title change before the publication of one of her texts: 'pour le *Journal de la ville*, qui était le journal extérieur, j'avais choisi *Anonymes*. Pascal Quignard n'a pas aimé. C'est devenu *Journal du dehors*' [for *Journal de la ville* (*City Journal*), which was the journal about the outside world, I had chosen *Anonymes* (*Anonymous*) as a title. Pascal Quignard didn't like it, so we changed it to *Journal du dehors* (*Exteriors*)].[18] At the end of his career at Gallimard, Quignard was a member of the reading committee, and he also held the post of secretary general. Throughout those years, he led the highly social lifestyle of an *éminence grise* of the French literary scene. Rekindling his relationship with music, he took on high-profile responsibilities, taking part in the creation of the Centre de musique baroque in Versailles and becoming president of the orchestra Le Concert des Nations.[19]

These types of public engagement ended in 1994, when Quignard suddenly resigned from all his professional activities and social roles. This second act of renunciation, after the abandonment of music, painting and his philosophy studies in 1968, corresponds to a deeper involvement with literature. As Veinstein puts it, it was motivated by the realization that 'la désocialisation que provoque l'écriture [...] en est aussi la condition' [the dissocializing effect of literature [...] is also one of its conditions].[20] For Quignard, the affirmation of his identity as a writer, as an 'homme du livre', calls for the renunciation of society, suggesting that absence from the world is what enables the presence of literature. As he stated in an interview given in 2002, 'parler, c'est faire figure. Écrire, c'est disparaître' [speaking means appearing. To write is to disappear].[21] By cancelling his social existence, the writer intends to free himself from the multiple forms taken by social interaction, and by doing so, also rid himself of the fixed identities that necessarily come with them.

The definition of writing as the voluntary decision to leave behind social existence in the name of literature is dependent on a specific conception of language. By opposing disappearance to the act of appearing, which points to what Quignard sees as the postures forced upon him by society, he also opposes writing and speech. The recourse to literature is seen as a way to exit not only society, but also language. In the text *La Barque silencieuse* (*Dernier royaume VI*) (*The Silent Crossing*), the question 'qu'est-ce-qu'un littéraire?' [what is a literary person?] prompts the following definition: 'celui pour qui les mots défaillent, bondissent, fuient, perdent sens' [someone for whom words falter, jump about, elude his grasp, lose their meaning].[22] Here, he clearly positions his writing as part of what Rabaté defines as 'la littérature de l'épuisement'. This conception of writing as a way of exposing the inherent faults of language is also indebted to the work of Blanchot, who argues that 'le langage n'[est] réel que dans la perspective d'un état de non-langage qu'il ne peut réaliser' [language is real only from the perspective of a state of non-language, which it cannot realize] and that:

> c'est à l'intérieur des mots que ce suicide des mots doit se tenter, suicide qui les hante mais ne peut s'accomplir, qui les conduit à la tentation de la page blanche ou à la folie d'une parole perdue dans l'insignifiance [...]. La cruauté du langage vient de ce que sans cesse il évoque sa mort sans pouvoir mourir jamais.

> [it is inside words that the suicide of words must be attempted, a suicide that haunts them but cannot be achieved, that leads them to the temptation of the white page or to the madness of a word lost in insignificance. [...] The crudity of language comes from the fact that it endlessly evokes its death without ever being able to die].[23]

Quignard further defines writing as the paradoxical fulfilment of a vow of silence: 'la *mise au silence du langage*' [the act of *silencing language*].[24] This takes the form of the annihilation of verbal language as a system of signs that can never truly achieve communication, truth or knowledge. But, because literature is undeniably made of words — and Quignard's texts, which draw on a rich array of elements borrowed from culture, even more obviously — it is necessarily affected by the process of destruction it aims for. Quignard addresses this obvious paradox in *Vie secrète*, where the narrator asks: 'comment se dénuder du langage avec le langage? [...] Mais dans le même temps comment se guérir du langage sans lui?' [how do we get rid of language through language? [...] And, at the same instant, how do we cure ourselves from language without language?]. This question is followed by a possible answer, which implies a conception of literary writing as the attempt to 'ensauvager le [langage] domesticateur' [render savage the very language that domesticates us], to reverse the civilizing aspect of language and lead it back to the inhumanity Quignard sees as characteristic of its origins.[25] But can the writer really be defined as this self-styled 'bestial' figure who through destruction produces a victorious form of literature? Or is his work rather pulled into the very process of disappearance and annihilation it puts language through?

In one of his earliest published works, *La Parole de la Délie, essai sur Maurice Scève*, a critical study of Maurice Scève's *Délie*, Quignard recognized the impossibility contained in the act of writing. Whilst this text marks the start of a prolific career in literature for Quignard, it is presented in its first pages as a work 'ne prétendant à rien' [that lays no claim], an imposture and '[une] œuvre perdue' [a lost work].[26] Quignard produces a literary oeuvre that paradoxically draws its value from the relentless expression of its own disappearance.

The first chapter of this study concentrates on the most obvious form that disappearance takes in Quignard's oeuvre. Exploring his novels and other fictional texts, this chapter shows how disappearance is defined as an ideal lifestyle, and how self-writing is replaced by a dissolution of the self through writing. Drawing on claims made by critics and by Quignard both within and at the periphery of his work, I confirm the importance of solitude as a theme, and argue that its celebration is not based on the desire to put the writer's own voice forward but rooted in the longing for an erasure of the self. I first show that solitude, because it relies on a celebration of the reader figure, is paradoxically based on collaboration and directed towards others. I then contend that Quignard's solitude also amounts to the return to a primordial state of non-differentiation with the world.

The second chapter offers a detailed study of Quignard's *contes*: the literary fairy tales and rewritings of folktales he has published on their own or inserted into other texts. By drawing on the psychoanalytical literature surrounding the genre, and through references to authors such as Apuleius and Ovid, this chapter analyses various strategies by means of which the *contes* convey the disappearance of language. Here, I begin by arguing that Quignard relies on the distinctive metamorphic quality of literary fairy tales, which differentiates them from myths, to pursue further the process of dissolution already present in the novels. I then look at Quignard's collaborations with musicians, dancers and choreographers, to explore how his *contes* sustain a celebration of silence and hint at the physical disappearance of writing.

Following this exploration of music and dance, my third chapter concentrates on the relation between Quignard's work and the visual. It analyses the writer's multiple forays into visual arts — collaborations with contemporary artists, essays on painting, and fictional biographies of invented artists — to postulate that Quignard, by presenting reading as a plunge into darkness and writing as the literary production of obscurity, redefines his work as the quest for a vanishing point, an invisible and unreachable place of origins. I first demonstrate that, for Quignard, literature becomes the scene of a metamorphosis of text into image through the act of reading. I then define Quignard's writing as the creation of images, which, like the reader figure, ultimately remain out of sight.

This introduces a conception of the book as a place where the spatial and the temporal are merged; an obscure space that lures the reader into a fall towards an unreachable point of origin. The latter is referred to in the work as the *Jadis*, a key term that occurs again and again in Quignard's work. Chapter Four details the meanings of this term and explores its various representations, in particular by drawing on the characteristics it shares with the Lacanian real. Quignard's texts focus on subjects that mainly concern past figures and eras, which are put through a process of obscuration: by sabotaging the possibilities of grasping the past, the writer attempts to shorten the distance that separates it from the *Jadis*. I argue in the first instance that Quignard is more concerned with accessing underground ruins than bringing them back to the surface. This literary form of archaeology is part of a larger attempt to put forward the advantages of obscurity over those of knowledge, which reveals a paradox at the heart of Quignard's work: how can his writing, which is of an undeniably erudite nature, possibly sustain this definition? I then explore the implications of this paradoxical stance, and how the work relies on erudition to develop a representation of the writer as a hunter and of the text as his prey.

The relation to the *Jadis* redefines writing as a form of hunting and a mimicry of the predatory practices of animals. But such a posture is based on an irresolvable issue: the rejection of culture it implies relies exclusively on intertextual material extracted from this very culture. This relates to the larger impossibility at the heart of Quignard's writing, which is both productive and destructive: it is a work in continuous expansion, yet it is also filled with literary representations of destruction and disappearance. My final chapter first deals with this impossibility by arguing that production happens not in spite of destruction but because of it. This self-destructive nature takes its most complete form through two complementary motifs borrowed from Blanchot: fragmentation and fire. Finally, by looking at the theme of childhood, I attempt to determine whether Quignard's writing is ultimately defined by the way it reaches towards a vanishing point, or whether a glimmer of hope remains amongst the surrounding devastation.

This book follows the career of a living and working author who is at home in the present times and yet constantly yearning to arrive at a destination he knows to be unreachable. The issues at the heart of Quignard's writing are undeniably contemporary and they are shared by other French writers of his generation. It is the specific tactics Quignard uses to deal with them, and the way in which his work exposes, rather than resolves, these tensions that carve out his distinctive place within the current French literary landscape. His posture resembles that of the young man buried in Paestum, and his work takes the form of the tomb in which his body rests. Underground and outside the world, walled up in an obscure space, the writer is both alone and in the company of selected friends. Art forms such as music and painting are constantly at his side. Like the painted diver suspended in his descent, Quignard's writing is always transitory, caught between affirmation and renunciation, freedom and despair, and between presence and absence.

Notes to the Introduction

1. R. Ross Holloway, 'The Tomb of the Diver', *American Journal of Archaeology*, 110 (2006), 365–88 (p. 365).
2. Ibid., p. 381.
3. Pascal Quignard, *Vie secrète (Dernier royaume VIII)* (Paris: Gallimard, 1998), p. 39.
4. Roland Barthes, 'La mort de l'auteur', in *Le Bruissement de la langue* (Paris: Seuil, 1984), pp. 63–69. 'The Death of the Author', in *The Rustle of Language*, trans. by Richard Howard (Oakland: University of California Press, 1989), pp. 49–55.
5. In his essay (pp. 175–84), Rabaté explains how his use of the notion of 'épuisement' relates to the concept of 'exhaustion' developed by John Barth in: 'The Literature of Exhaustion', *Atlantic Monthly*, 220 (1967), 29–34 and 'The Literature of Replenishment, Postmodernist Fiction', *Atlantic Monthly*, 245 (1980), 65–71.
6. Dominique Rabaté, *Vers une littérature de l'épuisement* (Paris: José Corti, 1991), p. 9.
7. Dominique Rabaté, 'Figures de la disparition dans le roman contemporain', in *Un Retour des normes romanesques dans la littérature française contemporaine*, ed. by Marc Dambre and Wolfgang Asholt (Paris: Presses Sorbonne nouvelle, 2011), pp. 67–75 (p. 67).
8. Ibid., p. 68.
9. Ibid., p. 70.
10. Pascal Quignard, 'La Déprogrammation de la littérature', in *Écrits de l'éphémère* (Paris: Galilée, 2005), pp. 233–49 (pp. 242–43).
11. Alain Veinstein, 'Tout autre, purs pluriels et dehors', in *Pascal Quignard, ou la littérature démembrée par les muses*, ed. by Mireille Calle-Gruber, Gilles Declercq, and Stella Spriet (Paris: Presses Sorbonne nouvelle, 2011), pp. 257–66 (p. 266). And Jérôme Garcin and Pascal Quignard, 'Les Pensées de Pascal (Quignard)', *Le Nouvel Observateur*, 4 October 2011 <http://bibliobs. nouvelobs.com/romans/20110928.OBS1315/les-pensees-de-pascal-quignard.html> [accessed 12 November 2015] (para. 29 of 34).
12. See the obituary of Jean Bruneau by Julian Barnes: 'World Within Words', *The Guardian*, 28 June 2003 <www.guardian.co.uk/books/2003/jun/28/classics.julianbarnes> [accessed 1 November 2015].
13. Pascal Quignard and Chantal Lapeyre-Desmaison, *Pascal Quignard le solitaire* (Paris: Flohic, 2001), p. 24.
14. *LS* p. 26.
15. *LS*, p. 28.
16. *LS*, p. 32.
17. Veinstein, pp. 260, 266.
18. Claire-Lise Tondeur, 'Entretien avec Annie Ernaux', *French Review*, 69 (1995), 37–44 (p. 41)
19. *LS*, p. 35.
20. Veinstein, p. 260.
21. Pascal Quignard and Catherine Argand, 'Entretien', *Lire*, 1 September 2002 <http://www.lexpress.fr/culture/livre/pascal-quignard-goncourt-2002_806807.html> [accessed 12 December 2015] (para. 5 of 29).
22. Pascal Quignard, *La Barque silencieuse, Dernier royaume VI* (Paris: Seuil, 2009), p. 7. *The Silent Crossing*, trans. by Chris Turner (Calcutta: Seagull Books, 2013), p. 1.
23. Maurice Blanchot, *La Part du feu* (Paris: Gallimard, 1949), p. 30. *The Work of Fire*, trans. by Charlotte Mandell (Stanford, CA: Stanford University Press, 1995), pp. 22–23.
24. *VS*, p. 215.
25. *LS*, pp. 103–04.
26. Pascal Quignard, *La Parole de la Délie, essai sur Maurice Scève* (Paris: Mercure de France, 1974), p. 20.

CHAPTER 1

❖

A Vanishing Act

In many of his texts and in the interviews he has given over the years, Pascal Quignard consistently portrays himself as a solitary writer. In the unambiguously entitled *Pascal Quignard le solitaire* (*Solitary Pascal Quignard*), which he co-wrote with Chantal Lapeyre-Desmaison, he explains his decision to leave all social roles behind and devote himself to a life of reading and writing. In *La Barque silencieuse* he defines this voluntary solitude as an exit from the social realm and as a form of commitment to literature: 'la capacité d'être seul est le but de la vie [...], le fondement de la créativité' [the ability to be alone is the purpose of life [...], the basis of creativity], borrowing a statement attributed to the British psychoanalyst Wilfred Bion.[1]

Quignard is far from being the only writer to idealize solitude as a necessary condition of writing. At first glance, he appears in a similar light to some of his contemporaries — one thinks especially of Modiano's discretion and of Houelle-becq's exploitation of the misanthropic author figure — whilst participating in a wider and older tradition of celebrating solitude in the artist's life. In the recent text *Sur l'idée d'une communauté de solitaires* (*On The Idea of a Community of Solitaries*), Quignard bases his conception of solitude on the way of life experimented by a community of self-proclaimed 'Solitaires', who settled in the grounds of the abbey of Port-Royal des Champs in the seventeenth century: 'des hommes [...] quittaient la cour pour franchir vingt kilomètres et se retrouver dans un bois. [...] Ils ne se guidaient sur aucune règle extérieure, n'obéissaient à personne, jaloux seulement de leur retrait du monde' [men left court to settle in the woods, twenty kilometres away from Paris. They followed no outside rules and did not obey anyone's orders. Their retreat from the world was all that mattered, and they guarded it with jealousy].[2] This experiment, led by noblemen and artists influenced by Jansenism, such as the French dramatist Jean Racine, ended abruptly when Louis XIV, prompted by the Jesuits, ordered its dissolution. Quignard's representation of a solitary form of existence goes hand in hand with a celebration of past and present outcast figures. In a study devoted to his friend Michel Deguy, the writer borrows a passage from one of the latter's poems, which presents the artist as a recluse, taking a step back from ordinary life better to comment on it: 'le poète s'exclut de l'usage, il n'est pas partie prenante de l'échange' [the poet does not trade; he excludes himself from customs].[3]

But what sets Quignard apart from his elders and his contemporaries is a representation of solitude that goes beyond the expression of the artist's individual voice and subjectivity. His idealization of solitude is rooted in a longing for the disappearance of self, which takes place first through the dissolution of all forms of identity, including that of writer. Quignard explains this in an interview with Jean-Louis Pautrot, where he states: 'les statuts je les ai tous délaissés en démissionnant de toutes les fonctions sociales que j'ai pu exercer' [when I resigned from all my jobs and positions I also lost any sense of social ranking], before adding: 'le statut d'écrivain est [un] autre statut que je trouve à vrai dire misérable dès l'instant où s'y recherche un rôle ou un honneur ou une supériorité dans le groupe' [the writer's social position is another one I find despicable as soon as it becomes a role, a reputation, a way of feeling superior to the group].[4] Such a clear-cut rejection is based on a wider critique of subjectivity and selfhood, both seen as mere products of discourse. In *L'Être du balbutiement, essai sur Sacher-Masoch* (*A Being in Infancy: Essay on Sacher-Masoch*), Quignard borrows a rhetorical question formulated by Jacques Lacan: 'comment ne pas voir que le sujet, s'il est le sujet qui parle, ne s'y soutient que par du discours' [how can we fail to see that the subject, assuming he is the subject who speaks, sustains himself there only on the basis of discourse].[5] While Quignard's position towards verbal and spoken language will be discussed in the following chapter, it is worth noting here that discourse is for the writer the object of deep mistrust: like Frédéric Molieri, the protagonist of a short story by Louis-René des Forêts, Quignard 'rejoint la solitude et le silence par répugnance à l'égard du mensonge, et par un refus farouche opposé au caractère démoniaque des langues' [sides with solitude and silence because lying is for him a source of disgust, and because he is fiercely opposed to the diabolical nature of languages].[6]

This reluctance to be defined socially as a writer paradoxically gives way to self-representation as a reader: 'c'est la lecture qui est pour moi vitale', as he tells Pautrot, 'plutôt que l'activité conquérante ou volontaire d'écrire' [it is reading that matters most for me, not the voluntary and belligerent act of writing].[7] This self-portrait as a reader is intended as a further blow to the concept of identity. The reader is for Quignard an empty shell, a figure marked by disappearance and absence. While writing reveals a will to conquer, reading becomes synonymous with a relinquishing of the self. In *Le Lecteur*, the reader's name is borrowed from Homer's *Odyssey*: like Odysseus facing the Cyclops Polyphemus, his name is 'Personne', which in French can mean both 'somebody' and 'nobody'.[8] As this chapter will show, Quignard's conception of the reader suggests that the solitude he seeks is paradoxically based on collaboration and directed towards others. As the identity of reader replaces that of writer, the very idea of identity is exchanged with that of 'being in debt', and the written work appears as an empty vessel invaded and taken over by the presence of others: not only other artists, but also various types of revenants the texts are meant to host.

Write, Hide, Seek

Lycophron et Zétès (*Lycophron and Zetes*), which Quignard published in 2010, contains a French translation of a canonical Greek poem, Lycophron's *Alexandra*. It also includes two series of fragments: the first is attributed to a Greek writer named Zetes and the second to Quignard. Because of its hybrid nature, *Lycophron et Zétès* provides a good illustration of Quignard's ambivalence towards literary genres, styles of writing and even art forms.

His various activities as a writer, translator and critic first appear as a postmodern embrace of the multiple possibilities allowed by a rejection of fixed identities and statuses. Quignard's frequent use of pseudonyms and avatars seems to confirm this: about Zetes's fragments, he states that 'ces fragments dérivés du grec [...] n'étaient pas vraiment de moi [...]. Je pris le pseudonyme de Zétès qui veut dire en grec celui qui cherche' [these fragments, derived from the Greek, are not really by me. I used a pseudonym, Zetes, which in Greek means 'the one who seeks'].[9] A fictional authorial figure is also used in *Les Tablettes de buis d'Apronenia Avitia* (*On Wooden Tablets: Apronenia Avitia*) where what is explicitly presented as a suite of literary fragments by a Latin woman writer named Apronenia Avitia is in fact written by Quignard. The invention of Zetes and Avitia has led several critics to identify Quignard as the real author of two texts published under the name Agustina Izquierdo, which is a near-anagram of Pascal Quignard.[10] Izquierdo, who remains an obscure figure in the current literary landscape, published two texts in the 1990s, *L'Amour pur* (*Pure Love*) (1993) and *Un Souvenir indécent* (*An Indecent Memory*) (1992), the style and the themes of which are reminiscent of Quignard's work.[11] The writer has refused to confirm that he is the author of these texts, even claiming that he does not use pseudonyms: 'on m'a imputé quatre pseudonymes. Tous sont faux' ['four different pseudonyms have been attributed to me: they are all false].[12] The ambiguity of this statement is of course revealing: after all, a pseudonym is necessarily false, and Quignard has admitted to writing under the guise of invented authors, such as Apronenia Avitia and Zétès, and the art historian Grünehagen in *Terrasse à Rome* (*Terrace in Rome*).

If this use of pseudonyms seems to invite readers to a game of hide and seek, it also plays a part in a larger enterprise of dissolution in which writing amounts to the disappearance of the self. As the following passage indicates, to write, for Quignard, is to disappear:

> Toute œuvre à laquelle on consacre ses jours est profondément *encapuchonnante*. C'est cette même possibilité d'invisibilité qui attire celui qui s'y plonge afin d'y soustraire son visage et d'y protéger sa vie. [...] Peu importe qu'il s'agisse de la rédaction d'une traduction, ou de la méditation d'un traité, ou de la notation d'une partition, ou de la contraction d'un conte. On vit dans l'œuvre qu'on traduit comme Persée dans son loup.

> [Any working day is spent making a hood. One is attracted to the possibility of becoming invisible: by diving into a book we are able to cover our faces and protect our lives. Composing a translation, notating a musical score, or compressing a long tale are all ways to achieve this. One lives inside the work one translates like Perseus in his hood.][13]

In this passage, Quignard carefully avoids the word 'écrire' and assigns various activities — 'rédaction', 'méditation', 'notation' and 'contraction' — to the overall production of invisibility. The literary realm is defined as a hood and likened to a mythical object, the 'Cap of Invisibility' that Hades gives to Perseus to help him defeat the Gorgon Medusa. This conception of writing could be defined as *cuculliform*, from *cucullus*, the Latin word meaning 'cap' and 'hood', not only evoking the idea of a hood in the sense of a protective cover but also of an enclosed and delimited space where one can retreat and disappear.

The motif of a retreating space is relevant to Quignard's representation of solitude, which is associated in his texts with a particular space: the writer's own home in Burgundy. *La Barque silencieuse* offers a description of its immediate surroundings: 'sur le bras mort de l'Yonne' [on a branch of the Yonne], '[à] l'ouest de l'île de Sens' [to the west of the île de Sens] and on the 'Quai de la fausse rivière' [Fake River Quay].[14] Here, Quignard situates his home outside the borders of both society and reality. The text also explores the poetic possibilities offered by geographical details, suggesting that it is not only a real but also a fictitious place: a magical island situated on a 'fake' river and outside the symbolic realm, on the borders of 'Sens' which plays on the name of the town and the French word *sens* [the meaning conveyed by language].

This description of the writer's home pushes it out of reality and into the realm of literature. In *Lycophron et Zétès*, the translated text is defined as 'une cabane [...] établie dans un mûrier' [a hut built in a mulberry tree] with reference to the spatial setting of another text, *Tous les matins du monde (All the World's Mornings)*.[15] Literary work is represented as a space where solitude and disappearance are made possible, yet Quignard is reluctant to label himself as a writer and to identify his own work as literary writing. It is as translator, scribe, and especially as reader that he intends to exploit fully the possibilities of invisibility and disappearance offered by the *cuculliform* book he produces. To become a reader is defined as the entry into a state of emptiness and absence: this is the subject of *Le Lecteur*, Quignard's first literary text. Published in 1976, after years spent working as a publisher's reader, critic and translator,[16] *Le Lecteur* marked Quignard's entry into literary writing. Yet it is centred on the figure of the reader. The text begins with an enigma, as it announces the disappearance of its main figure, and gives a possible explanation for its absence:

> L'idée suivant laquelle sa disparition serait due à quelque échange sans doute monstrueux avec le corps péri d'une âme relativement ancienne constitue l'hypothèse, si prestigieuse qu'elle puisse paraître, à laquelle si j'étais vous je me rangerais pourtant sans hésiter.

> [The idea that the reader's disappearance has been caused by an undoubtedly monstrous transformation into the dead body of a relatively ancient soul is an impressive hypothesis. If I were you, I would nonetheless believe it without question.][17]

In *Le Lecteur*, the reader takes centre stage but never appears in the text, where he remains defined by absence. If the reader is missing, it is because he has been exchanged for 'le corps péri d'une âme relativement ancienne'. Quignard favours reading because it enables him to represent writing as a metamorphic process, where his own disappearance — as a writer turned reader — gives way to the resurgence of 'relatively ancient soul[s]'. The solitude supposedly achieved in the texts, and the disappearance of the self it implies, is thus paradoxically defined by the presence of others, whom the reader, turned into an empty vessel, is meant to host.

At a seminar in 2010 at the Sorbonne Nouvelle-Université Paris 3, Quignard presented his conception of identity in telling terms:

> J'ai une loyauté avec ce que je n'ai pas été. C'est le contraire de l'identité, être en dette. Plutôt qu'un témoignage autobiographique, écrire pour être fidèle à ces possibilités, remercier les morts qui m'ont aidé. Ne pas avoir à choisir entre ce que je suis et ce que je n'ai pas été.

> [I have a loyalty towards what I never became. To be indebted is the opposite of identity. Instead of an autobiographical account, my writing is devoted to such possibilities; to showing gratitude towards the people who helped me and who have died. I do not want to choose between what I am now and what I never was.][18]

The relinquishing of identity and the celebration of an undetermined form of self are rooted in a loyalty towards others, and more specifically towards dead friends. Quignard defines his texts not only as places of solitude but also as literary *tombeaux*, where the self is buried under the remains of celebrated but absent figures. In *Lycophron et Zétès*, Quignard recalls the experience of translating *Alexandra* for the first time by comparing it to an Orphic quest: 'Je préparais la traduction en commençant par chercher l'étymologie de chaque mot. Je voyageais. J'allais dans l'autre monde. [...] J'abordais le pays des morts' [I started working on the translation by looking up the etymology of each word. This took me on a journey to the underworld. I was reaching the kingdom of the dead].[19] The translated text, earlier likened to the artist's home as a solitary retreat, becomes a point of access to the realm of the dead, confirming the metamorphosis described in *Le Lecteur*: as the writer becomes a reader and vanishes into the book, the book becomes host to those who have disappeared. Quignard's solitude is 'complètement immergé[e] par ce qui est autre' [fully invaded by the presence of others].[20] Pautrot sees in the use of shadows and voices — those of obscure and forgotten artistic and literary figures — a form of false modesty on the part of Quignard. As he argues, 'en affectant de se placer sous la tutelle des méconnus, [il] fait de l'humilité une audace. Il entend être, en quelque sorte, un grand écrivain anonyme' [by seemingly hiding under the protection of unknown figures, Quignard turns humility into boldness. In a way, he means to become a great but anonymous writer].[21]

Voices are put forward in the texts through multiple borrowings and quotations, biographical narratives and fragments, and an extreme form of intertextuality. Quignard's writing first appears similar to that of many modern and postmodern writers: aware of its allusive nature, and of the fact that, as Barthes stated, 'le texte est un tissu de citations, issues des mille foyers de la culture' [the text is a fabric of quotations, resulting from a thousand sources of culture].[22] But the specificity of Quignard's work lies in the way these voices are convened. As he told Jean-Pierre Salgas, 'tous les textes que je tente de mettre en avant sont des textes d'inconnus' [all the texts I try to promote are from obscure sources], adding: 'Je lis le *Traité du vide parfait*, Kong-souen Long y est mentionné comme trop difficile à traduire, je m'y précipite, comme je me passionne pour Albucius parce que Pétrone le méprise' [I am reading a text attributed to Lie Yukou, where Gongsun Long is mentioned as a writer difficult to translate: I immediately turn to Gongsun Long's texts. Similarly, I love Albucius because Petronius hates him].[23] Texts such as *Lycophron et Zétès*, *Albucius* (*Albucius*), a translation of Gongsun Long's *Sur le doigt qui montre cela* (*On Pointing at Things*) and *Tous les matins du monde*, relate to authors marked by relative obscurity. Other texts focus on forgotten writers and artists: the Roman rhetorician Gaius Albucius Silus, M. de Sainte-Colombe — a seventeenth-century French composer overshadowed by the success of his better-known student Marin Marais — and the French Baroque painter Georges de La Tour, whose work was overlooked for more than three centuries until its rediscovery in the first part of the twentieth century. Quignard intends his books to be hosts to the dead, yet his texts do not to breathe new life into these figures, but pay tribute to the obscurity they are shrouded in, fusing the idea of being indebted to others and the celebration of anonymity over identity. The idealization of anonymous writers is not only, as Pautrot suggests, a display of false modesty meant to draw attention to the writer indirectly. Its goal is also to erase the self as writer and author by using intertextuality as well as actual and active collaborations.

In *Albucius*, which presents the life of Gaius Albucius Silus and includes some of the Latin author's surviving literary fragments, the more the writer's own self is buried in invisibility, the more Albucius gains in presence. Not only does the latter's name feature on the cover, implicitly challenging Quignard's own, but, in the sections devoted to Albucius's life, a first-person narrative is often used in lieu of the external point of view expected in biographies, making it difficult for the reader to know whose voice is being heard. When a clearly autobiographical statement by Quignard appears, it is presented as a slippage, caught and incorporated in a narration otherwise exclusively focused on Albucius. In the following passage, for instance: 'Enfant, je descendais au métro Alésia. Je ne savais pas que je rejoignais la terre meuble au pied de la ville entre les murs des Gaulois et les fossés de César' [When I was a child, I'd go down to the metro at Alesia station. I didn't realize I was penetrating the loose soil at the base of the city between Gallic walls and Caesarian ditches],[24] the autobiographical information is kept to a minimum, and the descent into the Paris metro becomes an image for the Orphic quest, a reference to myth rather than personal memory. Reading *Albucius*, Simon Kemp argues that '[through] confessional asides and fragments of personal memory [...] a picture of Quignard's life gradually emerges, which often suggests a personal, private dimension to topics presented in the text as neutral or universal'.[25] But the process can also be read as the reverse of what Kemp describes. In *Albucius*, references to the self depart from the realm of the real and the subjective to serve as a transition to the era of Albucius.

Les Tablettes de buis d'Apronenia Avitia, published six years before *Albucius*, displays a similar structure and intent. It is a biography of Apronenia Avitia, a Roman writer of the turn of the fourth century AD, with translations of her literary fragments. Yet, as mentioned earlier, Avitia is an invention on the part of Quignard. This is never explicitly stated in the text, which relies on precise, genuine sources to convince readers of Avitia's actual existence, stating for instance that:

> Il n'existe qu'une édition des lettres et des tablettes de buis. Elle figure dans la réédition parisienne de 1604 du recueil de Fr. Juret [...]. Les *Epistolae* d'Apronenia Avitia figurent aux folios 342 à 481 de la réédition parisienne de 1604.

> [There exists only a single edition of the letters and the wooden tablets. This appears in the Paris 1604 reissue of Father Juret's collection [...]. Apronenia Avitia's *Epistolae* appear in folios 342 to 481 of the Paris 1604 reissue.][26]

In an interview recently published, Quignard explains that this text was written in honour of his maternal grandmother, 'Marie Bruneau [qui] m'a appris à lire [...]. Quand elle est morte, j'ai écrit ce récit' [Marie Bruneau, who taught me how to read. I wrote this text after she died].[27] A personal event, the death of Marie Bruneau, is what triggers the production of a text rather than what defines its significance. On top of this autobiographical base, a game of shadows is played, which dissolves the figure of the maternal grandmother beyond recognition, and gives Avitia a universal quality, amplified by her fictitious rather than real nature. The content of her tablets is also universal because their material is purely intertextual, made from a multitude of voices borrowed from various eras and civilizations: that of the Roman man of letters Quintus Aurelius Symmachus, the Chinese poet Li Shangyin, and the Japanese author Sei Shōnagon.[28]

The hypothetical support for this intertextual content — Avitia's wooden tablets — introduces another dimension to the text by endowing the act of writing with an evident materiality. This is repeated and amplified throughout Quignard's work, especially in his collaborations with contemporary visual artists. In *Pierre Skira, Marie Morel & Valerio Adami*, a text devoted to three contemporary artists Quignard has worked with, he describes what his participation in a painting by Marie Morel entails: 'je notais des groupes de mots sur des petits cartons qu'elle avait découpés et peints en gris' [I would jot down groups of words on small pieces of cardboard which she had previously cut up and painted grey].[29] Rather than a text containing meaning, the writer talks of a physical intervention applied to a predominantly visual object, which highlights the dimensions, the colour of the words, and their position in the final painting.

Furthermore, Quignard's projects with visual artists allow his writing to become a physical act devoted to the production of invisibility. The etcher Pierre Skira defines his collaborations with Quignard as a series of 'monuments', a term which gives them a clear material and physical presence. Writing about a collaborative work entitled 'Ultima', Skira describes 'un monument de presque trois mètres cinquante de haut et de quatre mètres de large, [qui] réunit quinze panneaux comme quinze rayonnages d'une bibliothèque où la couleur de la nuit a envahi les livres' [a monument three and half metres high and four metres long, composed of fifteen panels like library bookshelves, where books are shrouded in darkness].[30] The main subject of this work is thus the obscuration of literature: books are represented in a painting that renders them invisible. The transformation of the text into a visual presence paradoxically leads to the representation of its absence.

Quignard's collaborations, from projects with contemporary artists to the prac-tice of an extreme form of intertextuality in texts that host a series of obscure or invented authors, illustrate how his desired solitude is fundamentally immersed in the presence of others. This is the idea at the heart of his text *Sur l'idée d'une commu-nauté de solitaires*, which is divided in part into brief chapters each devoted to an obscure figure, such as Georges de La Tour and M. de Sainte-Colombe. Moreover, it regroups two texts 'Les Ruines de Port-Royal' ('The Ruins of Port-Royal') and 'Compléments aux ruines' ('In Addition to the Ruins'), originally written to be read in public in collaboration with musicians. The act of writing is characterized by a devotion to others also visible in Quignard's collaborations with artists such as Morel and Skira, and with contemporary composers and musicians like Jordi Savall, Michèle Reverdy, the choreographer Angelin Preljocaj, and the dancer Carlotta Ikeda. By welcoming others into his texts, Quignard's intention is to abandon the status of writer and adopt the ultimately empty and absent position of reader. His attitude also implies that writing amounts to a vanishing act: the disappearance of writing into other art practices, and the dissolution of the self to make space for other lost figures.

Self-Dissolution

Some critics have argued that Quignard's paradoxical reliance on the works of others is driven by the desire to produce a form of veiled self-writing, and they identify autobiography as the main discourse hiding behind such collaborations. But as the first part of this chapter has shown, if autobiographical elements are indeed used as textual materials, they seem to be included in texts that aim for the impersonal. Whilst the extreme form of intertextuality and the collaborative dimension of the work imply the disappearance of writing in a visual sense, the recourse to fiction allows the elaboration of another type of vanishing. The protagonists in Quignard's novels share a tendency towards solitude and they are often driven by the same desire to retreat from society that Quignard has expressed. This is portrayed through various themes in different works: depression in *Carus* (*Carus*), love in *Vie secrète*, an extreme form of mourning in *Les Solidarités mystérieuses* (*Obscure Solidarities*), and a voluntary disappearance in *Villa Amalia* (*Villa Amalia*). Just as the obscure figures in Quignard's texts are not mere avatars whose function would be to allow an oblique form of self-writing, the characters in the novels are not merely fictional doubles of the writer's self. The representation of fictional disappearances is associated rather with a desire to erase the self and to return to a complete fusion and non-differentiation with the outer world.

Villa Amalia is the novel that deals most directly with the theme of disappearance. It tells the story of Eliane Hildenstein, a composer and pianist working under the stage name Ann Hidden, who decides to leave her old life behind. At the opening of the novel, Ann begins a process that starts with the break-up of a relationship, the sale of the house she shared with her partner, and the destruction of her personal belongings.[31] Ann also resigns from her various professional activities, giving up the stage and leaving a job in a record company. As she finally leaves, making sure that no one will find her, she settles in Ischia, an island in the Bay of Naples. Whilst her life there is one of retreat, Ann is not alone. She forms new relationships: with Leonhart, a man she meets in Italy, with Magdalena, his infant daughter, and with Juliette and Charles Chegogne, a couple on the brink of separation whom she befriends on the island. She also returns to her home town in Brittany, first to visit her ailing mother and later to bury her. At the funeral, she is reconciled with her father, from whom she has been estranged since he abandoned her as a child. Finally, she maintains a constant contact with Georges, a childhood friend who, having lost both his mother and his partner, is affected by a more obvious and constraining form of solitude than she is. After leaving Italy towards the end of the novel, Ann moves in with Georges on the estate he owns in Yonne, and lives there with him until his death.

Ann's initial disappearance and the life that follows is firstly represented in spatial terms. Interactions with people are not what matter most in *Villa Amalia*, and Ann's decision to vanish is shown as an evolution rather than a sudden resolve: she is described from the start as a distant figure, somewhat aloof and disconnected. Despite the plot's clear progression, a sense of stillness is instilled in the novel as Ann's existence is defined by retreat. Moreover, she remains completely alienated from the reader: her interiority is never revealed by a narrative voice that operates in a constantly deceptive way. The first parts of the novel are told by what seems to be an omniscient exterior narrator, although neither Ann's thoughts nor her actions are explained. The clue to this maintained distance is given in the fourth part of the text, where the narrator's identity is suddenly revealed: it is Charles Chegogne, one of *Villa Amalia*'s secondary characters, who is also the protagonist of *Le Salon du Wurtemberg* (*The Salon in Württemberg*), an earlier novel by Quignard.

This revelation creates an obvious confusion for readers. As they follow Ann through the various events of her life, the awareness that the story is told from the point of view of Chegogne creates constant doubt as to what is being told and highlights the fictional status of the text. Ann's ungraspable nature is further underscored by her fluid identity, and the various names she adopts throughout the story. Her real name is Éliane Hildenstein, yet she is also 'Anne [...] celle qui ne voulait pas qu'on l'appelle Éliane' [Anne [...] who doesn't want to be called Éliane],[32] Anna in Italy, and Ann Hidden on the stage. This stage name, which clearly reveals her preference for solitude and retreat, also makes her seem like one of Marguerite Duras's heroines, highlighting her identity as a fictional and literary character. The use of motifs such as the piano and the sea, and the relation between Ann and the young child Magdalena, evoke Duras's *Moderato Cantabile* and its main character Anne Desbaresdes.[33] In *Villa Amalia*, the meaning of the name 'Hidden' is presented as a reference to a past situated outside the story: it was chosen for Ann by an ex-lover, who named her after a mountain, the Hidden Peak situated on the border of China and Pakistan.[34] For Ann — as for Quignard — loyalty to the dead and the fictional replaces pre-existing forms of identity.

The fact that Ann is named after a geographical location points once more to the importance of places and their names in the novel. *Villa Amalia* can be read as a series of moving-outs and moving-ins: a succession of metaphors. As Quignard

notes, *metaphora,* 'transport', is used for the act of moving house in modern Greek.[35]
The journeys back and forth between Ann's homes function as metaphors for her
various states of mind, making up for the text's lack of narrative insight. It is when
standing outside his lover's home that Ann becomes aware of her partner's infidelity.
It is also there that she meets her childhood friend Georges, just as he is going into
the house of his deceased mother. Similarly, Ann's departure for Italy is dependent
on the emptying-out and sale of her own home, almost directly followed by the
purchase of the one located on Georges's estate. Finally, Villa Amalia, the house
where Ann lives in Ischia, gives the novel its title, and stands for Ann's desire to
vanish.

The villa is described as being almost unreachable, situated at the end of a long
and impracticable pathway: secluded, sitting on an island and carved directly into
the rock of a cliff, it is lost amongst nature. It is portrayed as a haunted place, built
in the nineteenth century for a woman named Amalia, who died before she could
inhabit it.[36] Dedicated to a dead figure, it stands not only as a place of solitude but
one where self-dissolution becomes possible:

> [Ann] aimait de façon passionnée, obsédée, la maison de zia Amalia, la terrasse,
> la baie, la mer. Elle avait envie de disparaître dans ce qu'elle aimait. [...] Mais ce
> n'était plus un homme qu'elle aimait ainsi. C'était une maison qui l'appelait à la
> rejoindre. C'était une paroi de montagne où elle cherchait à s'accrocher. C'était
> un recoin d'herbes, de lumière, de lave, de feu interne où elle désirait vivre.

> [Ann was passionately in love, obsessed even, with Zia Amalia's house, with
> its terrace, with the bay, with the sea. She wanted to disappear into what she
> loved. [...] It wasn't a man she loved any more. It was a house and it was calling
> to her. It was a rock wall she was trying to climb. A grassy recess, filled with
> light, lava, and internal fire: this was where she wanted to live.][37]

The house's field of attraction is explicitly presented as a replacement for human
relations. The specific nature of this attraction is modelled on the death drive,
defined by Freud as 'the task of which is to lead organic life back into the inanimate
state'.[38] Villa Amalia is literally a fusion of water and rock, standing for the
possibility of reaching an inanimate state. Rock is used as a poetic motif throughout
the novel, to express the figurative transformation of the protagonist into a lifeless
and natural object. Just as Ann's chosen name comes from a mountain, the novel's
final chapter portrays the protagonist with a mineral vocabulary: 'la vieillesse et la
solitude la rendirent plus osseuse. Son corps était devenu raide. Sa chevelure était
devenue entièrement blanche' [as old age and solitude became part of her life, she
became bonier. Her body was stiff, and her hair had turned completely white].[39]

Water is also part of the representation of the death drive that consumes Ann:
whilst the mineral theme expresses the return to an inanimate organic state, the
liquid realm represents a matrix-like place of origins, where the idea of self is
dissolved. Water is linked to the maternal, and Villa Amalia, buried within a cliff
and surrounded by the sea, is a womb-like space. The desire to be immersed within
this space calls for the return to a primitive fusion with the mother's body, one that
precedes parturition and the creation of the self. Birth is defined in Quignard's
work as the original event of separation, simultaneous with the end of a pure

synthesis with the rest of the world. In *Boutès* (*Butes*), the narrator states that: 'nous ne venons pas du sec [...]. La vie que nous menons est comme une terre étrangère à cette mer ancienne qui n'était que mouvement dans la pénombre' [we do not come from dry land. Our lives take place on foreign land, away from that ancient sea, which was nothing but movement and darkness].[40] As Rabaté notes, *Villa Amalia* offers a fictional representation of the oceanic feeling defined by Freud.[41] To try and return to this state, characterized as infancy's primitive ego, where the limits between the self and the outer world do not yet exist, has deathly consequences. As Elisabeth Roudinesco notes, 'when [the individual] regresses to primary narcissism, he is lost in a maternal and deathly imago'.[42] Quignard implicitly refers to this idea when he writes, in *Boutès*, that 'rejoindre la condition originaire c'est mourir' [going back to our original condition means dying].[43]

In *Villa Amalia,* water stands as a space where death is a necessary horizon. This idea ripples through Quignard's work as a whole, where it is expressed through the recurring theme of drowning. *Villa Amalia*'s fourth part opens with a scene in which Ann almost drowns but is saved by the arrival of Charles Chegogne. *Boutès* for its part centres on the obscure and mythical Butes, defined in the text as an anti-heroic figure. Unlike Odysseus, Butes, one of the Argonauts, did not resist the song of the Sirens and dived in the water to join them. The proximity of water and death is also developed into an idealization of suicide, for instance in *La Barque silencieuse*, which dwells on what is described as 'le mot magnifique et liquide de suicide' [the magnificent, liquid word 'suicide'],[44] defined also as 'la pointe extrême de la liberté humaine' [the outermost point of human liberty].[45] Similarly, melancholia, which through its etymological root contains the idea of liquidity, is a favoured motif. For example, the novel *Carus* tells the story of a musician named A. who, as Jean-Pierre Richard puts it: 'découvre qu'il est vide à l'intérieur' [discovers the void within him].[46] Richard notes how depression is presented in Quignard's work as 'une sorte d'être au monde, même si elle s'acharne à détruire l'idée de monde et à ruiner celle d'être' [a way of being in the world, despite its intent on getting rid of both the world and the self].[47] In *Lycophron et Zétès*, depression is presented not only as a way of life but also a way of writing for Quignard, who mentions 'la dépression nerveuse durant laquelle j'écrivis *Le Lecteur*' [the period of mental breakdown during which I wrote *Le Lecteur*].[48] This revelation regarding the text that marks Quignard's entry into literary writing suggests that depression — and the desire to leave the social realm and to dissolve the self which it implies — is inextricable from the act of writing. This is perhaps because writing, and especially the production of fiction such as *Le Lecteur, Carus*, and *Villa Amalia*, offers the possibility of achieving forms of disappearance that in reality could only be experienced through death or acute mental suffering. It is as such that Quignard's fictional texts express the desire to explore, outside of real existence and through the specific means allowed by literature, the possibility of making the self disappear.

The novel *Les Solidarités mystérieuses,* published in 2011, illustrates this by taking up many of the elements and themes developed in previous texts and developing them further. As Jerôme Garcin puts it: 'Claire, l'héroïne des *Solidarités mystérieuses*, est du même sang qu'Ann, la pianiste de *Villa Amalia*: ce sont des femmes qui abandonnent tout et partent un jour de chez elles sans se retourner' [Claire, the protagonist of Quignard's *Solidarités mystérieuses*, and Ann, in *Villa Amalia*, are birds of the same feather. They are women who one day decide to leave everything behind, without ever turning back].[49] The two texts form a diptych, which portrays two complementary female figures. Like Ann, Claire grew up by the sea in Brittany, and the land of her childhood is marked by the same presence of rock and water that characterizes Ann's Italian home. In the beginning of the novel, Claire's return to her childhood village is conveyed through an enumeration that fuses solidity and liquidity: 'elle reconnaissait les blocs de granite, les buissons, les sentiers, les vieux murs, les escaliers escarpés, la mer, le vacarme de la mer' [she recognized the granite boulders, the bushes, the coastal paths, the old decrepit walls, the steep stairs leading towards the roaring sea].[50]

Another similarity between Ann and Claire is their estrangement from family. Like Ann, Claire is marked by solitude: her parents and little sister died when she was a child and, at the beginning of the novel, she has no contact with Paul, her brother and the only remaining member of her immediate family. A voluntary form of abandonment follows this initial isolation, as the reader learns that Claire abandoned her own family just after the birth of her second daughter.[51] The extreme form of independence that Claire and Ann embody is typical of a larger trend in Quignard's texts, where, as Lapeyre-Desmaison notes, 'les personnages redoublent [...] l'exclusion dont ils ont été victimes par une exclusion seconde, délibérément choisie celle-ci' [an imposed form of exclusion precedes a further exclusion, this time voluntary rather than endured].[52] The characters' refusal to form or belong to a family is symbolized, in *Les Solidarités mystérieuses* as in *Villa Amalia*, by the protagonist's frequent name changes. As stated by one of the characters, Claire is 'Marie-Claire, ou Claire, ou Clara, ou Chiara'.[53] In the course of the novel, Madame Ladon, who taught her to play the piano as a child, legally adopts her so she can pass on her house to Claire after her death, implying another name change for the character. Ladon's farmhouse is also, like Villa Amalia, a secluded and liminal space:

> Le chemin qui conduisait à l'ancienne ferme s'était effacé dans l'herbe. [...] C'était une petite cour devenue un pré, un grand verger à demi mort, une grosse mare près de la barrière entourée d'un demi-cercle de grands roseaux vivaces.
>
> [The path leading to the old farmhouse had become buried in the grass. The courtyard was now a field, a large orchard on the brink of death. Next to the gate, tall and healthy reeds formed a half-circle around a large pond.][54]

Water from the nearby ocean invades the land on which the house stands. The latter, lost in the highlands, is an in-between space ('à demi', 'demi-cercle') marking the fusion between life and death, earth and sea, and the human and natural realms. As Claire moves into the house, she begins a process of transformation, which sees her becoming more and more immersed in nature, until the end of the novel, where her mysterious disappearance is announced.

Whilst Claire's vanishing remains unsolved in the novel, Quignard came back to it in 2013, with the publication of *La Suite des chats et des ânes*, co-written with Mireille Calle-Gruber. There he describes *Les Solidarités mystérieuses* as the story of 'une femme qui devient un chat' [a woman who turns into a cat].[55] This belated intervention by the author, who retrospectively closes his novel's open ending, ultimately obscures more than it clarifies. It suggests a shift from the merely uncanny to the wondrous, to echo Tzvetan Todorov's definition of the fantastic genre,[56] and moves the novel away from a sense of reality and verisimilitude. The irrationality this supposes is implicitly suggested in *Les Solidarités mystérieuses* through the use of different internal narrative voices, which successively shed a partial and subjective light on the events that make up the text. The novel is divided into five parts, each bearing the name of a different protagonist. They form a series of characters taking charge of the same story: Claire, Simon [Claire's first love, with whom she is reunited after her return to Brittany], Paul [Claire's brother who comes live with her after she moves into the farm], Juliette [her estranged daughter who appears towards the end of the novel], and finally 'voix sur la lande' [voices on the heath].

The distancing effect created by the sudden appearance of Charles Chegogne as the narrator in *Villa Amalia* is repeated and intensified in *Les Solidarités mystérieuses*. Claire's own voice never intervenes, and the part bearing her name is told in the third person. The succession of several narrative voices in the novel's last section, instead of offering the reader a better insight into the protagonist's mindset, only obscures the story further. This peculiar narrative structure echoes Louis-René des Forêts's work *Les Mendiants* (*The Beggars*), which is also told through various narrative viewpoints. According to des Forêts, they function as monologues, with each of the narrative voices existing independently of others and without any possibility of communication between them:

> Chacun de mes personnages est enfermé dans une solitude inexorable [...] son destin est d'avancer dans la vie comme dans un étroit tunnel d'où il cherche désespérément à sortir et où il ne parle que pour lui seul. En ce sens le monde profond de leur langage est bien le monologue: ce ne peut être le dialogue.

> [My characters are prisoners of an inexorable solitude. They are destined to live as if stuck in a narrow tunnel, which they are desperately trying to exit and where no one can hear them. It is in that sense that the linguistic world they share is a monologue rather than a dialogue.][57]

This description could be applied to the narrators in *Les Solidarités mystérieuses*, who take turns to tell the story of Claire's metamorphosis and final disappearance. Juliette explains how 'le paysage, au bout d'un certain temps, [...] venait vers [Claire] et c'est le lieu lui-même qui l'insérait en lui, la contenait d'un coup, venait la protéger [...] comme si elle n'était plus un être humain' [after a while the landscape came towards Claire; she felt suddenly wrapped up by the surrounding space; incorporated and protected by it, it was as if she was no longer human].[58] As each secondary character describes Claire's vanishing, the novel takes on a mythical nature. If, according to Quignard, *Les Solidarités mystérieuses* is the story of a woman transformed into a cat, it can also be read as a rewriting of the myth of Narcissus and Echo found in Ovid's *Metamorphoses*. In this mythical tale, Echo, a mountain nymph in love with an oblivious Narcissus, slowly withers away, until — to borrow a phrase from Quignard's *Le Sexe et l'effroi* (*Sex and Terror*) — 'il ne resta plus de l'amoureuse que la voix et les os [et] les os se transformèrent en rochers' [all that remains of the impassioned nymph is her voice and her bones. The bones turn into rocks].[59] In Ovid's myth, Echo's voice is the only thing that remains, yet Claire's own voice stays silent throughout *Les Solidarités mystérieuses*. This hints at questions the following chapter will explore, such as the opposition to language and the celebration of silence in Quignard's work, and the rewriting of collective forms of narrative such as myths and fairy tales. It appears for now that novels such as *Villa Amalia* and *Les Solidarités mystérieuses* are not purely about an expression of individuality or a veiled form of self-writing. Through the lack of character psychology, associated with a repeated use of periphrastic names and a reliance on collective forms of narrative and mythical imagery, Quignard's novels lean towards the universal rather than the personal. Myths, folk tales and fairy tales allow the writer to portray self-disappearance in a more condensed and effective way than in the novels: the former genres allowing more to be said than the latter, but with fewer words.

Coming back to the question of self-writing and the importance of solitude in Quignard's work, a final example, taken from *Villa Amalia*, involves the narrator Charles Chegogne and a revealing self-portrait:

> un civil au visage glabre, maigre, ridé, s'appuyait sur le mur. [..] Il était chauve, de rares cheveux blonds autour des oreilles, des lunettes rondes cerclées de fer, des grands yeux pâles. [...] Il allait mourir. C'était moi.

> [A civilian whose face was smooth, thin and wrinkled, was leaning on a wall. He was bald, except for some flecks of blond hair around his ears, with round metal-framed glasses in front of his big pale eyes. He was going to die. He was me.][60]

The sudden change from 'il' to 'moi' has a striking effect on the reader; an effect intensified by the fact that this portrait corresponds to both Charles Chegogne and Pascal Quignard. This could suggest that fiction is used to offer an indirect reflection of the writer's self. But the features that Chegogne displays, and which are modelled on Quignard's own, are typical not of the writer but of a certain type of man, embodied by the figure of a lost parent, 'l'oncle admirable, rescapé du camp de Dachau' [Quignard's admired uncle, a Dachau survivor]:

> Lorsque mon père est mort, je me suis mis à ressembler [à cet oncle] jusqu'à avoir son crâne chauve et porter ses lunettes rondes. J'adoptai le physique de l'intellectuel par excellence. Cet oncle, qui était le frère de ma mère, Anne Bruneau, s'appelait Jean Bruneau, [...] Eh bien voilà, je voulais devenir Jean Bruneau, c'est-à-dire un érudit absolu, je voulais être un homme du livre.

> [When my father died, I began to look like my uncle: I too was bald and I wore the same round glasses. I adopted the quintessential look of the intellectual. My uncle, who was my mother's brother, was named Jean Bruneau: well, I wanted to be Jean Bruneau — that is to say I wanted to become a perfect scholar, a bookish man.][61]

By describing his own metamorphosis, the writer shows once more how fidelity to the dead can replace other forms of identity. His physical traits, he tells us, are not truly his but his uncle's, and beyond the figure of Jean Bruneau hides the more general type of the scholar. Here, Quignard mentions 'l'homme du livre' as one would 'l'homme des cavernes' [a caveman]; suggesting that the book becomes a space, a territory by which to be defined, in direct opposition to reality and to social existence. Quignard is not Narcissus, a man obsessed with his own reflection, but the nymph Echo, whose existence, marked by invisibility and her final disappearance into nature, is devoted solely to the act of calling out to the one she has lost.

Notes to Chapter 1

1. *LBS*, p. 63. *LBSe*, p. 72.
2. Pascal Quignard, *Sur l'idée d'une communauté de solitaires* (Paris: Arléa, 2015), pp. 28–29.
3. Quoted in Pascal Quignard, *Michel Deguy* (Paris: Seghers, 1975), p. 60.
4. Jean-Louis Pautrot, 'Dix questions à Pascal Quignard', *Études Françaises*, 40 (2004), 87–92 (p. 87).
5. Quoted in Pascal Quignard, *L'Être au balbutiement, essai sur Sacher-Masoch* (Paris: Mercure de France, 1969), p. 139. See Jacques Lacan, *Écrits* (Paris: Le Champ freudien, Seuil, 1966), p. 709; *Écrits: The First Complete Edition in English*, trans. by Bruce Fink (New York: Norton, 2006), p. 594, where it is preceded by the following: 'the points at which the subject disappears under the being of the signifier; whether it is a question, indeed, of being oneself, being a father, being born, being loved, or being dead [...]'
6. Pascal Quignard, *Le Vœu de silence sur Louis-René des Forêts* (Fontfroide-le-Haut: Fata Morgana, 1985), p. 47. This is a reference to Louis-René des Forêts, 'Les Grands Moments d'un chanteur' in *La Chambre des enfants* (Paris: Gallimard, 1960), pp. 104–54. 'The Great Moments of a Singer' in *The Children's Room*, trans. by Jean Stewart (London: John Calder, 1963), pp. 131–71.
7. Pautrot, 'Dix questions à Pascal Quignard', p. 87.
8. Pascal Quignard, *Le Lecteur* (Paris: Gallimard, 1976), p. 125.
9. Pascal Quignard, *Lycophron et Zétès* (Paris: Gallimard, 2010), p. 154.
10. See Bruno Blanckeman, *Les Récits indécidables, Jean Echenoz, Hervé Guibert, Pascal Quignard* (Villeneuve d'Ascq: Presses Universitaires du Septentrion, 2000), p. 167. Also Jean-Louis Pautrot, 'Pascal Quignard et la pensée mythique', *French Review*, 76 (2003), 752–64 (p. 754).
11. 'L'énigme Agustina Izquierdo. Est-ce Quignard qui narre ?', *Le Nouvel Observateur*, 15 April 1993, p. 96.
12. *LS*, p. 105.
13. *LZ*, p. 149.
14. *LBS*, p. 12. *LBSe*, p.7. My translation for 'Quai de la fausse rivière'.
15. *LZ*, p. 149. In *Tous les matins du monde*, the protagonist M. de Sainte-Colombe composes and plays music in a small hut in his garden next to a mulberry tree.
16. Chantal Lapeyre-Desmaison, *Mémoires de l'origine* (Paris: Flohic, 2001), p. 291.
17. *LL*, p. 11.
18. Marc Dambre and Bruno Blanckeman organized a guest lecture with Pascal Quignard, as part of the series 'Écrire la modernité' and the research group *'Proses narratives en France, 2001–2010'* set up by the CERACC at the Sorbonne Nouvelle-Université Paris 3 in 2010. As the proceedings were not published, this reference is based on personal notes taken at the time.
19. *LZ*, p. 138.
20. Jean-Louis Cros, dir., *Pascal Quignard, 'Tous les matins du monde'* (Futuroscope/SCEREN-CNDP, 2011) [DVD].
21. Jean-Louis Pautrot, *Pascal Quignard ou le fonds du monde* (Amsterdam: Rodopi, 2007), pp. 9–10.
22. Roland Barthes, 'La mort de l'auteur', p. 67. 'The Death of the Author', trans. by Richard Howard, p. 53.
23. Jean-Pierre Salgas and Pascal Quignard, 'Écrire n'est pas un choix mais un symptôme', *La Quinzaine littéraire*, 565 (1990) <http://www.quinzaine-litteraire.presse.fr/articles/entretiens/pascal-quignard-ecrire-n-est-pas-un-choix-mais-un-symptome.php> [accessed 4 June 2015] (para. 8 of 45).
24. Pascal Quignard, *Albucius* (Paris: P.C.L, 1990), p. 45. *Albucius*, trans. by Bruce Boone (Venice, CA: The Lapis Press, 1992), p. 33.

25. Simon Kemp, *French Fiction into the Twenty-First Century, The Return to the Story* (Cardiff: University of Wales Press, 2010), p. 54.
26. Pascal Quignard, *Les Tablettes de buis d'Apronenia Avitia* (Paris: Gallimard, 1984), pp. 15–16. *On Wooden Tablets: Apronenia Avitia*, trans. by Bruce X (Providence, RI: Burning Deck, 2001), p. 12.
27. Chrystelle Claude, 'Les Stèles du recueillement, un dialogue avec Pascal Quignard', *L'Esprit Créateur*, 52 (2012), 3–11 (p. 4).
28. Camilo Bogoya, '*Les Tablettes de buis d'Apronenia Avitia*, à la recherche du manuscrit perdu', *L'Esprit Créateur*, 52 (2012), 12–21 (pp. 18–19).
29. Pascal Quignard, *Pierre Skira, Marie Morel & Valerio Adami* (Paris: Éditions des cendres, 2010), p. 9.
30. Pierre Skira, 'De l'amitié', in *Pascal Quignard ou la littérature démembrée par les muses*, pp. 101–03 (p. 103).
31. Pascal Quignard, *Villa Amalia* (Paris: Gallimard, 2006), p. 89.
32. *VA*, p.15.
33. Quignard has noted the influence of Marguerite Duras on his writing in *LS*, p. 96, where he answers the question 'Quel autre écrivain vous serait proche?' [Which writer do you feel close to?] by naming, among others, Marguerite Duras.
34. *VA*, p. 218.
35. *LS*, p. 121.
36. *VA*, p. 130.
37. *VA*, p. 136.
38. Sigmund Freud, 'The Ego and the Id', in *The Standard Edition of the Complete Psychological Works of Sigmund Freud*, ed. by James Strachey, 24 vols, (London: Vintage, 2001), XIX, pp. 3–68 (p. 40) (first publ. 1923).
39. *VA*, p. 295.
40. Pascal Quignard, *Boutès* (Paris: Galilée, 2008), pp. 22–23.
41. Dominique Rabaté, *Pascal Quignard, étude de l'œuvre* (Paris: Bordas, 2008), p. 115.
42. Elisabeth Roudinesco, 'The Mirror Stage, an Obliterated Archive', trans. by Barbara Bray, in *The Cambridge Companion to Lacan*, ed. by Jean-Michel Rabaté (Cambridge: Cambridge University Press, 2003), pp. 25–34 (p. 30).
43. *BO*, p. 72.
44. *LBS*, p. 78. *LBSe*, p. 90.
45. *LBS*, p. 92. *LBSe*, p. 109.
46. Jean-Pierre Richard, 'Sensation, dépression, écriture', in *L'État des choses, études sur huit écrivains d'aujourd'hui* (Paris: Gallimard, 1990), pp. 39–66 (p. 42). This article was first published in *Poétique*, 71 (1987), 357–74.
47. Ibid., p. 41.
48. *LZ*, p. 208.
49. Jérôme Garcin and Pascal Quignard, 'Les Pensées de Pascal (Quignard)', *Le Nouvel Observateur*, 28 September 2011 <http://bibliobs.nouvelobs.com/romans/20110928.OBS1315/les-pensees-de-pascal-quignard.html> [accessed 4 June 2015] (para. 9 of 34).
50. Pascal Quignard, *Les Solidarités mystérieuses* (Paris: Gallimard, 2011), pp. 23–24.
51. *LSM*, p. 36.
52. *LS*, p. 9.
53. *LSM*, p. 106.
54. *LSM*, p. 52.
55. Pascal Quignard and Mireille Calle-Gruber, *La Suite des chats et des ânes* (Paris: Presses Sorbonne nouvelle, 2013), p. 12.
56. Tzvetan Todorov, *The Fantastic: A Structural Approach to a Literary Genre*, trans. by Richard Howard (Cleveland, OH: Case Western Reserve University Press, 1973).
57. Louis-René des Forêts, *Lettre sur 'Les Mendiants'* (Paris: La Bibliothèque Littéraire, 1991), p. 8. This letter was written by des Forêts in 1943 to the critic Roger Vincent, in response to an article published by Vincent that same year in *Demain*.
58. *LSM*, pp. 216–17.

59. Pascal Quignard, *Le Sexe et l'effroi* (Paris: Gallimard, 1994), p. 257. *Sex and Terror*, trans. by Chris Turner (Calcutta: Seagull Books, 2011), p. 147.
60. *VA*, p. 193.
61. Garcin and Quignard (para. 29 of 34).

CHAPTER 2

❖

From Language to Silence

'Tu vas devenir un personnage de conte' [You'll soon turn into a fairy tale character].[1] This sentence, from a dialogue between Ann and Georges in *Villa Amalia*, could apply more widely to the protagonists found in Quignard's novels. As the previous chapter discusses, *Villa Amalia* and *Les Solidarités mystérieuses* lean towards the universal rather than the subjective, and towards the fantastic rather than the realistic. In other words, as novels centre on the self-dissolution sought by their protagonists, the novelistic genre is emptied of a defining specificity, namely its representation of an individual subjectivity. In his 1936 essay 'The Storyteller', Walter Benjamin focuses on the work of Nikolai Leskov, a Russian writer of the nineteenth century, to determine what distinguishes novelists from storytellers. According to Benjamin, 'the birthplace of the novel is the solitary individual' while 'the teller of fairy tales [as] the first true storyteller' is by contrast involved in the collective sharing of experiences.[2] Because Quignard's novels function simultaneously as places of solitude and of universal experience, they create a bridge between the genres of the novel and the tale as Benjamin defines them. Just as Ann Hidden is portrayed as a budding fairy tale character, *Villa Amalia* is a novel in the process of becoming a *conte*.[3]

Contes as stand-alone texts are a recurring presence in Quignard's ongoing oeuvre. He has published several of them individually, such as *L'Amour conjugal* (*Conjugal Love*), *L'Enfant au visage couleur de la mort* (*The Child With A Face The Colour Of Death*), *Triomphe du temps* (*Triumphant Time*), and *Ethelrude et Wolframm* (*Ethelrude and Wolframm*). Others are included in larger works: in the volumes of *Dernier royaume*, in texts such as *Vie secrète*, and in critical studies, with, for instance, the publication of 'La Voix perdue' ('The Lost Voice') alongside proceedings from a conference on Quignard held in Bologna in 1998.

The absence of psychological insight as a typical quality of *contes* offers a first clue to explain Quignard's predilection for the genre. This absence, already visible in the novels, is even more obvious in the purer, more condensed fictional form of the *conte*, as he explained in a recent interview:

> Le conte permet l'absence totale de subjectivité (il extermine toute considération psychologique). [...] Cette forme narrative est prélinguistique, est prélittéraire. Dans le conte l'expérience intérieure n'est même plus intime: elle est comme l'expérience que les chats ou les merles éprouvent dans le rêve qu'ils font. Narration hors sujet. [...] Le roman, lui, au contraire du conte, dérive de la littérature.

[The writing of *contes* allows a complete absence of subjectivity (by getting rid of any psychological considerations). Such a narrative form is both pre-linguistic and pre-literary. In *contes*, inner experiences are no longer personal: they are no different from what cats or blackbirds experience in their dreams. This is a narration that is literally off the subject. Novels, on the other hand, derive from literature.][4]

By highlighting a lack of subjectivity in storytelling, Quignard confirms what Benjamin states in 'The Storyteller'. He also goes further in giving *contes* a pre-linguistic and non-human nature, likening it to the content of animal dreams. This proximity between the genre and the realm of the unconscious is an idea borrowed from psychoanalysis, and more specifically the work of Bruno Bettelheim, who writes in his *Uses of Enchantment, the Meaning and Importance of Fairy Tales* that:

Applying the psychoanalytical model of the human personality, fairy tales carry important messages to the conscious, the preconscious, and the unconscious mind, on whatever level each is functioning at the time. By dealing with universal problems, particularly those which preoccupy the child's mind, these stories speak to his budding ego and encourage its development, while at the same time relieving preconscious and unconscious pressures.[5]

Whilst Quignard borrows from Bettelheim the idea that the fairy tale and by extension the *conte* function at a non-conscious level, his view of the genre does not involve a constructive contribution to the child's 'budding ego'. Rather, Quignard's *conte* aims for a primitive and undetermined form of self, a connection with nature rather than society, and a realm that sits outside of literature and language.

This conception of the genre as alien to both literature and language is paradoxical. Storytelling is, by definition, a doubly linguistic act: found in written and literary forms, it is also a specifically oral type of narration. Folktales have been told out loud since time immemorial, and the fairy tales Bettelheim sees as being essential to the child's development are first experienced through hearing. Despite this, Quignard asserts that his *contes* constitute an attack on both speech and writing, in line with a conception of literature defined as 'cet engagement de plus en plus profond, depuis sa source jusqu'à sa fin, dans le silence' [engaging, more and more deeply, from beginning to end, with silence].[6] Quignard first relies on the distinctive metamorphic quality of *contes*, which differentiates them from myths, to pursue further the process of dissolution already in the novels. It is also through the exploitation of their specific orality, intertextuality and traditional intimacy with other art forms that literary fairy tales correspond to the wish to annihilate speech and work towards the physical disappearance of writing.

Tales of Disappearance

As already noted, Quignard's novels point not only to the realm of the fairy tale, but also to the mythical. The protagonists of *Villa Amalia* and *Les Solidarités mystérieuses* evoke Ovid's depiction of Echo, and their deadly attraction to water echoes themes developed in *Boutès*, a text devoted to the mythical Argonaut. Critics have commented at length on the strong mythical influences in Quignard's texts, especially insisting on the predominant presence of the Orphic myth. Pautrot discusses 'l'omniprésence orphique chez Quignard' [the omnipresence of the Orphic myth in Quignard's work],[7] and presents *Le Salon du Wurtemberg, Les Escaliers de Chambord* (*The Chambord Staircase*), *Tous les matins du monde*, and *Terrasse à Rome* as rewritings of the same myth, retelling 'la quête d'une patrie originelle perdue' [the quest for a lost primeval land].[8] He describes an intertextual dialogue between Quignard and Claude Lévi-Strauss, who famously stated that 'les mythes n'ont pas d'auteur' [myths are anonymous].[9] Quignard's conception of myths is indeed indebted to Lévi-Strauss, as his use of the mythical reveals 'moins un désir de véracité historique que la nécessité de garder le fil, d'entretenir une filiation depuis l'origine' [less a wish for historical truth than the necessity to keep track and maintain a link with our origins].[10]

In Pautrot's view, 'l'écriture de contes [...] ressemble fort [...] à une entreprise de production de mythes' [the writing of *contes* is akin to a process of myth production].[11] They both share an absent and unidentified author, and the capacity for constant renewal noted by Lévi-Strauss. Yet the *contes* play a different role from myths in Quignard's work. In *Lycophron et Zétès*, Quignard states that 'les contes ne sont pas les mythes, mais ce qu'il en reste' [*contes* are not myths but what they leave behind].[12] This refers back to Benjamin's 'The Storyteller', where the fairy tale appears as 'a need created by the myth', which 'tells us of the earliest arrangements that mankind made to shake off the nightmare which the myth had placed upon its chest'.[13] In other words, myths express the anguish caused by an absence of connection with the world and the inability of men to make sense of it. They produce a discourse that can only comment on this irresolvable loss. This mythical discourse, as Benjamin and Quignard suggest, differs from the one produced by *contes* and fairy tales, which deal with the consequences of the anguish first expressed through myths. This is achieved, according to Benjamin, by 'liberating magic'.[14] Fairy tales rely on the wondrous and, as Rabaté notes, *contes* belong to 'le monde des métamorphoses [the world of metamorphosis]', where they are 'toutes permises, possibles' [always allowed, always possible].[15] Quignard's various *contes* illustrate this defining use of metamorphosis, drawing on not only on tales of transformation but also dissolution and disappearance.

Le Secret du domaine (*The Secret of the Domain*), republished in 2006 under the title *L'Enfant au visage couleur de la mort*, offers a narrative development of the metamorphosis and subsequent disappearance of the reader that *Le Lecteur* first introduced. Set in the undetermined time and place typical of fairy tales, it tells the story of a protagonist only known as 'l'enfant' ['the child']. This unnamed character undergoes a series of metamorphoses, triggered by the departure of his father, who leaves to fight in an unidentified war. The child first becomes an avid reader, and this transformation changes his physical appearance: the more he reads, the weaker his body becomes. Later, the child turns into a monster: he becomes a Medusa figure condemned to kill anyone who meets his gaze. The events that follow anchor the text deeper into the realm of the fairy tale. The child asks for a wife and his mother presents him with three potential spouses. His encounter with the third triggers a new metamorphosis, which turns the child into 'la page enluminée de mille couleurs vives' [a book page illuminated with thousands of vivid colours].[16] At this point, the *conte* seems to have reached the typical fairy-tale happy ending, yet the text continues, describing an ultimate transformation. The child-turned-book is thrown into a fire and the final image is one of immolation, marking the complete annihilation of the protagonist. As this ending shows, metamorphosis in Quignard's *contes* serves a specific purpose: to make the characters of his texts disappear.

L'Enfant au visage couleur de la mort focuses on metamorphosis as a means of disappearance and as such holds a special place in Quignard's work. In this *conte*, the motif of fire clearly functions as the catalyst for disappearance. Yet in others, Quignard relies on the motif of water — already present in his novels — to depict the self-dissolution of his characters. 'La Voix perdue' tells the story of a young man named Jean. His parents die in an accident at the beginning of the text, and Jean decides to settle in the town where the accident took place. From then on, it becomes clear that the *conte* is an adaptation of the nineteenth-century classic fairy-tale 'The Frog Prince' in the version by the Brothers Grimm. This tale tells of a young princess who one day drops a ball at the bottom of a well. A frog appears and promises to retrieve it in exchange for her companionship. The princess accepts, but when it visits her the following evening and climbs into her bed, she throws the frog violently against a wall. By doing so, she unknowingly breaks a spell and allows the handsome prince who had been turned into a frog to take back his original form.[17] Quignard's version borrows some of the tale's original features, but modifies them. In 'La Voix perdue', the frog is a queen rather than a prince, and her kingdom a lake and not a well. 'La Voix perdue' also relies on themes borrowed from myth. Jean is seduced by the frog-queen because of her 'voix irrésistible' [irresistible voice].[18] In a reference to Odysseus' encounter with the Sirens in Homer's *Odyssey*, Jean ties himself to the frame of his bed to hear the queen's song: 'la bouche ouverte, l'oreille dressée, cherchant à se mouvoir [...] sous le charme de sa voix, il désirait se diriger vers elle' [with an open mouth and pricked up ears, he was trying to move [...] under the spell of her voice, he yearned to be near her].[19] When, later in the text, Jean dives into the lake to be with the queen, the reference is to Butes rather than Odysseus. Here, the *conte* uses a reference to myths to underline what they leave behind: in this case, the obscure figure of Butes and the dark, deadly impulse he stands for.

In 'La Voix perdue', water symbolizes the return to an original bond with the maternal realm, as the queen strictly forbids Jean to dive into the lake: 'L'eau est faite pour les petits des hommes. Pas pour les hommes qui sont sortis du ventre de leur mère' [Water is meant for the young of men. Not for those who have already left their mother's womb]. Soon after the burial of Jean's parents on the lake shore, a storm blows up and creates a mudslide, washing the buried bodies into the nearby water. One of the villagers describes the frog-queen as a 'revenante verte' [green spirit], because 'les morts noyés deviennent des rainettes' [the drowned corpses turn into tree frogs].[20] The frog Jean falls in love with is thus implicitly designated as his dead mother, and his love the expression of a death drive — the desire to come back to a primitive form of ego and to the fusion with the maternal it supposes. As in

'La Voix perdue', readings of Quignard's *contes* often rely on the reader's awareness of the psychoanalytical references they contain, yet they reverse the therapeutic role psychoanalysis ascribes to the genre. Rather than enabling the development of the child's self and preparing his or her entry in the social realm, Quignard's *contes* offer adult readers the possibility through fiction to return to origins which in reality could only be reached through death.

This function of the genre is confirmed by two further texts: the story of Nukar included in *Vie secrète* and the tale of the Countess of Hornoc in *La Barque silencieuse*. The former is the rewriting of an Icelandic folktale, transcribed in a collection of folktales published by the Occitan writer Henri Gougaud in 1996.[21] 'Nukar' is the story of 'un vieux garçon [qui] s'appelait Nukar [qui] ne parlait jamais, sauf quand il était seul' [a bachelor named Nukar who never spoke, except when he was alone].[22] In Quignard's version, the initial characterization is expanded through an enumeration of details:

> Nukar [...] ne se lavait plus. [...] il ne chassait plus. Il ne pêchait plus. Il ne parlait plus. Ou du moins il ne parlait que quand il était sûr d'être seul. Et même, alors, il se parlait à lui-même en ayant soin de ne pas utiliser le même langage que celui qui avait cours chez les autres membres du groupe.

> [Nukar no longer washed himself. He no longer hunted or fished. He no longer spoke. Or rather he spoke only when he was certain to be alone. And even then, even though he only spoke to himself, he did so in a language that was different from the one used by his community.][23]

As with 'The Frog Prince' in 'La Voix perdue', Quignard modifies an existing story. In his version, Nukar's initial solitude is turned into an acute form of aloofness the protagonist's unwashed body is the mark of his refusal to live for and with others, and his rejection of communication is doubled by the use of an unintelligible language. In Gougaud's version, sudden news of a beautiful woman living in the next village prompts Nukar to change. He decides to try and find her. When he finally does so, he is so struck by her beauty that he falls senseless: 'si beaux étaient son corps, son regard, sa figure, qu'il tomba à genoux, le front contre le sol, et là perdit le sens' [her body, her gaze, her face were so beautiful that he fell to his knees, his forehead pressed against the ground, and lost consciousness].[24] Later, Nukar and the woman make love, and the bachelor suddenly feels his body disappearing into hers. The story ends the following morning when the young woman wakes up alone, her lover nowhere to be seen. Quignard's version follows broadly the same narrative structure, although it expands the final scene, where love-making is presented as an act leading to self-dissolution. Whilst Gougaud's Nukar merely vanishes, Quignard adds a last twist to the story: the woman wakes up in the morning and urinates in the snow, marking through the excretion of liquid the completion of Nukar's disappearance.[25]

In *La Barque silencieuse*, the story of the Countess of Hornoc is a rewriting of a seventeenth-century cautionary tale, first published as 'Histoire miraculeuse et admirable de la comtesse de Hornoc, flamande, estranglée par le diable, dans la ville d'Anvers, pour n'avoir trouvé son rabat bien godronné, le quinziesme avril 1616' [The miraculous and admirable story of the Countess of Hornoc, a Flemish woman strangled by the devil in the town of Antwerp because her collar was not sufficiently well starched, on the fifteenth of April 1616]. It can be found in one of the volumes of the nineteenth-century writer and historian Edouard Fournier's 'recueil de pièces volantes rares et curieuses en prose et en vers' [collection of rare and unusual ephemera written in prose and in verse].[26] Marianne Closson describes this tale as one of many *canards*, or hoax stories, published in the seventeenth century to scare women away from the sin of vanity and to remind them that God punishes those who disobey him. She notes that the tale is based on the model of the *exempla*, or moral anecdotes, found in medieval literature.[27] This intertextual dimension, in which Quignard participates by recycling the tale, reminds us that *contes* rely on metamorphosis not only for their content but also their form. In *La Barque silencieuse*, the writer transforms a text with a clear moral and religious dimension into an erotic *conte*.

The seventeenth-century version clearly states its edifying function in a moral at the end:

> Cecy doit servyr de miroir exemplaire à tant de poupines qui ne désirent que de paroistre des mieux goderonnées, mieux fardées, avec des faux cheveux et dix mille fatras pour orner ce misérable corps, qui n'est à la fin que carcasse, pourriture, pasture de vers et des plus vils animaux. Dieu leur doint la grâce que ceste histoire leur profite et les convie à amender leurs fautes! Ainsi soit-il.

> [May this serve as a cautionary mirror to all these dolled-up females whose only wish is to appear to have the best starched clothes, the best make-up, adorned with false hair and a jumble of other things on top of a miserable body, which in the end is nothing more than a rotting carcass, food for worms and the vilest of animals. May God grant them grace that from this story they may profit and learn to mend their ways! Amen.][28]

According to the text, the Countess of Hornoc was famous for her vanity. She is presented as someone who really existed, probably better to impress the tale's intended readership. One day, she is invited to a feast, and requests that one of her collars be starched for her. Unhappy with the result, she asks for a second collar, which she also rejects. At this point, the devil appears in the guise of a mysterious and handsome tailor, who presents her with the most beautiful ruff she has ever seen. But when she puts it on, she suffocates and is strangled to death. The tale ends with a metamorphosis, which serves as a second punishment for the countess: her dead body is turned into a black cat — a traditional symbol of prostitution — and the sinful woman is thus deprived of a burial.

In the version included in *La Barque silencieuse*, this posthumous transformation is suggested in an initial description: 'la comtesse de Hornoc avait les yeux noirs. Ses cheveux étaient noirs. Elle était maigre et velue. C'était de longs poils noirs qui n'avait jamais été coupés ou rasés' [the Countess of Hornoc had black eyes. Her hair was black. She was thin and hirsute. She had long, black body hair that had never been cut or shaved].[29] Whilst the first tale uses the motif of animality to condemn the countess's vicious nature, Quignard's *conte* uses it to celebrate Hornoc as a feral and carnal figure. She embodies an inhuman form of violence, biting and kicking to death the two tailors when they fail to prepare her collar. The arrival of the devil, named 'Monsieur de Hel' in Quignard's version, pursues the subversion of the cautionary tale, which slowly transforms into an erotic *conte*. The piece of clothing created by Monsieur de Hel strangles the countess but does not kill her instantly, as first:

> Il se passa quelque chose qui la fit rougir. Au fur et à mesure que son col se resserrait elle sentait que les lèvres de son sexe se distendait à chaque nouveau pas de danse qu'il lui fallait faire. [...] Elle se mit peu à peu à couler. Elle le vit par les traces qu'elle laissait sur le plancher en dansant.

> [Something happened that made her blush. As her collar tightened, she felt the lips of her genitals distend with each new dance step she had to take. [...] Her juices began to flow. She noticed this through the liquid trails it left on the floor.][30]

Hornoc's sexual desire manifests itself through water: as in Nukar's tale, disappearance takes place through the protagonist's transformation into a liquid entity. The reliance on such a psychoanalysis-infused motif, the insistence on physicality over psychology, and the encounters between humanity and animality the *contes* put forward, imply that they are situated in a location Quignard has defined as 'prélinguistique' [pre-linguistic]. This suggests that the effort to produce disappearance is not only aimed at the characters but also, through them, at the content of the *contes* and the words that constitute them. Writing *contes* belongs to a larger enterprise aiming for the destruction of language, both as speech and as written words. It is one of the tactics deployed by the writer to escape language, by expressing its annihilation and by drawing on other forms of art, such as music and dance.

The Vow of Silence

Quignard writes *contes* for adults rather than children. Through these texts, both the writer and his readers can approach the earliest stage of childhood, when separation between the infant and the mother is not consciously accepted, the ego not formed, and language not acquired. The *contes* are dedicated to the memory of this lost primeval state and, as such, are inhabited by a specific figure that haunts and hovers over them: the figure of the silent child. It appears in *L'Enfant au visage couleur de la mort* and in 'Petit traité sur la Méduse' ('Little Treatise on the Medusa'), a brief and explicitly autobiographical text included in Quignard's *Le Nom sur le bout de la langue* (*The Name On the Tip of the Tongue*).[31] This treatise discusses the narrator's childhood and a specific period when, as a child, he decided to keep silent in order to resist what was perceived as an invasion of the self by language.[32] This episode is mentioned in other texts, such as the short essay *Sarx*, which offers a fragmented and poetic reflection on *sark*, the Greek word for flesh, and sarcasm, from *sarkazein*, the tearing of that flesh. A harsh diatribe against language, it defines national tongues as '[des] raclures de violence' [scrapings of violence], and the image of a bloody mouth, 'au milieu du visage nos lèvres sont rouges' [right in the middle of the face, our lips are red], is used to present the entry into the linguistic realm as an irreparable mutilation: 'le langage teint les lèvres comme les mûres' [language stains the lips like mulberries].[33] In 'La Métayère de Rodez' ('The Tenant Farmer's Wife of Rodez'), language is characterized as a bully beating the subject into submission, and the narrator states how 'le corps se met à aimer son persécuteur' [the body starts to feel love for its tormentor].[34] A similar image is conveyed in the recent *Mourir de penser*, where the narrator evokes 'un enfant otage de la voix de la mère' [a child held captive by his mother's voice].[35] In the face of such aggression, the silent child becomes a warrior figure, an active combatant against the invasion of language.

Whilst Quignard presents his story of childhood mutism as autobiographical, it is also deeply indebted to Louis-René des Forêts, who has written about a similar figure. In Quignard's *Le Vœu de silence sur Louis-René des Forêts* (*The Vow of Silence: on Louis-René des Forêts*), literary writing is defined as the attempt to honour an impossible pact made during childhood, a primordial form of resistance against language:

> Un enfant fait vœu de se taire. 'Je jure, dit-il, de ne plus desserrer les lèvres. Plutôt mourir, qu'ils ne m'arrachent un seul mot. [...] Ce silence à la fois sera ma force et il me protègera.'
>
> [A child vows never to speak again: 'I swear never to say another word. I would rather die than letting them get another word out of me. From my silence will come strength and protection.][36]

Des Forêts writes about a child who decided to keep silent, and describes this as an act of defence against 'un adversaire trop puissant' [an all-too-powerful enemy], a way to escape the alienating, aggressive hold of language.[37] Quignard's descriptions of his own experience of mutism draw on the same idea. In 'Petit traité sur la Méduse', for instance, he writes: 'à dix-huit mois, je me suis tu [...]. Je devins ce silence, cet enfant en 'retenue' dans le mot absent sous forme de silence' [I stopped speaking at eighteen months. I became silence itself, a child 'in detention', rooted in the silence created by the absence of words].[38] The narrator's age suggests that what is rejected is not the intelligible, rational and verbal language, but the physical act of speaking itself. Yet for des Forêts as for Quignard, the battle against language can only be sustained for so long, and the childhood pact of silence is doomed to fail. This is because it is based on an obvious and inescapable paradox: as Quignard writes, 'la contradiction est irréductible; c'est comme le ver est dans le fruit que le langage réside dans le vœu de silence' [there is an irreducible contradiction: like the worm in an apple, language resides in the vow of silence].[39] For des Forêts and Quignard, it is precisely this initial dilemma that motivates a later engagement in literature.

This idea is outlined in *Le Vœu de silence sur Louis-René des Forêts*: if the vow of silence made as a child is necessarily broken, because 'qui se tait est "mort" et qui parle "parjure"' [refusing to speak is to 'die' but to speak is to 'betray'], literature is seen as a way to honour one's vow whilst surviving within the realm of language: 'parler en se taisant, parler en silence, s'enfoncer dans le silence tout en demeurant dans le langage [...] tout cela c'est en effet "écrire"' ['writing' means to speak without uttering a word, to speak in silence, to bury oneself in silence whilst still living with language].[40] By defining writing as a way to repair the initial defeat experienced in childhood, Quignard implies that it must also become an offensive act. The writer is presented as a double agent, penetrating the field of the enemy in order to attack it from within. This destruction of language through writing relies on two main stratagems:

> D'une main, parler en se taisant. De l'autre: parler pour ne rien dire. [...] quant à la profération, écrire, quant à la signification, soustraire une à une, à mesure qu'elles se présentent, les thèses avancées dans l'écrit, détruire un à un, à mesure qu'ils prennent corps, les personnages que l'intrigue suscite. D'une part, le sacrifice de la voix, de l'autre, le sacrifice du sens.

> [On the one hand, speaking without saying a word. On the other hand, speaking yet saying nothing. Writing solves the issue of utterance. Regarding the question of signification, one should bring down one by one, as soon as they are presented, the hypotheses presented by the text. One should also break down, one by one, as soon as they start taking shape, the characters created by the plot. On one hand, sacrificing speech, on the other, sacrificing meaning.][41]

The last tactic corresponds to what has been discussed in the first part of this chapter: by making their protagonists disappear, Quignard's *contes* are emptied of their own content, suggesting that they are constituted by absence rather than presence. The first tactic is aimed at speech, as the mere fact of writing down words instead of speaking them amounts for Quignard to a silencing act. It is through the genre of the *conte* that this attack takes place; by perpetuating the idea that most of the genre's material comes from oral culture, its writing can stand for the borrowing of something spoken to turn it into a written, and therefore silent, product.

Quignard's *contes* include in their plots the deficiency of spoken language, and they offer fictional and meta-fictional representations of the destruction of speech they stand for. *Ethelrude et Wolframm*, published in 2006, is a good illustration of this. It contains three protagonists: a young woman, her suitor and a wise older woman. Following the conventions of the genre, Ethelrude, the young woman's name, is periphrastic: because it sounds like *est-elle rude* — which can be read in French as a a question or an exclamatory phrase commenting on the protagonist's abrupt nature — it contains the savagery and violence found in the characters of Quignard's *contes*. It is also a variation on 'Ethelred', a medieval name, whilst Wolframm recalls Wolfram von Eschenbach, the German poet of the late twelfth century. Whilst the text is set in the undefined time and place typical of fairy tales, these names suggest a medieval context for the story. The text begins with the description of a scene frozen in time, where the narrative gaze moves from a broad view encompassing the sky and a countryside landscape, to a close-up of a young blonde girl and of 'les ciseaux posés dans le creux de sa robe, sur la toile tendue entre ses cuisses' [the pair of scissors held in the hollow of her dress, on top of the fabric stretched out between her thighs].[42]

Embroidery, a familiar motif in fairy tales, is also common in medieval texts such as the *Lais* of the twelfth-century French poet Marie de France, where it appears as representation of a specifically feminine type of writing.[43] This is implicitly referred to in the *conte*: whilst Ethelrude is clearly on the side of writing — in the first scene she is shown embroidering a name onto a cloth — Wolframm, the male protagonist, is stuck in a relentless oral discourse, a form of language that creates separation from and within the world. His courtship of Ethelrude takes the form of a series of visits during which he asks her impossible questions, which Etherlude answers with more unanswerable questions. Their exchanges read as a Socratic dialogue gone wrong, which leads to division and suffering rather than truth. The specific content of their conversations exposes language as that which produces separation. To do so, it mimics philosophical discourse's typical assertive tone and abstract vocabulary: 'Pourquoi le désir et la peur ne sont-ils jamais séparés? [...] Pourquoi dans le monde le propre et le sale se sont-ils un jour séparés?' [Why is desire never free from fear? [...] Why did cleanliness one day get separated from dirtiness?].[44]

Whilst Wolframm appears as a defeated and passive figure, Ethelrude, is portrayed as a potent force in the text. Embroidery appears in the *conte* as a form of writing situated outside the realm of the symbolic. It implicitly refers to Julia Kristeva's notion of a pre-linguistic and bodily domain, 'la *chôra* sémiotique' [the semiotic *Chora*]. Borrowed from Plato's *Timaeus*, this 'chôra' is '[une] fonctionnalité pré-verbale, qui ordonne les rapports entre le corps (en voie de se constituer comme corps propre), les objets, et les protagonistes de la structure familiale' [a preverbal functional state that governs the connections between the body (in the process of constituting itself as a body proper), objects, and the protagonists of family structure].[45] In other words, it is a mode of expression that precedes separation from the world and from the mother, the most essential part of the 'protagonists of family structure'. Embroidery becomes an activity that is simultaneously feminine, silent and visual rather than textual: Ethelrude echoes the mythical Penelope, whose weaving is also a tool used to keep her suitors at bay whilst she awaits the return of her husband. To put an end to Wolframm's endless flow of speech, Ethelrude, armed with her scissors and needle, stabs his ears. She turns into a figurative earwig, a *perce-oreille* in French, literally an 'ear-piercer'. This fusion of the maternal and the animal echoes the representation of women in 'La Voix perdue' and in the story of Hornoc. It also turns the confrontation between Ethelrude and Wolframm into the opposition between weaving as a form of non-rational, bodily and animal language on the side of creation, unity and silence, and a masculine and verbal discourse useless in the face of the division that language creates. Ethelrude's true achievement is not a piece of embroidery but rather the destruction of spoken language; the conception of writing she stands for does not aim to produce meaning but to make language disappear. The *conte*, which ends with Wolframm's cries of pain, is a narrative representation of Quignard's definition of literary writing as the sacrifice of speech.

As suggested by the parodic use of the Socratic dialogue in *Ethelrude et Wolframm*, *contes* also entail a sacrifice of meaning. This is achieved through a narrative voice that relies on authority to expose the impossibility of language to produce truth. As Rabaté notes, 'la force assertive de l'œuvre, sa puissance extraordinaire d'affirmation et de définition lui viennent précisément du défaut de vérité qu'elle ne cesse de vouloir nommer' [the work's assertive power, its extraordinary ability to define and affirm, can both be traced back to an enduring will to denounce the impossibility of truth].[46] In Quignard's *contes*, the storyteller is not there to exchange experiences or to engage in a collective form of sharing, but to work against language's pretension to truth and communicability. In *L'Enfant au visage couleur de la mort*, the story begins with a pact made with the reader: 'je prête serment que je ne mentirai pas' [I swear that I will not lie].[47] The narration that follows, seemingly led by ideals of truth and justice, uses a judicial form of speech also found in 'La Métayère de Rodez'. The latter is adapted by Quignard from a legal statement written in 1777, which he defines as 'peut-être le plus beau texte français' [perhaps the most beautiful French text ever written], because of its 'style antipsychologique par excellence' [perfect anti-psychological style].[48] Here, Quignard's use of judicial speech obscures rather than reveals, and aims for the absence of psychology in lieu of truth and justice.

L'Enfant au visage couleur de la mort relies on a language that bans access to its characters' internal lives, and which pretends to be truthful the better to seduce, in the etymological sense of the word: *seducere*, to mislead. Quignard adopts the tactics of a rhetorician and whilst his texts imitate the model of the Socratic maieutic, they follow a Gorgiasian form of rhetoric. The statement at the beginning of the *conte* is an implicit reference to the Greek sophist Gorgias and his *Encomium of Helen*, translated into French by Michel Deguy — a translation quoted by Quignard in his critical essay on the poet. In *L'Enfant au visage couleur de la mort*, the storyteller wishes to 'mettre fin à la mauvaise renommée qui entache [...] [d]es lieux' [put an end to the notorious reputation that tarnishes the land] whilst Gorgias, in his eulogy of Helen of Troy, aims to 'effac[er] par ce discours la mauvaise renommée d'une femme [...] faire disparaître l'injustice du blâme et l'ignorance de l'opinion' [to free the slandered woman from the accusation and to demonstrate that those who blame her are lying; to show what is true and put an end to their ignorance].[49] By adapting Gorgias's words, the *conte* relies on language as a tool of power rather than knowledge and uses the force of language against itself. The authority displayed by the storyteller at the beginning of the story is gradually relinquished as the tale progresses. At the end, it appears that truth can no longer be guaranteed, and the storyteller admits his incapacity to distinguish his own voice from the collective hearsay. In place of the moral usually found at the end of fairy tales, *L'Enfant au visage couleur de la mort* ends on a 'sacrifice of meaning' through writing. The narrator intervenes to comment on the general impossibility of truth, and states his indecision concerning the authenticity of the story that has just been told.

This sacrifice is also achieved in the *conte* through the exploitation of a specific characteristic of the literary fairy tale genre: its reliance on intertextuality. It is typical for writers to capitalize on the illusion that fairy tales are originally oral, collective and uncultured. Charles Perrault in the seventeenth century concealed the highly literary nature of his *Contes* by presenting them as old- wives' tales transcribed by a child — a strategic move in the quarrel that opposed him, and the other Moderns, to the Ancients.[50] Similarly, the Brothers Grimm claimed a nationalistic and folkloric origin for their *Children's and Household Tales*, which actually borrowed from an array of literary sources, including Perrault's *Contes*. Jack Zipes confirms this when he writes that a literary tale 'can only be understood and defined by its relationship to the oral tales as well as to the legend, novella, novel and other literary fairy tales that it uses, adapts and remodels'.[51] Quignard's *contes*, which are explicitly presented as part of a continuous process of textual metamorphosis, exploit this intertextuality to fight against language. As seen previously, his tales display a large range of references, from Icelandic folklore through Greek mythology to seventeenth-century cautionary tales. This intertextuality, and the self-awareness with which it is exposed, highlight the artificial nature of these textual productions. As stated in *Le Vœu de silence sur Louis-René des Forêts*, to write means 'speaking yet saying nothing'; in other words, to use a self-imposed form of *bavardage*. In his critical study on Maurice Scève, Quignard describes a 'secrète, vertigineuse, et fondamentale complicité entre bavarder et écrire' [a secret, dizzying and fundamental complicity between chattering and writing],[52] and borrows a statement from Maurice Blanchot: 'quand on bavarde on ne dit rien de vrai, même si l'on ne dit rien de faux, car l'on ne parle pas vraiment' [when one chatters, one says nothing true, even if one says nothing false, for one is not truly speaking].[53] The performative language of literary fairy tales offers an ideal illustration of *bavardage*,[54] and their intertextual nature enables the writer to use words from a wide array of sources; in 'La Voix perdue' for instance, references to the Brothers Grimm, Homer and Ovid are mixed with forays into science and general knowledge.

The reliance of *contes* on other works of literature shows how the process of disappearance undertaken by writing extends to the texts themselves. By aiming for the destruction of language, the *contes* are not only emptied of their own content, but also subjected to a series of metamorphoses that lead to their disappearance. Quignard's *contes* are frequently the subject of dialogue with other forms of art, especially music and dance. 'La Voix perdue' was written as part of a collaborative project with the choreographer Angelin Preljocaj, and turned into a ballet entitled *L'Anoure (Anura)* in 1995. *Le Nom sur bout de la langue* and the *conte* it contains were produced in collaboration with the composer Michèle Reverdy.[55] This transformation of *contes* into musical works shows how the fight against verbal language affects the texts themselves. Despite the claims made in *Le Vœu de silence sur Louis-René des Forêts*, literature can hardly reconcile the use of language with the wish for its destruction. As a result, Quignard's texts are constantly on the verge of becoming something else, and they are drawn outside the borders of literature towards other arts. Music, especially, plays an essential but ambiguous role, as it is both condemned and embraced in the work. Quignard's *La Leçon de musique (The Music Lesson)*, a 1987 essay in which music is generally idealized, was followed almost ten years later by *La Haine de la musique (Hatred of Music)*, which, as the title suggests, contains a re-evaluation and denunciation of musical expression.[56]

La Leçon de musique can be read as a non-fictional counterpart of *Tous les matins du monde*, as both texts focus on the French baroque composer Marin Marais and portray music as a way to repair the loss of a primeval voice. The primordial state that precedes the formation of the self is symbolized not only by water but also by sound. In 'La Voix perdue', it is primordially the voice of the frog, 'voix tenue, merveilleuse, invisible' [that fine, wondrous and invisible voice],[57] that Jean is attracted to. *Boutès* also contains an association of water with a primordial form of sound, through a reference to the philosopher and musicologist Vladimir Jankélévitch: 'Jankélévitch a écrit: la musique nous enveloppe [...] car elle est vaste

et infinie comme la mer. C'est bien là l'image du premier monde [...] vieille eau
étrange' [Jankélévitch wrote that music surrounds us [...] because it is as vast and
infinite as the sea. This is what the origin of the world looks like [...] an ancient
and strange sea].[58] Music rather than literature appears here as the art form that best
allows an escape from the verbal; a form of refuge into another language, which,
if not silent, is 'un système de signes sonores qui ne signifient plus' [a system made
of acoustic signs that signify nothing].[59] Yet this conception of music as a possible
alternative to both speech and writing is challenged in *La Haine de la musique*, which
sees the musical realm as tainted by a necessarily authoritative nature.

In this text, a discussion of Primo Levi's classic *If This Is a Man*, based on the
Italian writer's detention in Auschwitz during the Second World War, represents
music as inherently violent and oppressive: 'la musique est le seul, de tous les arts,
qui ait collaboré à l'extermination des Juifs organisée par les Allemands de 1933
à 1945. Elle est le seul art qui ait été requis comme tel par l'administration des
Konzentrationslager' [Of all the arts, music is the only one to have collaborated in
the extermination of Jews organized by the Germans between 1933 and 1945. It
was the only form of art to be specifically requested by the administration of the
Konzentrationslager].[60] This conception of music evokes Kristeva's definition of
musical language as a 'système algébrique' [algebraic system] based on order and
rules. According to her, this system originally required 'une obéissance stricte aux
règles du code [...] considéré comme donné et sacré' [strict obedience to the rules of
the musical code, which is considered as a given and as sacred] and, in its modern
form, is organized internally as 'un système réglementé' [a regulated system].[61]
La Haine de la musique's redefinition of music leads to Quignard's complete and
seemingly final rejection of the art form: 'l'expression *Haine de la musique* veut
exprimer à quel point la musique peut devenir haïssable pour celui qui l'a le plus
aimée' [The expression *Hatred of Music* is meant to convey to what point music can
become an object of hatred to someone who once adored it beyond measure].[62]

As tactics used to try and destroy language, the writing of *contes* and the practice of
music ultimately fail. *Contes* are successful in expressing the annihilation of the self
and of speech, but they also subject themselves to a process of textual disappearance.
Similarly, recourse to music is only partly satisfactory, as it too carries with it the
values of order and authority that Quignard rejects in verbal language. Katherine
Kolb, in her article 'Music and the Feminine in Pascal Quignard', highlights the
specific relationship between Quignard's female characters and what she defines as
the idealization of music. These women, Kolb argues, 'cannot be composers because
they are musically and emotionally too powerful', and as such are not concerned
with the equivalence between *la mue*, the voice breaking that happens at puberty,
and the act of composing. Ann Hidden in *Villa Amalia* is used as an example of
the work's 'scantiness about women composers', because she gave up her career
as a pianist and composer.[63] Yet it could also be argued that this very nature —
marked by retreat, discretion and sparseness — is what gives value to Ann's life
and work. Following *La Haine de la musique*, musical expression does not disappear
from Quignard's work, which contains literary representations of female musicians
like Ann Hidden, and collaborations with women who work as composers,

choreographers and dancers. In *Boutès*, the narrator states how 'il faut peut-être tourner le dos à la musique orphique, occidentale, technologique et populaire' [one should probably turn away from Orphic music, which is occidental, technological and popular], to embrace another form: 'la musique qui est là avant la musique, la musique qui sait se "perdre"' [music that precedes music, music that can 'lose itself'].[64] Exemplified by the song of the Sirens that Butes is unable to resist, this form of music appears to be primordially feminine: from the frog queen's voice in 'La Voix perdue', through Ann Hidden's piano compositions, to the collaboration with Michèle Reverdy for *Le Nom sur le bout de la langue*.

Another recent example is Quignard's collaboration with the late Butoh dancer Carlota Ikeda for *Medea*, a work first performed in 2010 in Bordeaux. *Medea* contains a text by Quignard based on Euripides' tragedy, which accompanies choreography by Ikeda and a musical score by Alain Mahé. The three artists toured together from 2010 to 2013, in France, Belgium, Japan and Canada — the project is one of the last Ikeda worked on before her death in 2014. During performances, Quignard appeared onstage alongside the dancer. Whilst Ikeda danced at the front of the stage, the writer sat at a table, in a dimly lit corner. This collaboration is akin to the lecture-concerts given in 2012 and published in *Sur l'idée d'une communauté de solitaires* in 2015. When first considered, such performances could not seem further away from Quignard's quest for the vanishing of self, society, and verbal language. Yet these collaborative projects, and *Medea* in particular, become opportunities for the writer to stage a series of metamorphoses that lead to disappearance. The dialogue between the writer and the dancer presented onstage is a literal incarnation of the exchange in *Ethelrude et Wolframm*: between a female figure put forward as an embodiment of Kristeva's semiotic language, and a male voice, which, by uttering words, participates in the exhibition of their inherent inadequacy. Ikeda's Butoh is a form of dance developed in Japan in the aftermath of the Second World War. As mentioned in the introduction, Quignard often evokes his childhood in Le Havre, a port devastated during the war. In *Mourir de penser*, the narrator evokes 'le danseur de butô nu et couvert de cendres qui maintenant rampe dans le port d'Hiroshima en ruines sous le soleil d'août' [a naked Butoh dancer, his body covered in ashes, crawling through the port of Hiroshima in ruins, under the late summer sun].[65] Through this image, the shared imagery between Quignard's childhood and Butoh's origins is underlined. The writer's interest in a dance invented after World War II also positions this art form as a possible answer to what Quignard sees as the limitations of music, which he explicitly links to its role in Nazi oppression during the war. Moreover, as Vicki Sanders notes, Butoh was introduced by the dancer and choreographer Tatsumi Hijikata as 'a style of choreographic extremism he called *ankoku butō*, interpreted to mean "dance of darkness" or "dance of the dark soul", a term later abbreviated simply to *butō*'. This characterization echoes Quignard's own preference for obscurity and obscure figures: like his texts, Butoh was created to give recognition to Japan's 'nonpeople [...] all that was rejected by Japan's classical definition of beauty'.[66]

Through its historical origin, its embrace of darkness and outcast types, Butoh appears as the translation, in dance form, of what Quignard aims to express through literary writing. Yet *Medea* is not only a translation, but also a transformation from words to movement, and from voice to silence. Carlotta Ikeda was one of few women to dance and choreograph Butoh, a dance which is inherently violent and visceral. As Sondra Fraleigh, a dancer and academic, notes, Butoh is 'metamorphic and transformational' as well as 'an image-making process'.[67] Through the bodily images Ikeda presents onstage, she stands as a double not of the writer but rather of the female characters included in his texts. Ethelrude, Ann, the countess of Hornoc, Nukar's unnamed lover: all are feminine figures who achieve metamorphosis and disappearance through non-verbal means. Dance, like embroidery, appears as a form of creation that successfully belongs to silence and, as such, hints at Quignard's exploration of image-making processes through and beyond writing. As the next chapter will explore, he proposes to redefine reading and writing as visual acts, and by doing so, attempts to approach the primeval state towards which his work is directed.

Notes to Chapter 2

1. *VA*, p. 70.
2. Walter Benjamin, 'The Storyteller', trans. by Harry Zohn, in *Illuminations*, ed. by Hannah Arendt (London: Jonathan Cape, 1970), pp. 83–109 (pp. 87, 102).
3. The all-encompassing French term *conte* will be used throughout this chapter to designate the literary genre adopted by a specific group of texts written by Quignard. The word *conte* has no precise equivalent in English, as it applies to popular folk, cautionary and old-wives' tales, and to the literary fairy tales that appeared in seventeenth-century France, including the *contes de fées* written by Charles Perrault.
4. Pautrot, 'Dix questions à Pascal Quignard', pp. 90–91.
5. Bruno Bettelheim, *The Uses of Enchantment, the Meaning and Importance of Fairy Tales* (London: Thames and Hudson, 1976), p. 6.
6. *VS*, p. 215.
7. Pautrot, *Pascal Quignard ou le fonds du monde*, p. 157.
8. Pautrot, 'Pascal Quignard et la pensée mythique', p. 753.
9. Claude Lévi-Strauss, *Le Cru et le Cuit* (Paris: Plon, 1964), p. 13. *The Raw and the Cooked*, trans. by John and Doreen Weightman (Harmondsworth: Penguin, 1986), p. 18. As quoted in Pautrot, 'Pascal Quignard la pensée mythique', p. 759.
10. Ibid.
11. Ibid., p. 754.
12. *LZ*, p. 283.
13. Benjamin, 'The Storyteller', p. 102.
14. Ibid.
15. Rabaté, *Pascal Quignard, étude de l'œuvre*, p. 149.
16. Pascal Quignard, *L'Enfant au visage couleur de la mort* (Paris: Galilée, 2006), p. 63.
17. Jacob Grimm and Wilhelm Grimm, 'The Frog Prince', in *Grimm's Household Stories*, trans. by Lucy Crane (London: Macmillan, 1882), pp. 32–36.
18. Pascal Quignard, 'La Voix perdue', in *Pascal Quignard, la mise au silence*, ed. by Adriano Marchetti (Seyssel: Champ-Vallon, 2000), pp. 7–34 (p. 18).
19. 'LVP', p. 19.
20. 'LVP', pp. 31, 28.
21. Henri Gougaud, 'Nukar', in *Le Livre des amours* (Paris: Seuil, 1996), pp. 238–39.
22. Ibid., p. 238.
23. Pascal Quignard, 'Sur la disparition de Nukarpiatekak', in *VS*, pp. 331–34 (p. 331).
24. Gougaud, pp. 238–39.

25. *VS*, p. 334.
26. Edouard Fournier, *Variétés historiques et littéraires*, 10 vols (Paris: P. Jannet, 1855), I, pp. 163–67.
27. Marianne Closson, *L'Imaginaire démoniaque en France (1550–1650)* (Geneva: Droz, 2000), p. 255.
28. Fournier, p. 167.
29. *LBS*, p. 67. *LBSe*, p. 77.
30. *LBS*, p. 71. *LBSe*, p. 82.
31. Pascal Quignard, *Le Nom sur le bout de la langue* (Paris: P.O.L, 1993).
32. Pascal Quignard, 'Petit traité sur la Méduse', in *LNBL*, pp. 57–113.
33. Pascal Quignard and Gérard Titus-Carmel, *Sarx* (Paris: Maeght, 1977), pp. 38, 44, 51. *Sarx*, trans. by Keith Waldrop (Providence, RI: Burning Deck, 1997), pp. 28, 32, 37.
34. Pascal Quignard, 'La Métayère de Rodez', in, *Études Françaises*, 'Pascal Quignard ou le noyau incommunicable', 40 (2004), 9–11 (p. 11).
35. *Pascal Quignard, Mourir de penser (Dernier royaume IX)* (Paris: Grasset, 2014), p. 154.
36. *LVS*, p. 17.
37. Louis-René des Forêts, 'Une mémoire démentielle', in *LCE*, pp. 185–223 (p. 185). 'Disordered Silence' in *LCEe*, pp. 175–208 (p. 175).
38. *LNBL*, p. 62.
39. *LVS*, p. 19.
40. *LVS*, pp. 23–24.
41. *LVS*, pp. 30–31.
42. Pascal Quignard, *Ethelrude et Wolframm* (Paris: Galilée, 2006), p. 14.
43. See Simon Gaunt, *Retelling the Tale, an Introduction to Medieval French Literature* (London: Duckworth, 2001), pp. 60–61.
44. *EW*, pp. 28–31.
45. Julia Kristeva, *La Révolution du langage poétique* (Paris: Seuil, 1985), p. 26. *Revolution in Poetic Language*, trans. by Margaret Waller (New York: Columbia University Press, 1984), p. 27.
46. Dominique Rabaté, 'Vérités et affirmations chez Pascal Quignard', in *Études Françaises*, 'Pascal Quignard ou le noyau incommunicable', 40 (2004), 77–85 (p. 77).
47. *LEVCM*, p. 9.
48. 'LMR', pp. 9–10.
49. Quoted by Quignard in *Michel Deguy*, p. 139. First published as 'l'*Eloge d'Hélène de Gorgias*', trans. by Michel Deguy, *Revue de Poésie*, 90 (1964), 36–49. Gorgias, *Encomium of Helen*, trans. by Douglas Maurice MacDowell (Bristol: Bristol Classical, 1982), p. 21.
50. See the 1695 preface to Perrault's *Histoires ou contes du temps passé* signed by Pierre Darmancourt, which begins: 'Mademoiselle, on ne trouvera pas étrange qu'un enfant ait pris plaisir à composer les contes de ce recueil [...]' [Mademoiselle, people will not think it odd that a child took pleasure in writing the tales in this collection]. See also the preface to his *Contes en vers* (1695), where he defines them as '[des] bagatelles [qui] n'étaient pas de pures bagatelles' [trifles [that] were not mere trifles], adding that 'comme j'ai affaire à bien des gens [...] qui ne peuvent être touchés, que par l'autorité et par l'exemple des Anciens, je vais les satisfaire là-dessus' [since I am dealing with many people who [...] can only be persuaded by the authority and example of classical antiquity] and explains how 'les Fables Millésiennes si célèbres parmi les Grecs [...] n'étaient pas d'une autre espèce que les Fables de ce recueil' [The Milesian tales so famous among the Greeks [...] were no different from the stories in this collection]. Charles Perrault, *Contes*, ed. by Marc Soriano (Paris: Flammarion, 1989), pp. 245, 185. *The Complete Fairy Tales in Verse and Prose*, trans. and ed. by Stanley Appelbaum (Mineola, NY: Dover, 2002), pp. 113, 3.
51. Jack Zipes, 'Introduction, Towards a Definition of the Literary Fairy Tale', in *The Oxford Companion to Fairy Tales* (Oxford: OUP, 2000), pp. xv–xxxii (p. xv).
52. *LPD*, p. 168.
53. From Blanchot's essay on des Forêts's *Le Bavard*: Maurice Blanchot, 'La Parole vaine' in *L'Amitié* (Paris: Gallimard, 1971), pp. 137–49 (p. 145). 'Idle Speech', in *Friendship*, trans. by Elizabeth Rottenberg (Stanford, CA: Stanford University Press, 1997), pp. 117–28 (p. 124). As quoted by Quignard in *LPD*, p. 168.
54. The notion of 'bavardage' is also a reference to des Forêts, whose work 'presents language as an imperfect tool capable only of impure recollections, and irremediably tied up in the intertextual

and the "fabulaic"'. James Petterson, *Postwar Figures of L'Éphémère* (Lewisburg, PA: Bucknell University Press, 2000), p. 73.

55. *LNBL*, p. 7.
56. Pascal Quignard, *La Leçon de musique* (Paris: Hachette, 1987) and *La Haine de la musique* (Paris: Calmann-Lévy, 1996).
57. 'LVP', p. 18.
58. *BO*, p. 76.
59. *LS*, p. 144.
60. *LHM*, p. 215. *The Hatred of Music*, trans. by Matthew Amos and Fredrik Rönnbäck (New Haven, CT: Yale University Press, 2016), p. 129.
61. Julia Kristeva, *Le Langage, cet inconnu* (Paris: Seuil, 1981), pp. 306–07. *Language: the Unknown*, trans. by Anne M. Menke (New York: Columbia University Press, 1989), pp. 309–10.
62. *LHM*, p. 218. *LHMe*, p. 131.
63. Katherine Kolb, 'Music and the Feminine in Pascal Quignard', *L'Esprit Créateur*, 47 (2007), 101–14 (pp. 104, 112).
64. *BO.*, pp. 34, 18.
65. *MDP*, p. 98.
66. Vicki Sanders, 'Dancing and the Dark Soul of Japan: an Aesthetic Analysis of "Butō"', *Asian Theatre Journal*, 2 (1988), 148–63 (pp. 148–49).
67. Sondra Fraleigh, *Butoh: Metamorphic Dance and Global Alchemy* (Champaign: University of Illinois Press, 2010), pp. 41, 44.

CHAPTER 3

❖

Towards the Invisible

The previous two chapters have shown how Quignard's reliance on collaboration and an extreme form of intertextuality works against himself and against his texts. It takes part in a general effort towards self-effacement and a refusal of identification, considered a by-product of language and social belonging. As Quignard collaborates with writers, critics and artists, he demonstrates a desire to relinquish any rights over his own works and to decline authorial responsibility for the texts produced. He also makes clear the aim to abandon his own voice in favour of the voices, bodies and works of others. Moreover, he expresses the wish to be completely invaded by their presence, to let his texts be inhabited by departed or invented figures to the point of oblivion. This leads to a form of surrender, which for Quignard functions as the only possible identity he can adopt: that of the reader.

In *Pascal Quignard le solitaire*, he describes days spent writing, not sitting down at a writing desk, but lying in bed, immersed in the act of reading books. Writing is presented as the corollary of reading and reading as the root from which writing grows and develops, and without which it could not exist. Quignard also explains how he writes inside the books he is reading, on tiny sheets of paper kept inside their covers.[1] *Sur le désir de se jeter à l'eau* (*On Taking the Plunge*), a collaborative work with the critic Irène Fenoglio, uses Quignard's *Boutès* as a case-study of his writing process, and it contains reproductions from the original manuscript. In the introductory essay, Quignard explains how it came into being:

> Voici exactement comment je travaille, ou plutôt, comment je ne travaille pas; comment je vis; je lis dès que le sommeil me quitte, dans la fin de la nuit; puis je lis dans l'aube naissante. Je descends dès que la faim s'impatiente au fond de moi. Je fais couler le café, je mange un peu. L'aube est là. Les chats sortent. [...] Je regravis les escaliers, je remonte dans ma chambre, je me reglisse dans mon lit et j'y lis sans souci de finir, sous les nuages qui passent. Je lis, j'écris, je rêve, je médite, je respire, en même temps, sans que cela se distingue. Quand la faim me prend de nouveau, [...] alors la journée de travail est finie.
>
> [Here is a precise account of the way I work — or rather of the way I avoid working; of the way I live. I start reading from the moment I wake up, just as night begins to pass, and I am still reading when the dawn begins to break. When hunger strikes, I go downstairs: I make coffee, I eat a little. It is already dawn. The cats go outside. [...] I go upstairs again and slip back into bed, and I read without a care for time, under the passing clouds. I read, I write, I meditate, I breathe, as if it were all the same. When hunger strikes again, then my work is over for the day.][2]

Quignard refuses to represent himself as a labouring writer, and instead puts forward an idealized account of his life and work. He insists on the importance of solitude, in the form of a physical retreat from the outside world, where his only companions are decidedly non-human: cats and clouds. The writer's daily routine appears to be ruled by his bodily needs, mainly hunger and sleep. Quignard's working day is entirely centred on reading: reading done in a bedroom at the top of the stairs of what we can guess to be his home in Sens, and wrapped up in the nocturnal realm of dreams. In a later passage, the activity carried out in daylight is reduced to perfunctory and mindless typing, where a fully conscious and awakened Quignard becomes his own scribe, transcribing the notes produced as he was reading.

There are obvious questions as to the credibility of this highly stylized self-representation as a non-writer, firstly because what is described as non-writing still results in the production of text. But that material reality is brushed aside using specific tactics, the first being Quignard's insistence on a physical dissociation from the act of writing, through a preference for reading and for the state of near-unconsciousness it apparently calls for. He states for instance that he has never observed his own hand in the act of writing: 'donc si vous dites: "Avez-vous écrit?", je n'ai jamais écrit, vous me direz: "Vous avez publié tant de livres", je vous dirais: peut–être, je n'ai pas vu ma main écrire' [so if you say to me: 'Have you ever written anything?' No, I have never written a line. Your reply: 'But what about all of the texts you have published?' and mine: 'Perhaps, but I have never caught my hand in the act of writing'].[3] This stubborn refusal to be seen — and to see himself — as a writer is justified by the redefinition of writing as a process of rereading, correcting and removing text: '[je] recorrige, reretape. [...] rerecorrige, rereretape. Etc. C'est ma joie. Non pas écrire: lire, relire' [I re-read again, I type again, and again. [...] I re-read once more, I type once again. And so on. That is what gives me joy. Not writing but reading and re-reading].[4]

Pleasure is derived from reading and from the correction rather than the creation of text, suggesting once more that the work is fuelled by a paradoxical wish for its own vanishing. As this chapter will show, if writing amounts to the creation of disappearance, then reading becomes an act of immersion into the deadly content of the book. The figure of the reader quickly appears to be one that cannot be grasped. At first, Quignard's decision to take part in Fenoglio's project seems in contradiction with his refusal to be defined as a writer. *Sur le désir de se jeter à l'eau* stands for the larger issue in Quignard's oeuvre, which attempts to reconcile its offensive against verbal language with a continuous production and publication of texts. By exhibiting drafts normally subjected to a process of rewriting defined as non-writing, Quignard admittedly contradicts himself, but he also finds the opportunity to turn his creative process into a spectacle, a visual performance in which the materiality of the manuscript pages turns them into visual entities. They are not meant to be read, because they are, for the most part, unreadable: as Fenoglio's book shows, they are often obscured by indecipherable handwritten notes jotted down in red ink, and by the presence of drawings and doodles that cover entire pages of text. This collaboration with Fenoglio is thus used by Quignard as a chance to achieve a transformation of text into image. A similar intent lies behind the elevation of the figure of the reader, which serves a redefinition of the book as a visual product, situated in a space of darkness rather than light, belonging to night rather than day. As Lapeyre-Desmaison notes on the subject of Quignard's representation of reading: 'le premier acte de la lecture, son acte fondateur, est [...] de se vouer à reconnaître l'obscur qui voile les textes qu'elle veut aborder' [the founding act of reading is to become aware of the obscurity in which the texts are shrouded].[5] The study of the reader figure in this chapter will show how Quignard's writing takes place through the creation of images. Like the reader figure, these images will ultimately remain out of sight, as the writer attempts to achieve the disappearance of writing by defining it as a production of obscurity.

Reading in the Dark

Throughout his writing career, Quignard has promoted the status of reader over that of writer, both in a literal and symbolic manner. To read is paramount for him and this is especially visible in the triptych composed by *Le Lecteur*, *Le Secret du domaine* and *L'Enfant au visage couleur de la mort*. These three texts illustrate the prime position given to the reader figure, but also how it is subjected to a process of disappearance, and how reading is defined as a plunge into obscurity.

The predominance of reading over writing is present from the publication of Quignard's first truly literary work, which follows a long career devoted to the books of others, as reader and editor at Gallimard. This first fictional text clearly announced the need to be defined foremost as a reader through its unambiguous title: *Le Lecteur*. The text though, as Lapeyre-Desmaison notes, soon turns out to be a disappointing read: 'au lieu du témoignage attendu, ou du roman, voire de la romance, un ensemble de cinq chapitres relatant une bien énigmatique "disparition"' [instead of the expected testimony, novel or even romance, a series of five chapters telling the very enigmatic story of a 'disappearance']. Like Georges Perec's 1969 novel *La Disparition* (*A Void*), which does not contain the letter 'e', Lapeyre-Desmaison argues that Quignard's text deals with a central absence. It serves as *Le Lecteur*'s main plot and justifies its apparent depth: 'le tissu comme troué par cette absence qui pourtant paradoxalement fait masse' [this absence is like a hole in the textual fabric, but a hole that nonetheless gives matter to the text].[6] Yet Lapeyre-Desmaison's analogy between Quignard and Perec functions only up to a point. Firstly, Perec's novel maintains the illusion of a certain fulfilment by hiding the absence at its core, whilst *Le Lecteur* makes no secret of the loss it is based on, expressing it clearly from the first pages to then turn the text into the site of its own destruction. Moreover, the absence of the letter *e* in Perec's novel can be said to reveal the dazzling new possibilities offered by a playful deconstruction à language, while the disappearance of Quignard's reader originates from a presupposition of the deathly nature of language. Finally, *Le Lecteur* inaugurates a series of disappointing revelations: behind Quignard's new status of writer hides the figure of a reader, which, as soon as it is revealed, goes missing.

This text shows how reading allows access to a specific solitary state through continued reference to a specific source: a work entitled *De contemplatione*, also known as *Benjamin major*, written in the twelfth century by the theologian Richard of Saint Victor. Whilst often eclipsed by his better-known predecessor Hugh of Saint Victor, Richard is commonly recognized as one of the first Western writers to have considered the topic of contemplation. His *Benjamin major* influenced the later writings of Meister Eckhart, the German speculative mystic, and of Dante, whose *Divine Comedy* contains many references to Saint Victor's definition of contemplation.[7] In *Le Lecteur*, passages attributed to Saint Victor help define reading as an act of contemplation. The voices of Saint Victor and the narrator are merged together in what is both an adaptation in French of the medieval Latin text and a series of glosses provided by the narrator: a form of writing explicitly supported by a preceding act of reading. Saint Victor's *contemplatio* is divided into four stages: 'la *meditatio*, le *soliloquium*, la *circumspectio*, l'*ascensio*'. Through the narrator's commentary on Saint Victor's own exegesis, these steps become part of a process of disappearance. *Meditatio*, firstly, amounts to a clear separation from the world: 'le lecteur est deux fois seul. Seul comme lecteur, il est sans le monde. [...] Seul "avec" son livre [...] qui est le dénuement du monde' [the reader is twice alone. Alone as a reader, he is also cut-off from the world. Alone 'with' his book [...], which symbolizes deprivation from the world]. Whilst this is a common representation of reading, the second step, *soliloquium*, introduces the idea of a disappearance of the book itself: 'seul, sans le monde, sans le livre' [alone, without the world, without the book].[8] This disappearance is confirmed by the *circumspectio*, which amounts to a rejection of language and of the written content of the book. This rejection is defined as the main consequence of a previous separation from the world: 'l'engloutissement du monde, de soi, et du langage' [engulfing the world, the self and language].[9] Quignard expresses a similar idea elsewhere by characterizing reading as both 'la dimension de l'absence' [what absence encompasses] and 'un instant [...] dénué d'identité' [a moment [...] stripped of identity].[10] Finally, the last step, the *ascencio*, brings forth the image of a complete void in place of the book:

> le quatrième mode. La roue de la lecture, qui passait du dessaisissement du lecteur au livre, du monde au livre, de la loi au livre, du livre à son absence, de soi au seul et du seul au nul [...], la roue soudain s'excède: l'œil est tombé dans le livre tombé.

> [the fourth step: the wheel of reading, which removed the reader from the book, from the world to the book, from the book to its absence, from being a self to being alone and from being alone to being nothing [...]. Suddenly the wheel exceeds itself: the eye falls into the fallen book.][11]

This passage describes a force that causes the reader to be sucked into the book as into a vortex, where a spiralling movement — that circular spinning of the wheel of reading described above — accelerates into a whirlwind that makes both the book and the reader disappear.

The representation of reading introduced by *Le Lecteur* remains a constant thread in Quignard's body of work, and especially in the two texts *Le Secret du domaine* and *L'Enfant au visage couleur de la mort*. As mentioned in the second chapter, the latter is a republished and retitled version of the former, which was written around the same time as *Le Lecteur*. Both versions tell the story of a child who becomes a reader, a monster and a book, before turning to ashes. The most obvious difference between the two texts, apart from their title, is the inclusion in *Le Secret du domaine* of a series of illustrations by Jean Garonnaire that are absent from the 2006 version. Garonnaire's etchings show the nameless protagonist as a faceless figure, whose head is surrounded and obscured by an aureole.

As Lapeyre-Desmaison notes, *L'Enfant au visage couleur de la mort* 'thématise les dangers et les effets de la lecture' [provides a thematic representation of the dangers and other effects of reading].[12] As a *conte*, it implies constant reiteration: told through two different versions, it can also be read on several levels. The disappearance of the child reader can first be perceived through the implicit but dense psychoanalytical echoes it contains. Secondly, it can be taken, as Lapeyre-Desmaison suggests, as a moral tale, an *exemplum* meant to warn of the dangers of reading. Finally, when read literally, it becomes the story of the magical and visual transformations of a reader. All of these readings end with the same conclusion, which gives the act of reading a similar implication: presented as deadly, it leads towards the annihilation of the reader. In the *conte*, reading is primarily defined as the violation of an order formulated by the child's father, who forbids his son to read. This ban on books is presented as a secret passed on through generations: 'secret de ce qui illumine nos visages' [the secret that gives colour to our faces].[13] References to psychoanalysis, and more specifically to the Lacanian concept of a father figure 'representative of the social order',[14] irrigate the tale. A literal 'Law of the father', which stands for acceptance of social rules, is disobeyed through the act of reading, which becomes akin to a refusal of such social order. This reverses the usual conception of reading; books, because they undeniably belong to the symbolic realm, are expected to stand on the paternal side, and reading to be key to the child's entry into the symbolic realm. Defined instead as a way to resist this entry, reading becomes a form of death drive, allowing the return to a primeval state of being.

This is expressed in the father's prohibitive order, where the forbidding of books is a means to 'give colour to' one's face, or — echoing the *conte*'s final title — to not take on the colour of death. Obeying the father, turning away from books towards life with others would allow growth and a healthy form of development for the child. The somewhat mysterious paraphrase used in the title — 'l'enfant au visage couleur de la mort' — is clarified by the paternal decree, which is meant to protect the child from symbolic death. Lacan uses the concept of 'symbolic death' in his reading of Sophocles' *Antigone*, where he mentions 'une mort vécue si l'on peut dire d'une façon anticipée, une mort empiétant sur le domaine de la vie' [a death lived by anticipation, a death that crosses over into the sphere of life].[15] Antigone is exclusively referred to in the original Greek text as 'ἡ παίς', 'the child', and Lacan identifies her as a clear incarnation of an accomplished death drive.[16] By disobeying Creon's interdiction to mourn and bury her brother Polynices, she first opposes a law imposed by political authority, and, Lacan argues, the symbolic as a whole. Indeed, Polynices' body is deprived of burial because he is a traitor, whilst his brother Eteocles is a hero. His posthumous treatment is caused by language, which is responsible for opposing hero and traitor, good and bad.[17] The choice Antigone makes to defend her brother's honour, and to condemn herself to the punishment this entails, is not justifiable within the symbolic realm, but has to do with Polynices and Antigone's common origin in an incestuous primal scene, in their sharing of the same maternal matrix. Antigone buries her brother, and acquiesces in a form of symbolic death by being walled up alive, embodying, as Lacan puts it, 'cet inanimé où Freud nous apprend à reconnaître la forme dans laquelle se manifeste l'instinct de mort' [that inanimate condition in which Freud taught us to recognize the form in which the death instinct is manifested].[18] By doing so, she expresses the desire to return to a primeval state of being.

Lacan's reading of *Antigone* sheds light on the way the positions of child, mother and father (as Law) are distributed in Quignard's *L'Enfant au visage couleur de la mort*, and how this affects the definition of reading it offers. Reading is the expression of the child's desire to remain in his present fusion with the maternal body. Just as Antigone is walled up alive, the child, because his extensive reading has turned him into a monster, is locked up in a room at the top of a circular tower, built for him on his mother's orders. The child's symbolic death is a retreat from the world, similar to the one experienced by Antigone, who 'sans être encore morte [...] est rayée du monde des vivants' [although not yet dead, is eliminated from the world of the living].[19] It takes the form of an exclusive relationship with the mother: the child inhabits a space, a *domain*, literarily ruled by the maternal figure. As Agnès Cousin de Ravel notes, 'lire est le désir de s'approcher du secret de l'origine, du fœtal, du contact avec la mère' [reading is the desire to approach the secret of one's origins, towards the foetal realm, the maternal contact].[20]

This conception of reading, which paradoxically suggests that turning to books is akin to leaving rather than entering the symbolic realm, also relies on more general and traditional tropes. It associates reading with death, and presents the reader as a frail and somewhat morbid individual. In so doing, the *conte* takes the form of an *exemplum*, warning against the deadly power of books through the allegorical story of the child's transformations and of his final disappearance. Reading, the story suggests, leads not only to a symbolic death but also to an actual dissolution of the reader's vital forces. As Quignard states, 'c'est plus dangereux qu'on ne croit la lecture', adding, 'je comprends très bien qu'on déteste cela — que des civilisations entières aient détesté cela' [reading is more dangerous than we think. I understand why some are revolted by it — why entire civilizations have despised it].[21] The *conte* relies on a familiar representation of reading as an unsafe activity, and one that is the prerogative of the weak. In his *Petits traités* (*Small Treatises*), Quignard refers to the key scene in Stendhal's *Le Rouge et le Noir* (*The Red and the Black*), in which the protagonist Julien Sorel is punished by his father for reading.[22] In the same work, Quignard mentions the unease that parents feel upon seeing their children 'soustraits absolument au pouvoir de l'écriture et de la lecture [qui] leur paraît constituer un [...] indice d'imbécilité assez préoccupante' [completely under the spell of writing and reading, in a state they regard as a worrying sign of idiocy].[23] This representation of reading refers back to the eighteenth century, and in particular to medical theories developed in Samuel Tissot's *De la santé des gens de lettres* (*Treatise on the Health of Men of Letters*). Better known for his account of the 'diseases produced by onanism', Tissot also wrote on the dangers of excessive reading:

> Les inconvénients des livres frivoles sont de faire perdre le temps et de fatiguer la vue; mais ceux qui [...] élèvent l'âme hors d'elle-même, et la forcent à méditer, usent l'esprit et épuisent le corps.
>
> [Frivolous books waste time and damage our eyesight. Books that [...] elevate our soul and force us to meditate, exhaust the body and wear the spirit out.][24]

All books are dangerous, Tissot argues, even those that contain the most scholarly texts. The latter, which lead the reader towards meditation, have ill-effects, as proven by the example he later gives of a 'gentilhomme anglais qui, étant à Rome, se livra si fort à l'étude des mathématiques, qu'au bout de quelques mois il ne pouvait plus se servir de ses yeux' [an English gentleman who, in Rome, devoted himself so fully to the study of mathematics that, after a few months, he lost the use of his eyes].[25] A similar physical transformation affects Quignard's child after he becomes an avid reader:

> Tous tombèrent d'accord pour dire qu'il devint maigre; que ses os semblèrent se rétrécir [...] que son souffle se fit haletant, et inégal; sa voix hâtive et rauque; que ses yeux perdirent de leur éclat; mais surtout, [...] son visage, quand la méta-morphose fut complètement achevée, prit la couleur du visage de la mort.
>
> [Everyone said that he became thin, that his bones suddenly seemed to shrink, [...] that from then on his breath was always short and uneven, his voice raspy and hasty, his eyes without their usual glow, and also that his face, when the metamorphosis was over, took on the colour of the face of death.][26]

This passage shows how the metamorphosis of the child can be read as a metaphor of the fatal consequences, both physical and psychological, of reading. But this transformation is short-lived; the child, unlike Tissot's English gentleman, does not simply weaken. He is instead the subject of a second transformation, which turns his morbid body into that of a deadly monster. At this point, the child has stopped reading, and as in Saint Victor's *soliloquium* and the *circumspectio*, the book is not there any more: the reader is purely on his own, without the world, without others and without reading.

   In exchange for this solitude, the child has acquired a specific supernatural power, which turns his gaze into a deadly weapon. Like the mythical Medusa, he is capable of killing anyone who enters his field of vision: 'qui vivait un certain temps dans la proximité de son visage, on disait était entraîné peu à peu dans la mort' [it was said that those who remained too long in close proximity of his face were slowly dragged from life into death].[27] This second metamorphosis gives another, more literal, explanation for the expression 'to take on the colour of death' that gives its final title to the *conte*. The child has been filled with deathly matter, as if, by absorbing books through reading, their content had invaded his body, forcing it to emit a deadly halo. This echoes a passage from *Le Lecteur*, a reformulated quotation taken from the third-century biographer Diogenes Laertius, in the chapter of *The Lives and Opinions of Eminent Philosophers* he devotes to the pre-Socratic philosopher Zeno of Elea: 'il demanda à l'oracle à quoi il était préférable qu'il engageât sa vie, et [le] dieu lui répondit: SI TU DEVIENS DE LA COULEUR DES MORTS. Il comprit: il lut les auteurs anciens' [he consulted the oracle, as to what he ought to do to live in the most excellent manner, the God answered him that he ought to become of the same complexion as the dead, on which he inferred that he ought to apply himself to the reading of the books of the ancients].[28] Through the motif of a child-reader whose face, more and more exposed to the printed word, gains the colour of death, language is endowed with a deathly nature. What the *conte* suggests is that books contain and transmit death because they are made of words, defined as lifeless remnants left over from previous civilizations, which always predate the existence of the speaking, reading and writing subject. Acquiring speech, learning the meaning of words is to become aware of the finite nature of things and being.

Reading is thus endowed with a dual deathly nature, which makes it both desired and feared, because of the book's ability to transmit the deathly symbolic material it contains. But turning to reading is also to give in to the death drive, to follow the logic of desire and make reading the vector of an all-important relation to a lost origin. Quignard's ambiguous conception of reading turns his text into a dizzying puzzle, which fuses together familiar tropes, references to psychoanalysis, ancient authors and medieval philosophers, and the writer's personal statements on his own reading practice. Trying to solve the puzzle is a necessary but deceitful exercise, because the extremely self-aware nature of Quignard's writing means that readers always stay one step behind, lured by the promise of a revelation that never takes place. This attitude differs from the Oulipian game played by Perec in *La Disparition*. It suggests that language is not a fertile and playful realm of infinite possibilities, but a finite and dead land, a source of anguish rather than pleasure. Whether likened to the 'dark territory' of the unconscious through Quignard's self-representation as a reader, to the nocturnal state during which reading takes place, to the lost fusion with the maternal body or to a cultural realm inhabited by departed and forgotten figures, the book becomes a space where readers experience a never-ending fall: the paradoxical *ascencio* described by Saint Victor.

A Literary Black Manner

L'Enfant au visage couleur de la mort, *Le Secret du domaine* and *Le Lecteur* together put forward a portrait of the writer as reader and a representation of the book as a dangerous place, which is of a fascinating and deadly nature. The limits of language and the morbid content of the words it relies on are presented as causes for this hazardous nature of the book, suggesting that its linguistic content must be emptied out from within.

In the previous chapter, recourse to music and dance appeared as possible tactics deployed against verbal language. Yet, Quignard's collaborations with visual artists are as numerous as his interactions with musicians and dancers, if not more so: he has written on a large number of painters and draughtsmen, from Georges de La Tour to the Surrealist Hans Bellmer, and worked with several contemporary artists like Louis Cordesse, Pierre Skira and Marie Morel. Perhaps more telling is the way in which many of these collaborations enable a shift from the literary to the visual. *La Frontière* (*The Border*) is a narrative text that Quignard based on the *azulejos* — the painted ceramic tiles typically found in Spain and Portugal — featured on the walls of the Fronteira Palace in Lisbon. As the critic Midori Ogawa notes, this text 'renvoie le lecteur à un espace d'avant la narration' [takes the reader back to a place that precedes narration].[29] In this story of revenge, the Count of Mascarenhas wishes to avenge the death of his brother in arms. The King of Portugal, keen to avoid bloodshed, convinces Mascarenhas to accept the title of Marquis of Fronteira in exchange for giving up his right to retaliation. The count accepts, but still manages to tell the story by having it painted on the *azulejos* that adorn his palace. In addition to Quignard's text, *La Frontière* contains photographic reproductions of the *azulejos* in question, which illustrate the text and act as reminders of the power of images to transmit information without words.

Visual references summoned by Quignard are often linked to figures of obscurity. *La Frontière*'s painted tiles, for instance, are not figurative illustrations of events but shadows, indirect representations that are meant to fascinate the viewer rather than narrate a story: 'les azulejos qui représentent des personnages et des bêtes s'apparentent à des ombres bleues qui guettent les spectateurs' [the *azulejos* display humans and animals as lurking blue shadows awaiting the viewers].[30] Similarly, de La Tour's paintings, such as his *Nativity* scene, *The Newborn Christ* and *The Education of the Virgin*, all feature a lit candle obscured by a hand or an object. As the main source of light within the painted scenes, it is hidden from the viewer's gaze; its obscured presence seems motivated by the desire to highlight the darkness that surrounds it. The hardback editions of Quignard's *La Nuit sexuelle* (*The Sexual Night*) and *Le Sexe et l'effroi*, where the writer comments on artworks that are reproduced next to his text, are literally immersed in darkness, as both words and images are printed on black rather than white pages. One of the chapters in *La Nuit sexuelle* is devoted to the Lascaux cave paintings, plunging the reader into a literal and visual *mise en abyme*. The paintings embody the absent and invisible nature of images that Quignard wants to put forward. Discovered by chance in 1940, the caves had remained out of sight for more than seventeen thousand years. Their subsequent opening to the public in the early 1950s caused a grave process of deterioration, and general access to them was soon banned. Since then, the site in which Georges Bataille situated the origin of art has remained out of sight.[31] Moreover, the Palaeolithic paintings are located in sections of the caves where no sunlight can penetrate. Because the meaning of these paintings can only be the object of speculation and interpretation, the images they provide are fundamentally silent, as Quignard argues in *Vie secrète*: 'ce que nous [y] voyons [...], des dizaines de milliers d'années plus tard, ne sont pas des signes mais des vestiges d'actions' ['what we see, tens of thousands of years later, are not signs but traces of past gestures].[32] It is towards such primordial but ultimately absent and silent images that Quignard wants to lure his readers.

In *La Nuit sexuelle*, references to Palaeolithic paintings are accompanied by recurring evocations of the Freudian 'primal scene', as illustrated by the following passage:

> Je n'étais pas là la nuit où j'ai été conçu. Il est difficile d'assister au jour qui vous précède. Une image manque dans l'âme. Nous dépendons d'une posture qui a eu lieu de façon nécessaire mais qui ne se révèlera jamais à nos yeux. On appelle cette image qui manque 'l'origine'.

[I wasn't there the night I was conceived. It is difficult to witness the day that precedes you. An image is missing in the soul. We are the products of bodily positions that must necessarily have been adopted but will never be revealed to our eyes. We call this missing image 'the origin'.][33]

This 'nuit primitive' is seen as the origin of all art forms, both preceding and causing the birth of art in Palaeolithic times, and explaining the invention of the *chiaroscuro* in painting and the emergence of cinema. These art forms have in common the attempt to recreate, through their reliance on obscurity, the conditions of that missing scene. *La Nuit sexuelle*, as a work that combines both text and image, is fuelled by the desire to plunge into darkness towards the absent origin:

Je cherche à faire un pas de plus vers la source de l'effroi que les hommes ressentent quand ils songent à ce qu'ils furent avant que leur corps projette une ombre dans ce monde. Si derrière la fascination, il y a l'image qui manque, derrière l'image qui manque, il y a encore quelque chose: la nuit.

[I'm trying to take one step closer to the source of the terror human beings feel when they muse on what they were before their body cast a shadow in this world. If behind the fascination there is the missing image, behind the missing image there is something else — the night.][34]

This conception of art as directed towards primordial night implicitly refers to 'Le Regard d'Orphée' ('Orpheus's Gaze'), an essay by Maurice Blanchot where the Orphic myth is used to situate the origin of art in a total and dual darkness:

Quand Orphée descend vers Eurydice, l'art est la puissance par laquelle s'ouvre la nuit. La nuit, par la force de l'art, l'accueille, devient l'intimité accueillante, l'entente et l'accord de la première nuit. Mais c'est vers Eurydice qu'Orphée est descendu: Eurydice est, pour lui, l'extrême que l'art puisse atteindre, elle est sous un nom qui la dissimule et sous un voile qui la couvre, le point profondément obscur vers lequel l'art, le désir, la mort, la nuit semblent tendre.

[When Orpheus descends toward Eurydice, art is the power by which night opens. Because of art's strength, night welcomes him; it becomes welcoming intimacy, the harmony and accord of the first night. But it is toward Eurydice that Orpheus has descended. For him Eurydice is the furthest that art can reach. Under a name that hides her and a veil that covers her, she is the profoundly obscure point toward which art and desire, death and night, seem to tend.][35]

The Orphic myth is present throughout Quignard's work, where it stands for the desire — situated at the core of writing — to retrieve what has been lost. What art aims for, Quignard argues in *La Nuit sexuelle* by way of a Blanchottian reading of the Orphic myth, is always located beyond what can be said or seen, and concerned with a space that cannot be reached. Writing is thus based on the relentless staging of art's inherent impotence at representing what it truly wants to show or write. The writer, by relying on the works of others, exhibits his own powerlessness at achieving what others, like Blanchot, have already recognized as an impossible task. His work is immersed in the collective and the universal through its reliance on known images — the Lascaux paintings, Francisco Goya's 'black paintings' and the Japanese *shunga* that appear in *La Nuit sexuelle* — and on the borrowing of various genres such as *contes* and myths. In *La Nuit sexuelle*, reproductions of paintings and other artworks trigger references to biblical and mythical motifs, such as Lot and Noah, and Dido and Aeneas.

In *Pascal Quignard le solitaire*, Quignard notes that 'pour la part qui revient à l'écriture, le seul vrai Art poétique, c'est *Terrasse à Rome*. Ma manière est [...] la manière noire' [where writing is concerned, the real and only *Ars Poetica* is *Terrasse à Rome*. My manner is [...] the black manner].[36] *Terrasse à Rome* is clearly defined as a programmatic work, and writing as the literary equivalent of the etching technique used by its protagonist Geoffroy Meaume. 'Black manner', also known as mezzotint, first appeared in seventeenth-century Germany: its particularity is to reverse the usual order in which forms are produced. Instead of applying black or colour to a blank surface, images are created out of darkness. The first step is the roughening of a metal plate with a cradle, a spiked instrument that applies pressure on a plate by rocking back and forth until it is grated and covered with multiple holes, after which selected parts of the plate are polished. The latter is then covered with black ink and as it is pressed onto a piece of paper, the image appears. The softened parts, which have not been penetrated by the ink, create shapes that rise from the surrounding darkness to form recognizable images. For Quignard, this engraving technique stands for the idea that art has its origin in darkness. In *Terrasse à Rome*, the production of images through black manner is compared to childbirth. This passage uses visual and narrative devices also found in *La Nuit sexuelle*, as it groups together motifs such as the mother's womb, the Palaeolithic cave paintings (the black manner follows the same principle as the prehistoric negative hand-printing), and genres such as *contes*, legends and myths.[37]

These narrative forms are used in *Terrasse à Rome* to participate in an enterprise of disappearance deployed against its protagonist. The text first appears to be a historical narrative — a biographical account of the life of the seventeenth-century French etcher Geoffroy Meaume, from his departure from Bruges in 1639 to his death in Utrecht in 1667. A few of the companions he met during his travels appear in the text: the artist Claude Gelée, whom Meaume introduced to the art of depicting landscapes, and the etcher Abraham Bosse, who was Meaume's student for two years.[38] *Terrasse à Rome* gives a dense and precise account of Meaume's life that relies on several critical and biographical references. For instance, the narrator often quotes works by a certain Grünehagen.[39] This constant exhibition of facts is there to convince readers of the veracity of Meaume's existence, which they have no reason to doubt — except perhaps for the mention on the book's cover that *Terrasse à Rome* is a novel and not a biography.

But Geoffroy Meaume never existed. As Quignard indicates in a text published two years after *Terrasse à Rome*: 'j'inventais un eau-fortier préalablement défiguré par l'eau-forte: Meaume' [I invented an etcher whose face was destroyed by acid: Meaume].[40] No evidence of Meaume's existence can be located outside the novel, and no works by Grünehagen feature in the records of the Bibliothèque Nationale de France. Interestingly, the only instance in which the protagonist's name appears in relation to seventeenth-century art is through a nineteenth-century art historian, Edouard Meaume, who published several studies on etching and engraving.[41] This suggests that Quignard borrowed the name of an historian to invent a false historic figure, creating a slippage between the author and its subject. It illustrates how he himself blurs the borders between reading and writing, between the protagonist and the author, as part of his larger project of self-disappearance.

The effort deployed in *Terrasse à Rome* to deceive readers implies a primary concern for the creation of obscurity and the overall enterprise of destruction it demands. Meaume is an invented figure, as is Avitia in *Les Tablettes de buis d'Apronenia Avitia*, and he is subjected within the text to a literal form of effacement. A certain form of violence characterizes black manner, which relies on abrasive ingredients, and especially acid. Acid plays a key role in a central scene of the novel, where the artist and his lover, the young Nanni Veet Jakobsz, are brutally attacked by her fiancé, who throws acid on Meaume's face, rendering him both monstrous and unrecognizable. The instrument of this mutilation, the liquid used in etching, is diverted from the plate to the etcher's face, turning the latter into a work of art. This fusion of the artist and his oeuvre creates a *mise en abyme*, where Meaume's disfiguration becomes a representation of the destructive nature of his art, turning *Terrasse à Rome* into a literary form of black manner.

The attack on Meaume takes place at the beginning of the text, in a passage that is less the narration of an event than the depiction of a visual scene:

> Les amants [...] sont soudain couverts de débris de verre qui retombent. Le commis de ruelle de Jakobsz, qui s'appelle Vanlacre, s'est blessé en pulvérisant les carreaux de la fenêtre. Il titube. Sa lèvre saigne. [...] Le fiancé de la fille de Jakobsz a lancé l'eau-forte. Le menton, les lèvres, le front, les cheveux, le cou de Meaume sont brûlés.
>
> [The lovers [...] are suddenly covered with broken glass. Jakobsz's assistant, Valance, has injured himself smashing the window panes. He stumbles. His lip is bleeding. [...] Young Jakobsz's fiancé hurls the acid at Meaume's face. His chin, his lips, his forehead, his hair and his neck are burnt.][42]

The event is narrated through a series of fixed scenes. The use of the present tense, present participle and passive forms seems to describe a painting rather than tell a story. The gaze of Vanlacre, Nanni's fiancé, is key to the passage: his initial position as voyeur, as he watches Meaume and Nanni through the shop's window, is defined by prohibition. It breaks the cultural taboo attached to sexual acts in general — itself echoing the interdiction that rules the witnessing of the 'primal scene' in psychoanalysis — and also reveals the illicit and adulterous nature of Meaume and Nanni's relationship. Vanlacre's surveillance of this forbidden scene ignites a series of destructive events that begins with the breaking of the window, which wounds all three protagonists, and ends with the burning of Meaume's face.

A second event towards the end of the text completes the process of destruction initiated by this first attack. Once again, narration takes the form of *ekphrasis*, the textual representation of a visual work of art. Yet, this time, it is fused with references both to the myth of Oedipus and to one of the earliest German literary texts, the song of Hildebrand, which tells of the battle between Hildebrand and his unrecognized son Hadubrand. At that point in the novel, Meaume is an older man, and the scene begins with him resting under a tree. A young man, mistaking the artist for a criminal, confronts him and stabs him in the throat. The attacker is later revealed to be the son of Meaume and Nanni. The reference to the Oedipal myth is confirmed by the fact that the attack, not immediately fatal, results in Meaume becoming blind. The event is described as follows:

> Meaume le Graveur âgé de quarante-neuf ans fut agressé dans la campagne romaine le 8 du mois de juin 1666. Une déposition des archers de Rome, datée de ce jour, signée de onze noms, en porte témoignage. Il est assis dans la campagne, parmi les pierres ruinées, le dos portant contre le tronc d'un petit chêne vert, le grand chapeau de paille dérobant son visage et le protégeant du soleil. Il rêve. Un jeune homme le réveille, l'agrippe, le fait tomber dans la terre sèche, plante son couteau dans son cou pour l'égorger. Le graveur lève les yeux sur le visage du jeune homme qui l'égorge. Il le regarde, il est bouleversé par ses traits. Il le contemple. Il ne crie pas. Curieusement, il pense à une gravure sur bois de Jean Heemkers, qui était son maître à Bruges. Dans cette gravure Hildebrand se trouve devant Hadubrand qui lève son arme. Le père voit son fils qui s'apprête à le tuer. Il voit que son fils ne le reconnaît pas. Il voit le geste fatal qui se prépare dans le regard de son fils. Mais le père ne dit rien. Le jeune homme âgé de vingt-six ans enfonce la lame dans son cou. Le sang gicle.

> [Meaume the etcher, forty-nine years old, was attacked on the 8th of June 1666 in the Roman Campagna. This is attested by a deposition, written and signed by eleven Roman archers. Meaume is in the countryside, he is resting amongst the rocks and the ruins, his back leaning on the trunk of a small green oak tree, a large straw hat hiding his face and protecting him from the sun. He is dreaming. A young man wakes him up, grabs him by the collar, pushes him down on the dry soil, sticks a knife into his neck and slices it open. The etcher lifts his face up towards the young man who is cutting his throat. He looks at him and he is suddenly overwhelmed by what he sees. He gazes at his features. He stays silent. Oddly, he starts to think about a wood etching by Jean Heemkers, his master in Bruges. In the etching, Hildebrand faces Hadubrand with his weapon raised. The father looks at the son who is about to kill him. He can see that his son does not recognize him. He can see the fatal gesture that will follow by gazing into his son's eyes. But the father remains silent. The son, aged twenty-six, plunges the knife into his victim's neck. Blood spurts out.][43]

The ekphrastic quality of the passage is rendered explicit in its last part, which moves from the narration of an event to the description of an engraving, itself based on a written legend. Moreover, the progression leading from the first sentence to the end of the passage condenses the deceitful use of facts found in the rest of *Terrasse à Rome*. The passage starts as the retelling of a crime scene, with a reference to a supposed 'deposition' and ends with the legendary: it goes from the historically determined to the universal. Meaume's name, which sounds both like *homme* [man] and *môme* [young boy] in French, has the archetypal quality of names found in fairy tales: this highlights the passage from the personal to the general. Meaume's son and attacker is never aware that the victim is his father, and the scene pushes the artist further towards death and anonymity.

A similar logic is applied to the artist's body of work, which is detailed throughout the novel. Often described at length, Meaume's etchings function as doubly invisible works. Firstly, like the artist who produced them, they are fictional rather than real. Moreover, the text often presents them as having been destroyed or lost. The artist's erotic vignettes, for instance, are burnt on a public square in Rome, following their condemnation as obscene works.[44] The subjects depicted in these etchings suggest that Meaume's black manner, defined in the novel as a 'gravure à l'envers' [etching in reverse],[45] calls in its content for the representation of a Bakhtinian reversal of values, through an exhibition of the grotesque body.[46] The ekphrasis of Meaume's *Temptation of Saint Anthony* provides a clear example of this:

> Le saint ermite se tient assis au devant d'une grotte, le sexe dressé dans sa main. Ses yeux pleurent. Une rocaille sépare le saint d'une femme qui ouvre largement ses jambes, la tête penchée en avant sur sa nuit, qu'elle semble observer, mais qui est indiscernable. Près d'elle, un petit diable chie dans un livre qui est ouvert. À gauche de la gravure un Castillan joue du violon pour une laie.

> [The hermit saint is sitting down in front of a cave, his erect penis held in one hand. Tears roll down his face. A rock separates the saint from a woman whose legs are spread wide open, her face turned towards her night, which she seems to observe even though it remains indistinguishable. Next to her, a little demon is defecating into an open book. On the left of the etching, a Castilian is playing the violin for a wild sow.][47]

This description borrows elements from actual works of art. The presence of the cave and the hermit saint figure is a reference to the late medieval artist Hieronymus Bosch, and specifically his triptych *Temptation of Saint Anthony*, where, in the central panel, a half-ruined tower creates a grotto-like space in which is seen a crucified Christ. The musician evokes Jacques Callot — the French baroque printmaker on whom Meaume is most probably modelled — and his etching *La Tentation de Saint-Antoine*, whilst the naked female figure can be observed in Salvador Dali's 1946 painting of the same subject. Just as Meaume's story is made up of borrowed historical elements, his imaginary oeuvre is a collage of real visual works. But what sets his own etching apart is its accumulation of obscene motifs, two of which — the crying eyes associated with the erect penis and the defecating devil — represent an emptying of the body, echoing the dissolving process in Quignard's work and discussed in the previous chapter. Moreover, the central female figure, staring down an indistinguishable void, effectively plunges the etching into darkness. The female genitalia associated with the image of the crouched and faceless woman, works like a *mise en abyme* for the invisible etching, and also for the literary text that surrounds it. It can be read in reference to the Greek Baubo figurines mentioned in *Le Sexe et l'effroi*, where 'le trou du sexe féminin se confondait avec un large visage vu de face' [the aperture of the female sex organ merged into a broad face seen front-on] and 'l'exhibition de la *vulva* plonge celui qui voit dans la pétrification de l'érection' [the exhibition of that *vulva* plunges the one who sees it into the petrified state of erection].[48] It also refers to Quignard's conception, mentioned in the first part of this chapter, of the book as a means to communicate death rather than meaning, knowledge and culture. Here, literature becomes what Jean-François Lyotard has called 'une anamnèse du visible' with reference to painting, an art that '*travaille* [...] pour donner trace ou pour faire signe, dans le visible, d'un geste visuel qui excède le visible' [labors in the strong sense of the word, that used by obstetrics and psychoanalysis, to leave a trace or to make a sign in the visible of a visual gesture that exceeds the visible].[49] Meaume's etching is a bottomless void, in which the gaze of the etched woman stands for the reader's own, also falling into the abysmal space it looks towards. The latter can never be reached, and the text represents the indiscernible origin without ever showing it. It does so firstly by drawing on the description of a visual work that does not exist and thus cannot be seen. Secondly, it is shown in the etching by the woman's head placed in front of the void, which therefore obscures it.

Quignard's representation of reading and of the reader figure characterizes the book as a visual entity and writing as the production of an obscure space in which the book is immersed. He expressed this as early as 1973, in an essay entitled 'Le Manuscrit sur l'air' ('A Manuscript on Air'): 'tout ce qui peut se dire autant le taire. Cela qui ne vient jamais à être signifié [...] il faut tenter de le dire, tenter de le montrer. De le montrer [...] de la manière dont il se présente, c'est-à-dire obscurément' [everything that can be said is better left unsaid. We should always attempt to say and to show what signification leaves behind. Show it as it comes, in all its obscurity].[50] The recourse to a literary form of black manner shows how Quignard attempts to go beyond the limits of writing by relying on the visual. This in turn allows the exposition of the invisible and ungraspable nature of what is aimed at through literature: the 'Jadis' as the unreachable origin, towards which all forms of art are directed.

Notes to Chapter 3

1. LS, p. 88.
2. Irène Fenoglio and Pascal Quignard, Sur le désir de se jeter à l'eau (Paris: Presses Sorbonne nouvelle, 2011), p. 8.
3. Histoires d'écrivains, Pascal Quignard, dir by Loïc Jourdain and Benoît Canu, (La Cinquième MK2 TV, 2000) [DVD].
4. Fenoglio and Quignard, p. 9.
5. Chantal Lapeyre-Desmaison, 'Genèses de l'écriture', in Philippe Bonnefis and Dolorès Lyotard (eds.), Pascal Quignard, figures d'un lettré (Paris: Galilée, 2005), pp. 327–39 (p. 331).
6. Lapeyre-Desmaison, Mémoires de l'origine, pp. 287–88.
7. See Jean Grosfillier, 'Quelques considérations sur l'influence du De contemplatione de Richard de Saint-Victor', Sacris Erudiri, 52 (2013), 235–74; and Valentina Atturo and Alice Bourke, 'Contemplating Wonder: "ad-miratio" in Richard of St. Victor and Dante', Dante Studies, 129 (2011), 99–124.
8. LL, pp. 36–37.
9. LL, p. 39.
10. Pascal Quignard, 'Noésis', in Petits traités, 8 vols (Paris: Maeght, 1990), II, pp. 127–76 (pp. 164, 166).
11. LL, p. 40.
12. Lapeyre-Desmaison, Mémoires de l'origine, p. 273.
13. LEVCM, p. 19.
14. Dylan Evans, 'Father', in An Introductory Dictionary of Lacanian Psychoanalysis (London: Routledge, 1996), pp. 62–64 (p. 62).
15. Jacques Lacan, Le Séminaire, livre VII, l'éthique de la psychanalyse, 1959–60, ed. by Jacques-Alain Miller (Paris: Seuil, 1986), p. 291. The Ethics of Psychoanalysis (1959–1960). The Seminar of Jacques Lacan edited by Jacques-Alain Miller, Book VII, trans. by Dennis Porter (London: Routledge, 1992), p. 248.
16. Lacan, LSVII, p. 293. LSVIIe, p. 250.
17. 'C'est qu'à partir du moment où les mots et le langage et le signifiant entrent en jeu, quelque chose peut être dit [...] que l'un est le héros et l'ami, que l'autre est l'ennemi' [from the moment when words and language and the signifier enter into play, something may be said [...] that one is a hero and a friend, that the other is an enemy]. Lacan, LSVII, p. 324. LSVIIe p. 278.

18. Lacan, *LSVII*, p. 327. *LSVIIe*, p. 281.
19. Lacan, *LSVII*, p. 326. *LSVIIe*, p. 280.
20. Agnès Cousin de Ravel, 'La Peinture, pré-texte à l'écriture chez Pascal Quignard', *L'Esprit Créateur*, 52 (2012), 48–58 (p. 54).
21. *LS*, p. 73.
22. Julien Sorel is depicted as an archetypal reader, frail and delicate and despised for it by his father: 'rien n'était plus antipathique au vieux Sorel; il eût peut-être pardonné à Julien sa taille mince peu propre aux travaux de force, et si différente de celle de ses aînés; mais cette manie de lecture lui était odieuse' [Nothing was more antipathetic to old Sorel than this; he might have forgiven the slender build so little fitted to manual labour and so different from that of his brothers; but this mania for reading was odious to him]. Stendhal, *Le Rouge et le Noir* (Paris: Livre de Poche, 1997), p. 15 (first publ. 1830). *The Red and the Black*, trans. by Roger Gard (New York: Penguin, 2002), p. 25
23. Pascal Quignard, 'Chien de Lisart', in *PT*, v, pp. 23–56 (p. 26).
24. Samuel Auguste Tissot, *De la santé des gens de lettres* (Liège: Bassompierre, 1768), p. 15.
25. Ibid., pp. 15–17.
26. *LEVCM*, pp. 27–28.
27. *LEVCM*, p. 29.
28. *LL*, p. 77. The English translation is taken from Book VII of Diogenes Laertius, *The Lives and Opinions of Eminent Philosophers*, trans. by C.D. Yonge (London: Henry G. Bohn, 1853), p. 259.
29. Midori Ogawa, '*La Frontière*, un roman selon Pascal Quignard', *Gallia*, 42 (2002), 57–64 (pp. 57–58).
30. Ibid., p. 58.
31. Georges Bataille, 'Lascaux, ou la naissance de l'art', in *Œuvres complètes*, 12 vols (Paris: Gallimard, 1970–88), IX (1979) (first publ. 1955). *Lascaux or the Birth of Art*, trans. by Austryn Wainhouse (Lausanne: Skira, 1955).
32. *VS*, p. 352.
33. Pascal Quignard, *La Nuit sexuelle* (Paris: Flammarion, 2007), p. 11. *The Sexual Night*, trans. by Chris Turner (Calcutta: Seagull Books, 2014), pp. 1–2.
34. *LNS*, p. 11. *LNSe*, p. 2.
35. Maurice Blanchot, 'Le regard d'Orphée', in *L'Espace littéraire* (Paris: Gallimard, 1955), pp. 225–32 (p. 225). 'Orpheus's Gaze', in *The Space of Literature*, trans. by Ann Smock (Lincoln: University of Nebraska Press, 1982), pp. 171–76 (p .171).
36. *LS*, p. 131.
37. Pascal Quignard, *Terrasse à Rome* (Paris: Gallimard, 2000), pp. 93–94.
38. *TAR*, pp. 40, 161.
39. *TAR*, p. 46.
40. Pascal Quignard, 'Les Maîtres des ténèbres', in *EDE*, pp. 283–91 (p. 287) (first publ. 2002).
41. Edouard Meaume, *Recherches sur la vie et les ouvrages de Jacques Callot*, 2 vols (Paris: Jules Renouard, 1860).
42. *TAR*, pp. 21–22.
43. *TAR*, pp. 126–27.
44. *TAR*, p. 113.
45. *TAR*, p. 93.
46. Mikhail Bakhtin, *Rabelais and his World* (Bloomington: Indiana University Press, 1984).
47. *TAR*, p. 105.
48. *LSE*, pp. 109–10. *LSEe*, pp. 56–57.
49. Jean-François Lyotard, 'La peinture, anamnèse du visible', in *Misère de la philosophie* (Paris: Galilée, 2000), pp. 97–115 (p. 97). 'Anamnesis of the Visible 2', trans. by John Ronan, *Qui Parle*, 11 (1999), 21–36 (p. 21).
50. Pascal Quignard, 'Le Manuscrit sur l'air', in *EDE*, pp. 65–85 (p. 84) (first publ. 1973).

CHAPTER 4

❖

The Lure of the *Jadis*

Defining writing as a literary black manner creates the image of a book where the spatial and the temporal merge — the book as an obscure space luring the reader towards an unreachable point of origin. The various tropes used by Quignard fuse the spatial and the visual: the prehistoric cave and the maternal womb both situate a time of origins in a dark and inaccessible place. The extended Orphic metaphor running through Quignard's work signals a backward movement towards another space and another time. The Underworld of the Orphic myth offers the motif of a territory outside of life that also represents the temporal location towards which the texts are headed, which is situated not in the past but before it. Whilst the past is defined as '[le] monde des souvenirs, des mots, des noms, des reliques, de la brocante et de l'histoire' [the world of memories, words, names, relics, antiquities and history], Quignard's oeuvre is directed towards '[celui] du perdu, sans images, sans mots, sexuel, indomesticable' [the world of the lost, deprived of images and words; a world that is sexual and impossible to domesticate]. This world is what Quignard refers to as the *Jadis*, giving a substantive form to the adverb used in French to designate the erstwhile, the event that happened long ago, in former times.[1]

Quignard's *Jadis* shares many characteristics with the Lacanian real. It cannot be grasped through words or images, and stands outside both the symbolic and the imaginary. Necessarily experienced through its absence from these two realms, it is a virgin territory, alien to any concepts of differentiation. The *Jadis* is defined as a time that came before a primordial event of separation, which concerns both the individual and the universal. Its sexual nature hints at the image of the maternal womb and at the primitive stage of existence it represents, which starts with the primal scene and ends with parturition. Moreover, the idea that is it located outside of the domesticated world echoes the motif of the prehistoric cave favoured by the writer, and hints at a conception of humanity yet to be distinguished from animality. Finally, the relation to the *Jadis*, which stands as an impossible but necessary destination for the texts, is based on negation. The literary black manner explored in the previous chapter is a way for the writer to try and transform the book into an invisible image, an obscure and unreachable space. The quest for an unreachable *Jadis* means trying to annihilate all that does not belong to it: if it cannot be accessed, the elements seen as working against it can on the other hand be destroyed. Therefore, Quignard does not only attempt to make the book an invisible entity, but also tries to recreate a suitable environment for the *Jadis*, to produce artificially the nest of darkness in which the time of origins took place.

Works such as *La Nuit sexuelle, Le Sexe et l'effroi, Terrasse à Rome* and *La Frontière* all draw on a visual form of obscurity whilst concentrating on subjects that chiefly concern the past: prehistory, myths, the fall of the Roman Empire, and seventeenth-century European art. In these texts, interacting with the past is not an aim but a means. The past is what must be infiltrated in order to approach the *Jadis*, which can never be reached. The past belongs to the symbolic realm and can be accessed not only through material objects, but also through consciousness, memory and intellectual reasoning. But in order to get close to the *Jadis*, the past must go through its own process of obscuration. As this chapter will show, by sabotaging and destroying the possibilities of grasping past events and figures consciously, rationally and physically, Quignard attempts to shorten the distance that separates the past from the *Jadis*. Because the latter is fundamentally unreachable, it is through a backward motion that the texts are ultimately able to point towards this origin.

To create obscurity and to go back in time towards the *Jadis* both amount to the same enterprise. The quest for darkness in Quignard's work can be understood as a reversal of the quest for knowledge represented by Plato's allegory of the cave in *The Republic*. For Socrates, the philosopher walks away from the dark realms of shadows and illusions towards the sun as a metaphor for real knowledge. For Quignard, on the other hand, the writer must lure readers back into the darkness of the cave, where obscurity and the non-solar light of fire create non-palpable and non-graspable images, away from reality and knowledge. The obscurity that defines the *Jadis* is both visual and intellectual in a negative sense. The quest implies a process of obscuration that is the opposite of enlightenment: an exploration of the past that aims to bury it deeper by sabotaging knowledge and truth.

This attitude suggests an opposition to history and historiography taken as evidence of the need for a rational understanding of the past. Quignard's work is marked by a strong anti-historical and anti-historiographical stance, which relies widely on a limited conception of both the concept and discipline of history. Its specific relation to the past is built and expressed through the rejection of chronology and the idea of a linear progression of time. While history, as a scientific discipline, is seen as preoccupied with truth and knowledge, Quignard's writing on the past is infused with fiction: novels and myths are written as alternatives to historical discourses, by an author who identifies with the archaeologist rather than the historian. Implicit references to Michel Foucault sustain Quignard's attempt to define writing according to his own agenda, which positions him as an 'inventor' of the past, accessing underground vestiges rather than bringing them back to the surface.

This anti-historical stance is also part of a larger attempt to put forward the advantages of obscurity over that of knowledge. The quest for the *Jadis* implies the attempt to return to an undomesticated state, through an operation which Quignard refers to as 'l'é-érudition' [a de-erudition process], which implies scraping away cultural marks to reveal the animality that lies at the origin of mankind.[2] Literary writing becomes both anti-historical and anti-philosophical, on the side of rhetoric rather than philosophy. This reveals yet another paradox at the heart of Quignard's writing: how can its undeniably erudite nature cohabit with the wish for 'é-érudition'? The second part of this chapter will explore the implications of this paradoxical stance, and show how Quignard attempts to use erudition to develop a definition of the writer as a predator.

Writing as Archeology

The quest for the *Jadis* is not about recapturing or bringing back the past, but rather preserving the uncertainty, obscurity and remoteness of people, things and events that existed before us. Pautrot notes the importance of Quignard's opposition to history and historiography: 'chaque livre invective plus ou moins ouvertement l'Histoire comme récit constitué, exclusif, explicatif, voire prescriptif' [each work can be read as a more or less overt attack against history defined as an established, exclusive, explanatory and even prescriptive narrative].[3] Through this negative characterization of history's supposedly hierarchical, progressive and rationalizing nature, the writer joins ranks, as Pautrot goes on to argue, with thinkers such as Jean-François Lyotard and Jean Baudrillard. Both developed a conception of history as fiction disguised as scientific truth, and as the necessary product of a modernity obsessed with the idea of progress. Quignard's conception of history also relies on the belief that it is ruled by the idea of progress, and on the fact that, as he puts it in *Albucius*, historians are ruled by fear and 'font semblant de croire que ce qui arrive dans le monde des hommes est cohérent' [they pretend to believe the things that happen to humankind are coherent].[4] By favouring myths and literary tales — what Jean-François Lyotard's calls 'petit récits' [small narratives] — over history and its 'métarécits' [metanarratives], Quignard situates his work within a postmodern condition characterized by Lyotard as the rejection of progress, truth and knowledge.[5] But his opposition to history is also embedded in a quest for a time outside of the past and the present, preceding any notion of time.

To approach this paradoxical and impossible temporal space, Quignard first takes aim at the chronological and progressive logic that history is meant to impose, through both a literary and a personal desire to exit the present. In a text entitled '1640', he writes:

> En 1979 j'ai écrit: 'J'espère être lu en 1640'. Benjamin dans 'Zentralpark' dit que nous devons avoir devant la vie moderne l'attitude du XVIIᵉ siècle devant l'Antiquité. C'est-à-dire: Il faut vivre le présent comme la ruine qu'il prépare. Il faut découvrir le présent comme une ruine dont on recherche le trésor. La ruine du jadis qui se répète — ou plutôt qui ne cesse pas de commencer. La ruine qui ne cesse pas de jaillir. La Ruine jaillissante, voilà ce que je nomme le 1640.

> [In 1979 I wrote that I hoped to be read in 1640. Benjamin in 'Central Park' states that we should face modern life the same way people in the seventeenth century viewed Antiquity. In other words: experience the present as a ruin in the making. The present should be explored like a ruin under which lies a treasure. The ruin of the Jadis as a never-ending source. 1640 as a source that never stops gushing.][6]

Through a play on the exactitude of dates (1640, 1979) and on the reader's awareness that the text was published in 1999, the writer creates an effect of immobility and repetition. The fusion of 1979 and 1640 underlines the absurdity of his desire to be read in 1640. This resistance to chronology is pursued at the end of the passage, where 1640 becomes an object rather than a date inscribed in a chronological conception of time. Finally, by implicitly referring to Stendhal's well-known wish to be read in 1935, Quignard substitutes a temporal relation for a literary one. As he explains elsewhere: 'par cette boutade, en référence à Stendhal je nie la succession temporelle. Que le proche soit très lointain et le lointain extrêmement proche. Le rêve, ce serait de dire: j'écris pour l'origine' [I playfully refer to Stendhal as a way to reject the idea of time as a succession of events. My wish is for the very close to be very far and the very far to become extremely close. The dream for me would be to say: I write for the origin].[7]

1640 becomes, through a series of literary echoes, a simultaneous reference to Antiquity, the seventeenth century, Stendhal's vision of the twentieth century, and, with the mention of Walter Benjamin's 'Central Park', to Charles Baudelaire. What Quignard presents as general guidance was written by Benjamin as an observation on Baudelaire, who 'confronted modern life in a way comparable to that in which the seventeenth century confronted antiquity'.[8] This transformation of Benjamin's words into a universal model for dealing with the past is typical of Quignard. It allows a representation of the present as what should be experienced through the promise of the past it contains, to be treated as an upcoming ruin. It also refers to Nietzsche's conception of time as 'eternal recurrence', and to the idea that 'all truth is crooked [and] time itself is a circle' found in *Thus Spoke Zarathustra*.[9] Progress and the necessary sequencing of events are replaced by a circular representation of time, influenced by Nietzsche and, by extension, by Eastern philosophy. For Quignard, all events are a repetition of the same, because they are equal in their relation to the inaccessible *Jadis*.

Quignard's negation of time as a linear succession of events and its definition in relation to a point of origin lead to a second anti-historical tactic, which attempts to replace chronology with metamorphosis. Whilst the metamorphic process by definition implies change, and is thus not strictly about the repetition or the return of the same, Quignard seems to favour it because it allows distance from the rationality he associates with history. This is explicitly set out in *Le Sexe et l'effroi*, which begins with an ambitious project: to challenge the common historical view of the passage from Ancient Greece to Roman civilization and of the arrival of Christianity. The text's focus on the relation between civilization and sex introduces a point of comparison with the last two volumes of Foucault's *Histoire de la sexualité* (*The History of Sexuality*), which present the idea, borrowed in *Le Sexe et l'effroi*, of a continuity between the role of sex in Greek and Roman times and its function in contemporary Western culture. This reference is never explicitly stated, yet, as Arlette Farge notes, Quignard's texts 'emportent l'historien sur d'autres terres que la sienne [...] rejoindre un Nietzsche ou un Foucault' [lead historians away from familiar territories [...] towards Nietzsche and Foucault].[10] Foucault's intertextual presence is rooted in a larger enterprise aimed at debunking scientific claims of universal and objective knowledge. This is dependent on the conception of history as a tool used to show how accepted truths (such as the definition of madness as a mental illness in Foucault's work) are in fact products of specific social norms and of given eras and civilizations. Foucault's displacement of the historical into the 'archaeological' and the 'genealogical' is a potent reference for understanding Quignard's own attitude towards history. For Foucault, joining an archaeological and a genealogical study of history helps uncover structures and links left out by historiography. Quignard's opposition to knowledge is also in relation to Foucault's definition of knowledge as an instrument of power and domination. Unlike Foucault, however, Quignard uses historical and archaeological practices not to uncover hidden structures of knowledge, but to create obscurity and reveal an absence. What Quignard aims for is the *Jadis*, defined by its inaccessibility (physical, temporal and intellectual), and the debunking of knowledge becomes for him a way to approach this impossible destination.

In *Le Sexe et l'effroi*, the main narrative object is not a specific series of events or the customs and habits of a civilization, but rather the attempt, in Roman frescoes and other forms of artistic expression, to represent an invisible point of origin. *Le Sexe et l'effroi* focuses in large part on the frescoes adorning the walls of Pompeii's Villa of Mysteries:

> Les patriciennes représentées sur les fresques que les anciens Romains composèrent sont comme à l'ancre. Elles se tiennent immobiles, le regard latéral, dans une attente sidérée, figées jusqu'au moment dramatique d'un récit que nous ne comprenons plus.

> [The patrician women represented in the frescoes painted by the ancient Romans seem to be lying anchored to the ground. They stand stock-still in a state of thunderstruck anticipation, their eyes glancing off to one side of the picture; they are frozen just at the dramatic point of a story we no longer understand.][11]

The same frescoes are described elsewhere by the writer as 'des peintures de l'instant qui précède la mort' [paintings that capture the instant just before death];[12] presenting them both as presages of Pompeii's destruction and icons of a city that has been frozen in time. The frescoes show time as a continuous entity marked by the inescapable but deathly presence of the past. They also show art as the representation of the non-visible. According to Quignard, art has an indirect way of interacting with an absent scene of origins:

> il faut confier son regard à un détour qui arrache au face à face médusé et mortel avec ce qui n'a pas de nom. Il faut une 'réflexion' sur un bouclier, sur un miroir, sur une peinture, sur l'eau de la rivière de Narcisse [...]. Caravage disait dans les premières années du XVIIe siècle: 'Tout tableau est une tête de Méduse. On peut vaincre la terreur par l'image de la terreur. Tout peintre est Persée'.

> [one must trust to some roundabout avoidance of the petrified, lethal face-to-face confrontation with the nameless. One needs a 'reflection' on a shield, in a mirror or a painting, on the water of Narcissus' river. [...] In the early years of the seventeenth century, Caravaggio said: 'Every painting is a Medusa's head. You can conquer terror by the image of terror. Every painter is Perseus'.][13]

As visual artworks, the frescoes directly address the anguish and terror created by the void left by the scene of origins, which for Quignard is both impossible to gaze at and to return to. As the event of procreation, it is situated in a non-reachable anteriority. Because of what they actually represent — the patricians' 'lateral gaze' — the frescoes are also a *mise en abyme* of the way art expresses the void whilst avoiding the terror and death that staring at it would cause. The myths of Medusa and of Orpheus, present throughout Quignard's work, provide useful representations of this impossible gaze by representing the 'interdit de regarder en arrière (Orphée)' and the 'interdit de regarder en face (Méduse)' [prohibition both on looking back (Orpheus) and on looking directly in the face (Medusa)].[14]

Le Sexe et l'effroi's reading of Roman civilization borrows from myths, psycho-analysis, and from a Foucauldian use of archaeology: social and artistic practices merge to bring forth their common source, identified as the unconscious and irrational relation to an invisible and absent scene of origins. Elsewhere, Quignard goes further by suggesting that this relation is found again and again in different times and eras marked by a fascination for the Roman Empire. In a filmed interview, he describes 'un retour du monde romain qui hante l'Europe' [the Roman world coming back to haunt Europe] through three main examples: first the discovery, in 1748, of the ruins of Pompeii, and the subsequent development of a European-wide Roman trend, where artistic practices, political revolutions, and even fashion were all 'à la Romaine' [inspired by Ancient Rome].[15] The following illustrations are, respectively, the coronation of Napoleon, inspired by the reign of Caesar, and twentieth-century fascism. Quignard, in true Lacanian fashion, relies on the linguistic echoes between '*fascinatio*' and 'fascism' to make his point. This furthermore illustrates how the writer chooses to replace time as a rational succession of events with a series of periods united by a persistent return to a specific moment in time (the obsession with the Roman era), itself defined as a veil hiding the eternal lure of the *Jadis*. Beyond the excavations of hidden temporal links and structures — Quignard's interpretation of Foucault's 'archaeology' and 'genealogy' — hides the pure and unsolvable impossibility of knowledge.

As *Le Sexe et l'effroi* dwells on the image of the petrified painted patricians found in the Villa of Mysteries, the reader is reminded of the casts made from the bodies and objects found in Pompeii, forever fixed in their terrified and suffering states. On the one hand, the vestiges found in Pompeii and Herculaneum provided historians with a wealth of information about life in that period, therefore enabling the construction of a reliable historiography. On the other hand, these vestiges are artificial casts, which were made after nineteenth-century archaeologist Giuseppe Fiorelli noticed the cavities formed by corpses and decomposing objects in a sub-layer of mud beneath the destroyed sites. By injecting plaster into these holes, 'death itself [was] moulded and cast', as Thomas Henry Dyer puts it.[16] Through this example, archaeology appears as a practice that exposes absence, offering a neat symbol for the absent point of origin Quignard's work tries to reach. French archaeological terminology calls the discovery of a site an 'invention', which might explain Quignard's reliance on the practice to define his own literary enterprise. As he writes, 'il faut sans cesse ramener des preuves que l'on part prélever dans le sous-sol de la terre et l'ombre de l'histoire' [one must constantly bring back proof retrieved from underground and snatched from history's shadow].[17]

The perpetual return of the past, as illustrated by a recurring Western and modern fascination for Roman times, and the omnipresence, through its absence, of the *Jadis*, are sources of strength, of anguish and of death. To face the void is a fertile and powerful act, one that provokes a potent flow of force. Yet the submission to an eternal recurrence of the past is deathly and it creates suffering and distress. Writing might appear as a way of taking control of the pain induced by the loss of the *Jadis*: 'déjouer les conditions du passé en modifiant un peu les figures du passé, c'est perturber l'idée même d'avenir et [cela] m'intéresse' [by slightly modifying past figures I can escape from the conditions imposed by that past. This is what I am interested in, what enables me to disrupt the very idea of future].[18] Here Quignard acknowledges the deathly aspect contained in the invasive presence of the past and in the way it shapes both present and future. But he also hints at the manner in which his own writing, through a modification of the past, tries to undo the latter's morbid primacy. It suggests a positive conception of literature, seen as the powerful replacement of reality by fiction and of truth by invention. This is the view put forward by Lapeyre-Desmaison, who argues that, for Quignard, 'se tourner vers le passé est tout le contraire d'un acte nostalgique' [to reach towards the past is the opposite of a nostalgic act]; it is an attitude marked by a 'fécondité créatrice' [a nature that is both creative and fecund].[19]

The issues posed by defining Quignard's writing as fertile rather than destructive, and as an act of creation rather than disappearance, will be assessed in the last chapter of this book. For now, it is essential to understand how Quignard's rejection of history in favour of a literary form of archaeology is part of a larger opposition to the conception of language as truth. By attempting to modify the past, the writer removes any possibility of truth being gained or of knowledge being shared. History is processed through fiction; in *Le Sexe et l'effroi*, accounts of actual events, such as the destruction of Pompeii, are interwoven with the retelling of ancient myths. Quignard's work explores the gaps left by predominant historical discourses, both highlighting and denouncing the limitations it sees in such discourses. His 1994 novel *L'Occupation américaine* [*The American Occupation*] is set during an often overlooked period of recent French history: the 'occupation' by American troops of a number of French towns in the aftermath of the Second World War.[20] The choice of such a temporal setting illustrates the writer's desire to denounce the way historiography creates hierarchy and narration from the succession of events.

This obscuration of history is also visible in texts such as *Terrasse à Rome* and *Les Tablettes de buis d'Apronenia Avitia*, where the writing of fiction challenges and annihilates the writing of history. Meaume and Avitia are fictional characters, yet everything is done to fool readers into thinking that they really existed: the assertive nature of the erudition displayed, the preciseness of dates and places, all take part in the creation of a lie. As Michel Deguy notes: 'l'énonciation quignardienne [...] annonce en dénonçant, dénonce en annonçant' [Quignard's use of assertion asserts by denouncing and denounces by asserting], whilst 'l'érudition est art de raconter une histoire' [erudition becomes the art of storytelling].[21] Erudition is used as material for fiction, and beneath the assertive display of knowledge drawn from history is the desire to avoid any authoritative position. This is achieved through a conscious breach of trust and the creation of a new kind of reading pact. The reversal of usual functions of erudition and authority allows the writer to make controversial statements about his own reliance on culture and regarding the use of etymology. According to Quignard, it is not there to 'obtenir un effet de vérité [,] mais pour qu'on soit perdu complètement et qu'il y ait un effet de vide qui naisse du mot lui-même' [obtain a truth effect but to create a feeling of total loss, and to extract a feeling of lack from the word itself].[22] In other words, the idea is to replace the quest for truth with a misleading discourse whilst simultaneously pointing towards the *Jadis*. Quignard's readers find themselves in dangerous territory; they are forced to enter a space where the boundaries between truth and fiction are blurred and where erudition is manipulated to create deception. By mixing together truth and fiction, by creating an illusory trick and a fool's game for the reader, Quignard's work does not aspire to revelation or enlightenment, but darkness and obscurity.

'L'Homme Paré du Prestige de la Bête' [Man Clad in the Glory of the Beast][23]

Quignard's anti-historical stance entails two main tactics. The first is to redefine the past as a relation to time ruled by an omnipresent but ultimately absent point of origin, defined as the *Jadis*. The second is to attack historical discourse by using it against itself. The reliance on a literary form of archaeology implies that writing is an act of invention meant to create obscurity and fiction. This means that Quignard's quest for the *Jadis*, and the effort of obscuration it demands, is not only anti-historical but also anti-rational. The texts more specifically express a rejection of philosophy, based on a conception of literature as non-rational and non-human, allowing a return to an original state of savagery and animality.

It is important to note that the impossibility of communicating truth frequently found in Quignard's work relies mainly on structuralist and post-structuralist critiques of language, which challenge the idea of verbal and written languages as transparent and rational modes of communication. Quignard subscribes to the awareness of an inadequacy between the word and the thing it names and of a reality much wider than the system of signs that tries to give it meaning. But rather than acknowledging the influence of theories developed by his contemporaries, the writer consistently chooses to present this conception of language as rooted in a trend of scepticism that goes back to a Classical opposition between rhetoric and philosophy.

The Orphic descent into the *Jadis*, which can be opposed to the philosopher's ascent from the cave in Plato's parable, is a first image used to refute a Socratic belief in the accession to knowledge through rational thinking. In *La Raison* (*Reason*), the anti-Socratic figure depicted is the Roman rhetorician Marcus Porcius Latro, presented as '[le] seul penseur que la Rome ancienne ait produit' [the only thinker Ancient Rome ever produced], an opponent of 'ce que les Grecs appelaient "logos" et que les anciens Romains nommaient "ratio"' [what Greeks named *logos* and

the Ancient Romans called *ratio*].[24] *La Raison*'s attack on rationality is pursued in
Rhétorique spéculative (Speculative Rhetoric); both works, published in the early 1990s,
reverse the usual hierarchy between philosophy and rhetoric, to argue that 'la
philosophie n'est qu'une rouille sur le glaive [de la rhétorique]' [philosophy is merely
the rust on the sword of rhetoric].[25] Again, despite Quignard's relative silence on
his contemporary influences, by aligning himself with rhetoric he situates his
writing not only alongside Classical texts, but also within a tradition that goes
from the French thinkers Pascal and Jean-Jacques Rousseau, through philosophers
such as Kierkegaard, Nietzsche and Wittgenstein, to Lacan. This modern lineage
is identified by Alain Badiou, who regroups these figures under the banner of
'antiphilosophy', which he defines by means of three main characteristics. The
first is a critique of language used by philosophy, followed by a recognition that
behind the philosopher's idealization of truth lies the fact that philosophy is an act
of power, and finally a will to go beyond the philosophical act: 'l'appel fait, contre
l'acte philosophique, à un autre acte, d'une radicale nouveauté' [the appeal made,
against the philosophical act, to another, radically new act]. In Wittgenstein's case,
this means 'porter dans l'activité scientifique ou propositionnelle le principe d'une
clarté dont l'élément (mystique) est au-delà de cette activité, et dont le paradigme
réel est l'art' [bringing into scientific and propositional activity the principle of
a kind of clarity whose (mystical) element is beyond this activity and the real
paradigm of which is art]. Music is the ultimate horizon for Wittgenstein, yet, as
Badiou puts it: 'il ne s'agit pas non plus de substituer l'art à la philosophie' [it is not a
question of substituting art for philosophy].[26] If Quignard, by the dismissal of truth,
belongs to the tradition of 'antiphilosophy' defined by Badiou, he differs from
Wittgenstein in that, for him, art is in fact a substitute for philosophy. This is made
clear from the beginning of *Rhétorique spéculative*, which evokes a 'tradition lettrée
antiphilosophique' [a literary tradition of antiphilosophy], creating a direct line of
descent from the rhetorician to the writer. In that sense, Quignard's texts, which
constantly oscillate between essay and fiction, between assertion and narration,
serve a primarily literary purpose.

   In *Rhétorique spéculative,* and other texts such as *La Parole de la Délie, essai sur
Maurice Scève*, writing is explicitly situated within a tradition of rhetoricians and
sophists. It displays arguments of authority and a performative language influenced
by a Gorgiasian form of rhetoric. One section of the essay on Scève's 'Délie' opens
with a quotation attributed to Gorgias, which defines *logos* as 'un corps d'une telle
chétivité' [such a frail body].[27] In Plato's *Gorgias*, Socrates shows that rhetoric is
inferior to philosophy because it relies on opinions rather than knowledge, and
because it convinces its audience through tricks of flattery rather than rational
constructions: 'rhetoric is a part of something not at all fine [...] a practice, not of a
craftsman, but of a guessing, brave soul, naturally clever at approaching people'.[28]
Socrates also highlights how rhetoric relies on a physical rather than intellectual
use of words, and how rhetoricians have the power to convince crowds regardless
of the righteousness and truth of their discourses: 'the rhetor [...] doesn't know the
things themselves, what is good or bad, what is fine or shameful or just or unjust,
but has devised persuasion about them'.[29] By aligning literature with rhetoric,

Quignard positions Gorgias as a model to follow, basing his avowed preference for rhetoric on the opposition to philosophy it implies. This means reversing Plato's own treatment of Gorgias and — keeping Socrates's definition of the art of rhetoric — inverting the established hierarchy between the philosopher and the rhetorician. Quignard embraces the belief that language is incapable of communicating truth and subscribes to the ideas, presented in Gorgias's lost treatise *On the Nonexistent or On Nature*, 'that nothing exists; second, that even if it exists it is inapprehensible to man; third, that even if it is apprehensible, still it is without a doubt incapable of being expressed or explained to the next man'.[30]

The rejection of a Socratic view of knowledge as something to be accessed through discourse leads Gorgias — and Quignard — to embrace language as a powerful tool of seduction. According to Sharon Crowley, 'Gorgias [...] wants to free language from any ties to objective reality, in order that language may be exploited to its fullest potential as a medium for creating illusions and exciting emotions'.[31] The same can be said of Quignard, as exemplified by his claim of a 'modification' of the past and the replacement of history with invention. In *Rhétorique spéculative*, 'le littéraire' [the literary figure] is defined as 'un preux, un hardi, un menaçant' [fearless, bold and menacing].[32] Such a representation contradicts the simultaneous conception of writing as devoted to the creation of obscurity and disappearance. How can the claim of a destruction of language through writing coexist with this definition of literary writing as a productive and powerful act? Quignard resolves this paradox — and the next chapter will examine in turn the contradictions implied by his stance — by stating that literature does not belong to the realm of language as we know it, but to another domain, shared by dreamers, animals and rhetoricians:

> Les littéraires ne doivent pas s'identifier au langage *in flore* (les systèmes), ni même au langage *in herba* (la langue vernaculaire), mais au langage *in germine*, à la semence originaire. [...] La philosophie doit être rejetée parce qu'elle divertit de la prédation propre au langage.
>
> [Those who practice literature should not identify with language *in flore* (the language of systems) nor with language *in herba* (the language that we share) but with language *in germine* (the original seed of language). Philosophy should be rejected because it refutes this predatory nature of language.][33]

This idea of a primitive essence of language broadly corresponds to what Julia Kristeva sees as the language of prehistoric and primitive societies, defined as 'une *substance* et une force *matérielle*' [a *substance* and a *material* force]. As Kristeva explains:

> Si l'homme primitif, *parle, symbolise, communique*, c'est-à-dire établit une distance entre lui-même (comme sujet) et le dehors (le réel) pour le signifier dans un système de différences (le langage), il ne *connaît* pas cet acte comme un acte d'idéalisation ou d'abstraction, mais au contraire comme une *participation* à l'univers environnant [...]. Il participe comme un élément cosmique du *corps* et de la *nature*, confondu avec la force motrice du corps et de la nature.
>
> [While primitive man *speaks, symbolizes*, and *communicates*, that is to say, establishes a distance between himself (as subject) and the outside (the real) in order to signify it in a system of differences (language), he does not *know* this act

to be an act of idealization or of abstraction, but knows it instead as *participation* in the surrounding universe. [...] It participates as a cosmic element of the body and nature, and is joined with the motor force of the body and nature.][34]

When *in germine*, language takes on a certain materiality, a performative and magical power that is defined as predatory. Its use supposes the return to a primitive form of existence, giving a new signification to the quest for the *Jadis*. The desire to return to a primordial state of being becomes the wish to reclaim a primordial, undomesticated form of language and existence.

In *Rhétorique spéculative*, humanity is defined as 'la conversion en prédatrice d'une espèce qui figurait au titre de proie' [a species that from prey turned into predator] and its origins are located in the practice of 'prédation imitée' [the imitation of predation].[35] This conception of humanity as originating in the mimicry of animal habits implicitly refers to Bataille's seminal essay 'Lascaux, ou la naissance de l'art' (*Lascaux or the Birth of Art*). Literary writing, in Quignard's view, should recognize the predatory origin of mankind: the idea that 'le littéraire est cette remontée de la convention à ce fonds biologique dont la lettre ne s'est jamais séparée' [the literary lies in this ascent from convention to a biological terrain, which writing never truly left].[36] Situating literature in a primeval space and defining literary writing as a practice connected to a primitive and predatory form of existence relies on the deployment of a logic that is specifically metamorphic in nature. In *Rhétorique spéculative*, literary language is presented as being affected by a constant process of *metaphora*, of transport. Metaphors, which merge one element into another by implicit comparison, are seen as the linguistic and rhetorical embodiment of metamorphosis. Language, Quignard argues, can only function through metaphor: 'nous transmettons des mots auxquels le visage est impossible: la révélation ne séjourne pas dans le langage, qui manifeste en se transportant, en se déplaçant' [we transmit words that have no face: revelations cannot happen within a language that only manifests itself through transport and movement]. Here, the familiar trope of an impossible encounter between the word and the thing accompanies a characterization of the linguistic system as a form of transport. Because they can never fully capture the world, words go through a series of metamorphoses without ever becoming the things they stand for: 'sans qu'il puisse connaître un instant de pause, [le langage] se transporte, s'arrache, jaillit, passe' [language moves, tears itself away, gushes, passes without pause].[37] The idea that literary language is ruled by such metamorphic logic is what allows Quignard to represent the *Jadis* as a state of being in which humanity has yet to be separated from a purely animal nature. This anthropomorphic condition can be defined, using an expression found in Bataille's essay on Lascaux, as the paradox of 'man clad in the glory of the beast'.

According to Rabaté, 'l'œuvre dont se rapproche le plus celle de Quignard aujourd'hui est, sans doute, celle de Georges Bataille' [The oeuvre Quignard's work is probably closest to is Georges Bataille's].[38] In particular, Rabaté likens Quignard's 'totalizing enterprise' in the *Dernier royaume* series to Bataille's unfinished *Somme athéologique* (*The Atheological Sum*). Quignard's texts take up many of the themes featured in Bataille's work, including the prehistoric art in the Lascaux caves. In his essay, Bataille defines one of the cave paintings as 'l'une des premières figurations de l'être humain [et] l'une des plus significatives' [one of the most significant of the earliest known figurations of the human being].[39] This same painting, representing a creature half-man, half-bird, is described by Quignard as 'cet homme-oiseau érigé tombant sur le dos en transe [qui] forme pour l'humanité une extraordinaire première image d'elle-même' [a man-bird, erect yet falling backwards, which constitutes the first and most extraordinary image that humanity has of itself].[40] The remarkable nature of the painting comes from its representation of mankind in a transitional and metamorphic state. It is a cross between animal and man, caught in a movement that fuses both the erect position associated with humans and the crouching posture typical of animals. Bataille notes how the image's specificity also comes from its difference from the paintings around it. Whilst they show animal figures in a realistic manner, the man-bird painting appears to have been drawn hesitantly, with a unique ruggedness and naivety.

Kristeva, in *Langage, cet inconnu* (*Language: the Unknown*), defines the Lascaux paintings as geometrical figures, symbolizing the passage from a visual representation, imitative of nature, to a first attempt at abstraction — the birth of the sign:

> Il est frappant de constater que les représentations humaines perdent leur caractère 'réaliste' et deviennent abstraites, construites à l'aide de triangles, de carrés, de lignes, de points, comme sur les parois des grottes de Lascaux, tandis que les animaux sont représentés d'une manière réaliste, s'efforçant de reproduire leur forme et mouvement.

> [It is striking that representations of humans lost their 'realistic' character and became abstract; they were constructed with the help of triangles, squares, lines and dots, as on the walls of the Lascaux caves. Animals, however, were represented in a realistic manner that tried to reproduce their form in motion.][41]

Kristeva's reading of the anthropomorphic Lascaux paintings is reminiscent of the conception of language explored in Quignard's *Rhétorique spéculative*. It puts forward a language that is physical rather than abstract, and which belongs to the natural world. But Quignard's own reading of the 'man-bird' painting is closer to Bataille's than Kristeva's. Where she identifies the rise of an abstract form of language, Bataille locates the expression of a double loss, describing the confusion of the Lascaux painters created by their inherently transitive state, and their nostalgia for the animality they left behind:

> Avec une sorte de bonheur imprévu, ces hommes de Lascaux rendirent sensibles le fait qu'étant des hommes, ils nous ressemblaient, mais ils l'ont fait en nous laissant l'image de l'animalité qu'ils quittaient. Comme s'ils avaient dû parer un prestige naissant de la grâce animale qu'ils avaient perdue.

> [These Lascaux Men forcefully transmitted to us the fact that, being men, they resembled us, but as a means for telling us so they left us innumerable pictures of the animality they were shedding — as though they had felt obliged to clothe a nascent marvel with the animal grace they had lost.][42]

The Lascaux painters were ashamed of their human form because it alienated them from the animals they hunted and painted. A similar yearning for lost animality is expressed in Quignard's work, which relies on a reversal of the hierarchy between man and beast: according to *Rhétorique spéculative*, 'nous n'avons jamais connu le "détachement" du règne animal et du monde naturel que nous supposons. Au contraire, nous avons accru l'attachement' [contrary to what we may think, we never experienced a 'detachment' from the natural and animal realms. The opposite is true: we increased our attachment to it].[43]

This controversial claim is developed through a reliance on the motif of metamorphosis. Anthropomorphism is a liminal state of being, and metamorphoses are used to describe a return to animality, or at least a departure from what makes us human. This is the case in 'La Voix perdue', where the frog-queen symbolizes a primitive aquatic life form common to both animal and man. Another example can be found in Quignard's 1989 novel *Les Escaliers de Chambord* where the protagonist's frequent fantasies offer a fictional representation of the paradox evoked by Bataille. Edouard Furfooz, whose name evokes both 'fur' and 'fuzz', is described as being constantly cold. Pautrot notes how this name 'renvoie aux sites magdaléniens sur les rives de la Lesse, en Belgique près de Gand' [is a reference to the Magdalenian prehistoric sites in Belgium on the banks of the Lesse river near Ghent].[44] Furfooz's incessant need for warmth leads to recurring daydreams, where he sees himself wrapped up in 'un pull-over vraiment chaud, extrêmement chaud, angora, aussi doux que la fourrure d'un chat ou le ventre d'un enfant' [a very warm sweater, extremely warm, made of angora wool, as soft as a cat's fur or the belly of a child].[45] Furfooz's bodily craving for a carnal refuge relates more widely to his family history, and to a sense of loss and estrangement. The only lineage Furfooz can identify with is a long way back in time:

> Un temps très ancien et très froid, à l'aube du paléolithique [...] quelques hommes erraient, se nourrissaient d'hyènes, de mammouths et d'ours. Ils écorchaient avec des os, sur le cuir des bêtes vivantes et hurlantes la laine — cette laine qui avait été à l'origine de la fortune des Furfooz. Ils s'abritaient dans des grottes enfumées semblables à celles qu'il avait visitées souvent, enfant [...]. Jadis, il avait été l'un de ces hommes.

> [A very long time ago, in colder times, before the Paleolithic period [...] A few wandering men survived by eating hyenas, mammoths and bears. They used bones to tear the wool directly from the skin of live and screaming animals: the same wool the Furfooz family used to build their fortune. They took refuge in smoky caves, just like the ones he often visited as a child. Once upon a time, he had been one of these men.][46]

In this passage, temporal duration and linearity are rejected in favour of a personal myth of origins that skips back from present times to the *Jadis*, connecting the industrialized production of wool developed by his family and the customs Furfooz associates with his remote prehistoric ancestors.

The backward movement that allows Furfooz to skip through time and find refuge in an identification with prehistoric figures is also present in Quignard's definition of writing as a process of 'é-érudition' [de-erudition], which he defines in *Pascal Quignard le solitaire*:

> Je ne suis pas un érudit. *Rudis* est le sauvage. E-rudis est celui à qui on a ôté son aspérité, sa sauvagerie, sa violence originaire ou naturelle ou animale [...]. Je cherche encore à m'é-érudir. Je ne suis pas encore assez rude.

[I am not erudite: *rudis* is the savage. *E-rudis* is the one without savagery, without asperity, without the violence that defines our animal and natural origins [...]. I am still trying to become a de-erudite. I am not yet rough enough.][47]

One might wonder how such a process of de-erudition can actually be achieved. Claims of violence and animality attached to the definition of writing as a predatory practice are striking in a work that uses a complex layering of intertextual references as its prime material, and which has often been characterized as precious, highly cultured and — as it happens — erudite. To face this contradiction, Quignard first relies on the idea of erasure contained in the term 'erudition'. In the passage above, the process of learning is likened to an act of polishing, through which every trace of ruggedness and savagery is removed to create a perfectly smoothed and civilized individual. In order to reverse this process, the logic of metamorphosis is again used. In *Le Sexe et l'effroi*, 'logos', 'ratio' and 'ego' are defined as 'des mouches porteuses d'étranges virus' [flies carrying strange viruses] hovering above the backs of the preverbal and the pre-human.[48] To rid oneself of rational language is to chase away a dangerous nuisance, as an animal would an insect. The de-erudition process also relies on a representation of the writer as a warrior figure, and of writing as 'un double geste de rébellion et de revigoration' [both a rebellious and reinvigorating act].[49] Bénédicte Gorillot follows this lead when she defines the writer's use of Latin as the powerful reinvention of a dead language that also symbolizes a dry form of erudition. By embracing Latin, most notably in the poetic work *Inter ærias fagos*,[50] Quignard invests it with a savage nature: 'une réponse violente à la violence subie en langue maternelle [et qui] renvoie au "silence" murmurant des animaux qui grognent, mais ne parlent pas' [a violent response to the violence of the mother tongue and an echo of the 'silence' of animals who growl but do not speak].[51] Here, Gorillot implicitly refers to the motif of the scavenger evoked by Quignard in one of his essays, where the figure of the writer is shown as feeding on the dead, using their remains to gain energy and produce his own texts: 'sucer les os des cadavres, les trouer, souffler dans la mort de ce qui nous précède' [sucking on the bones of dead men, until they break, and breathing in the death of what precedes us].[52]

This representation of the writer as a potent figure relies on the redefinition of literary language as both performative and seductive, and of literary writing as situated on the side of illusion and invention rather than reason and truth. What Quignard seems to suggest is that language cannot produce truth, but its inherent authoritative power and violence should still be exploited. This serves as the basis for the many paradoxical claims made in his work, where literature appears as the realm where impossible things become possible. This is also typical of rhetoricians and sophists, figures Quignard uses as models to denounce and expose language as a tool of power. In Gorgiasian rhetoric, language is 'an art of illusion, deception and power' that does not have to conform to reality,[53] and this is used by Quignard to assert the antithetical alliance of erudition and savagery.

But if Quignard relies on rhetoric, its inherent deceptive logic corrupts all discourse it produces, including the claim of a possible coexistence between an erudite and a savage nature of writing. The latter remains necessarily deceitful; the belief in an ultimately potent and victorious writer can only amount to an illusion, which plays on the willingness of critics and readers to be seduced by Quignard's rhetorical tactics. In truth, the desire to return to an animal and primordial state of being seems irreconcilable with the erudite nature of the work. This desire is one of the consequences of the relation to the *Jadis*, which drives the body of work forward — or rather backward, whilst remaining, at all times, necessarily unreachable. As the *Jadis* and the past cannot be regained, and the impossibility at the heart of writing cannot be transcended, the literary work is doomed to disappear. In the final chapter, I shall argue that the 'predatory' language adopted by Quignard, part of his quest for the *Jadis*, is not victorious but self-destructive, and that its inherent violence is turned inwards, through acts of carving, fragmenting and burning that are applied to the texts themselves.

Notes to Chapter 4

1. Pascal Quignard, *Sordidissimes (Dernier royaume V)* (Paris: Grasset, 2005), p. 49.
2. *LS*, pp. 112–13.
3. Pautrot, *Pascal Quignard ou le fonds du monde*, p. 8.
4. *AL*, p. 107. *ALe*, p. 81. It is worth noting here that this question of truth has long been a topic of debate for historians. As the nineteenth-century French historians Langlois and Seignobos wrote 'par la nature même de ses matériaux, l'histoire est forcément une science subjective [qui] doit donc se défendre de la tentation d'imiter les sciences biologiques' [history, because of the very material it relies on, is necessarily subjective [and] should resist the temptation to imitate the natural sciences]. Charles-Victor Langlois and Charles Seignobos, *Introduction aux études historiques* (Paris: Hachette, 1898), p. 124.
5. Jean-François Lyotard, *La Condition postmoderne, rapport sur le savoir* (Paris: Minuit, 1979). *The Postmodern Condition: A Report on Knowledge*, trans. by Geoff Bennington and Brian Massumi (Manchester: Manchester University Press, 1984).
6. Pascal Quignard '1640', *Scherzo*, 9 (1969), 7–18 (p. 11).
7. Christophe Kantcheff and Pascal Quignard, 'La littérature est le langage qui ignore sa puissance', *Le Matricule des anges*, 10 (1994–95) <hhttp://www.lmda.net/din/tit_lmda.php?Id=3517> [accessed 4 June 2015] (para. 11 of 33).
8. Walter Benjamin, 'Central Park', trans. by Lloyd Spencer, *New German Critique*, 34 (1985), 32–58 (p. 32).
9. Friedrich Nietzsche, *Thus Spoke Zarathustra*, trans. by Reginald John Hollingdale (London: Penguin, 1969), p. 178 (first publ. 1885).
10. Arlette Farge, 'Brisures du temps', in *Pascal Quignard, ou la littérature démembrée par les muses*, pp. 241–47 (p. 242).
11. *LSE*, p. 9. *LSEe*, pp. ix–x.
12. 'Rencontre avec Pascal Quignard, à l'occasion de la parution de *Le Sexe et l'effroi* (1994)' <http://www.gallimard.fr/catalog/entretiens/01025213.htm> [accessed 13 May 2015] (para. 8 of 10).
13. *LSE*, p. 110. *LSEe*, pp. 57–58.
14. Ibid.
15. Paule Zajdermann and Pascal Quignard, 'Pascal Quignard, le latin', in *Vie et mort des langues*, dir. by Paule Zajdermann (Bibliothèque Publique d'information, 2007) [DVD].
16. Thomas Henry Dyer, *Pompei, its History, Buildings and Antiquities* (London: Bell & Daldy, 1867), p. 477.
17. Pascal Quignard, *Sur le Jadis (Dernier royaume II)* (Paris: Grasset, 2002), p. 18.
18. Jourdain and Canu [DVD].
19. Chantal Lapeyre-Desmaison, 'Pascal Quignard, une poétique de l'agalma', in, *Études Françaises*, 'Pascal Quignard ou le noyau incommunicable', 40 (2004), 39–53, p. 45.
20. This novel was the basis of an English-language film adaptation by Alain Corneau, entitled *Le Nouveau Monde [New World]*, released in 1995.

21. Michel Deguy, 'L'Écriture sidérante', in *Pascal Quignard, la mise au silence*, pp. 45–64 (pp. 49, 53).
22. Pascal Quignard and Valère Novarina, 'De l'espace', in *Pascal Quignard, ou la littérature démembrée par les muses*, pp. 213–19 (pp. 213–14).
23. Bataille, 'LNA', p. 62. 'LNAe' , p. 115.
24. Pascal Quignard, *La Raison* (Paris: le Promeneur, 1990), p. 13.
25. Pascal Quignard, *Rhétorique spéculative* (Paris: Calmann-Lévy, 1995), p. 15.
26. Alain Badiou, *L'Antiphilosophie de Wittgenstein* (Caen: Nous, 2009), pp. 17, 22. *Wittgenstein's Antiphilosophy*, trans. by Bruno Bosteels (London: Verso Books, 2011), pp. 76, 80.
27. *LPD*, p. 184.
28. Plato, *Gorgias*, trans. by Terence Irwin (Oxford: Clarendon Press, 1979), p. 31 (463a).
29. Plato, *Gorgias*, p. 27 (459b).
30. Rosamund Sprague, *The Older Sophists* (Columbia: South Carolina Press, 1972), p. 65.
31. Sharon Crowley, 'On Gorgias and Grammatology', *College Composition and Communication*, 30 (1979), 279–84 (p. 281).
32. *RS*, p. 62.
33. *RS*, pp. 30–31.
34. *LCI*, p. 56. *LCIe*, p. 50.
35. *RS*, pp. 37–39.
36. *RS*, p. 47.
37. *RS*, p. 24.
38. Rabaté, *Pascal Quignard, étude de l'œuvre*, p. 159.
39. Bataille, 'LNA', p. 64. 'LNAe', p. 117.
40. *LS*, p. 88.
41. Kristeva, *LCI*, p. 31. *LCIe*, p. 26.
42. Bataille, 'LNA', p. 62. 'LNAe' p. 115.
43. *RS*, p. 37.
44. Pautrot, *Pascal Quignard ou le fonds du monde*, p. 153.
45. Pascal Quignard, *Les Escaliers de Chambord* (Paris: Gallimard, 1989), p. 24.
46. *LEC*, pp. 24–25.
47. *LS*, pp. 112–13.
48. *LSE*, p. 204. *LSEe*, p. 115.
49. Michael Bishop, 'Préface du directeur de la collection', in Pautrot, *Pascal Quignard ou le fonds du monde*, n.p.
50. Pascal Quignard and Valerio Adami, *Inter ærias fagos* (Paris: Galilée, 2005) (first publ. 1979).
51. Bénédicte Gorillot, '*Inter ærias fagos*, le salut d'une écriture latine', in *Pascal Quignard, ou la littérature démembrée par les muses*, pp. 85–97 (p. 92).
52. Pascal Quignard, 'Dix ans après', in *EDE*, pp. 277–81 (pp. 280–81) (first publ. 2002).
53. Crowley, p. 282.

CHAPTER 5

❖

Incendiary Writing

Quignard's writing produces a series of paradoxical stances. His quest for solitude relies on collaboration and on reaching out to other forms of art — namely music and visual art — to try and express what writing and art in general cannot represent. Such untenable positions relate to the larger impossibility at the heart of Quignard's oeuvre, which is both visibly growing and filled with images of destruction and disappearance. Faced with this impossibility, this final chapter will show how writing happens not against or in spite of destruction but because of it, and how it is fuelled by the desire for its own annihilation.

It can be tempting for Quignard's critics and readers either to overlook or resolve the contradictions on which his texts are built. On the surface, the works seem defined by a glaring erudition. In most existing critical studies, this layer of erudition becomes both the veil and the basis for questioning language, and for challenging its hold on the individual subject. As Gilles Anquetil insists, 'il ne faudrait pas [...] enfermer Quignard dans l'image frivole du rat de bibliothèque ou de l'érudit mélancolique' [Quignard cannot be simply reduced to a bookworm or a mournful scholar].[1] This pushes critics to try and find, beyond the antithetical coexistence of erudition and savagery, a synthetic definition of Quignard's writing. Anquetil comments on an erudition that does not belong to a scholar, but rather takes its source in a 'fureur collectionneuse' [collector's fury], 'une passion violente' [a violent passion]. He suggests that the writer emerges victorious from the attack on language and culture, and that the contradictions this battle implies are ultimately transcended to produce a 'joie à la fois pure et impie' [joy both pure and profane].[2] This interpretation is representative of a critical tendency to praise Quignard's writing by defining it as sublime, powerful, and close to a Barthesian textual *jouissance*.[3] But such dialectic developments, which rely on synthesis to justify the existence of the work and its continuous expansion, leave behind an essential part of its nature. Quignard's writing expresses an awareness of the inescapability of language, and his attacks on language are first and foremost directed against the texts themselves.

Despite Quignard's self-representation as a predatory writer — his identification with forceful figures such as the Gorgiasian rhetorician and the prehistoric hunter — his texts are the setting for a ritualistic sacrifice of language. As literary objects made of culture, they are also necessarily subjected to this sacrifice. As the writer produces texts, by the same means he also condemns them to destruction. This is what Quignard implies when he writes that 'l'idée de ne rien laisser après soi [l]'habite vraiment — même si c'est directement contradictoire avec le fait de publier des livres' [he is haunted by the idea of leaving nothing behind — even if that is in direct contradiction with the publication of books].[4]

The notion that Quignard's work subsumes its own vanishing point is central to this book. It has been shown in previous chapters through his attempts to negate the very existence of his work. Quignard does so literally, through his effacement in favour of other voices, and figuratively, by refusing the position of author and writer, and by representing the book as a space of disappearance. Yet the self-destructive nature of the literary work takes its most complete form in two complementary motifs: fragmentation and fire. Both express Quignard's desire to achieve disappearance through writing, and to produce what Blanchot, with reference to Franz Kafka, describes as a work that 'comme la mort [...] n'a pu s'obscurcir, et au contraire [...] brille admirablement de ce vain effort qu'elle a fait pour s'éteindre' [like death, is not able to be dimmed; on the contrary it shines admirably from the vain effort it made to extinguish itself].[5]

Burning Books

The definition of the writer as predator supposes an insistence on the physicality of writing. It also suggests its representation as a form of inscribing, similar to practices such as etching and carving. Just as the etcher uses abrasive and sharp tools, the writer works with a 'stylus', and, as Quignard writes, 'le mot de style renvoie directement en latin au stylus, à l'épieu, à la pointe' [the Latin root of the word *style* directly refers to the stylus, the spear, the point].[6] The essence of writing is metonymically associated with the pointed tool used in etching and in the first known forms of writing. Quignard presents his practice as the continuation of Mesopotamian cuneiform writing, and of the carving of clay, wax, wood and leather surfaces that preceded the use of paper in the making of books.[7] The book is itself likened to a hunted animal, often appearing in the texts in the form it took prior to the invention and development of the printing press. In *L'Enfant au visage couleur de la mort*, the child reads illuminated manuscripts, which in medieval times were made of parchment, the skin of dead animals, which give a literal meaning to their deadly nature in the tale.

Les Tablettes de buis d'Apronenia Avitia focuses on a form of writing characteristic of the Greek and Roman ages. The tablets of the title refer to the flat slabs of wood used to inscribe text, by engraving words directly onto the tablet or onto a wax surface previously applied to it. The reference to this ancient form of textual production also introduces the key notion of fragmentation. Presented explicitly as a work of research and translation, *Les Tablettes de buis d'Apronenia Avitia* is centred on the reproduction of literary fragments defined as the surviving extracts of a 'lost' work. The term 'fragments' also points to their incomplete and broken-off form as a necessary consequence of the support on which they were created. Because the tablets are covered with wax, their content can be easily erased and replaced. Moreover, the tablets' physical dimensions impose brevity and the breaking of discourse into small and divided parts. This disrupted and disappearing nature is displayed in the second part of the text, which contains translations of Avitia's fragments. Numbered in Roman numerals and each given a title, the fragments are of an extremely brief nature, offering a clear illustration of fragmentary writing. Of course, the fact that Apronenia Avitia and her work are invented needs to be taken into account. The invention of a fictional Latin writer and her lost fragments perhaps shows how Quignard's writing aims at finding voices behind which to hide, as the first chapter has shown, and how Avitia's model of fragmentary writing remains an inaccessible ideal.

This is the main thesis developed in *Une gêne technique à l'égard des fragments* (*On The Technical Difficulty of Fragments*), which questions modern and postmodern uses of literary fragmentation by comparing them to a more authentic model, embodied by the writings of the seventeenth-century French moralist Jean de La Bruyère. The focus on La Bruyère is typical of Quignard's tendency to favour historical figures over contemporary ones: when presenting La Bruyère as an overlooked author, Quignard fails to mention that he is indebted to a previous essay by Roland Barthes. In 1963, Barthes wrote of La Bruyère, that 'il lui manque même ce dernier bonheur de l'écrivain: être méconnu' [he lacks even that final fortune of the writer: to be neglected].[8] Yet Quignard does not refer to Barthes, choosing instead to unearth a mostly negative portrait of La Bruyère made by one of his contemporaries.[9] This presentation of La Bruyère as a disliked figure serves as an implicit justification for Quignard's choice to defend him and to embrace his specific use of fragmentation. Despite what the title suggests, *Une gêne technique à l'égard des fragments* argues not for a rejection of fragmentation itself — in fact defined as the obligatory form taken by writing — but of uses of fragmentation that exist without the necessary awareness of the violence the practice entails. More precisely, what is denounced is the artificial practice of fragmentation exemplified by 'les modernes [...] de S. Mallarmé à M. Blanchot' [the moderns from S. Mallarmé to M. Blanchot].[10] This loosely defined group of writers is compared to a union of 'fabricants de faux débris antiques' [forgers producing copies of antique fragments].[11] They are accused of using fragmentation for its own sake and avoiding '[le] mouvement destructeur dont la fracture ne devrait être qu'une trace résiduelle' [the destructive movement of which fragmentation should only be the residual trace].[12]

This lengthy and detailed condemnation of 'modern' forms of fragmentation is followed by the description of a better model. The narrator praises La Bruyère's *Les Caractères ou les mœurs de ce siècle* (*The Characters*), which 'assure une discontinuité entre les fragments' [manages to produce discontinuity through fragmentation].[13] This praise of La Bruyère's work is followed by a confession on the part of the narrator, who admits his own failure to avoid the artificial fragmentation he denounces. He reveals that his first aim was to write in an ordered and non-fragmented manner — to avoid fragmentation altogether — but that his disgust for logic and linearity was stronger than the uneasiness caused by fragmentation:

> En commençant ces pages, je crus que je touchais du doigt une difficulté réelle [...]. Je pensai m'en défaire en la précisant, l'affaiblir ou du moins la débiliter en en analysant la figure. Mais j'attisai le feu. Plus j'ai exposé cette difficulté plus je me suis enfermé en elle, plus je fus impuissant à la lever.

[As I started writing, I felt I was within reach of a real difficulty. I thought I could solve this problem by pinning it down, or that I could at least weaken it, turn it into a frail figure through the power of analysis. But I was playing with fire. The more I highlighted the issue, the more I found myself alienated by it, and the less I was able to resolve it.][14]

The narrator finds himself at a dead end: he is caught in a vicious circle and in a position of complete impotence. This statement is at first surprising for its honesty, but it can also be read as a tactical move, part of the larger annihilation of language achieved through writing. The failure in question concerns not the writer but rather his reliance on theoretical discourse. His efforts of precision and analysis, the attempt to shed light on difficulties he encountered have only led to further obscurity. The defeat this creates cannot be overcome and it does not produce anything but destruction: 'j'attisai le feu'. This specific expression relies on the motif of fire to convey the idea of an increasingly destructive force produced by the text; a force presented as the unique outcome of this failed act of writing. The concluding statement it belongs to is essential to the understanding of *Une gêne technique à l'égard des fragments*, and of the logic deployed in Quignard's entire body of work. The writer does not appear as a predatory hunter of language, but rather as its entrapped victim. Writing is only successful in showing language's inherent insufficiency and the ultimate impossibility of escaping its hold. The only way out, as the end of this text suggests, is through self-destruction.

Literary writing seems to produce a self-consuming energy, which paradoxically fuels the work and explains both its existence and its growth. Just as Quignard fails to mention the Barthesian source for his reading of La Bruyère, his critique of modern fragmentation and the conclusion it leads to conceal an 'unavowable community' with the work of Blanchot.[15] Blanchot sees literary writing as fragmented, ultimately destructive and heading towards its own disappearance. As he writes in *La Part du feu* (*The Work of Fire*) about the work of Franz Kafka, who famously asked for his texts to be destroyed, literary writing constantly hesitates between hope and despair, between 'l'impossibilité d'en jamais finir' [the impossibility of ever being done with it] and 'l'impossibilité de continuer' [the impossibility of going on].[16] Whilst Blanchot's influence on Quignard's work is undeniable, it remains strikingly suppressed in texts that usually show no reluctance to reveal the intertextual references they contain. If Quignard does not conceal his debt for tactical reasons, he does so perhaps because he identifies with a certain 'ethics of discretion', to borrow the term Leslie Hill uses to characterize Blanchot,[17] and idealizes silence, obfuscation, and disappearance. There is perhaps also an unease towards Blanchot's participation in extreme-right magazines in the 1930s, before his retreat from public life and into literature. The echoes of Blanchot in Quignard's work function according to a silent and indirect logic, and firstly through the mediation of writers that have influenced both Blanchot and Quignard: des Forêts, Bataille, and Lévinas. Hill, in *Blanchot, Extreme Contemporary*, discusses at length Blanchot's personal and theoretical relationship with Lévinas. Quignard, for his part, studied under Lévinas as a university student at the end of the 1960s, when he abandoned a doctoral project that was to have been supervised by the philosopher. This did not end their relationship, and they both frequently contributed to des Forêts's *L'Ephémère*. Lévinas's influence on Quignard is visible in the distrust of language developed in his work. It is also present in Quignard's use of a Jewish and Kabbalistic conception of concealment and disappearance, which I will explore later in the chapter.

The use of fragmentation, for both Blanchot and Quignard, has its roots in a specific conception of language, and in the celebration of silence that this conception produces. In *L'Espace littéraire* (*The Space of Literature*), Blanchot dwells on Mallarmé's opposition between essential and crude language. The former, he explains, 'n'est ni brute, ni immédiate. Mais elle donne l'illusion de l'être' [is neither crude nor immediate. But it gives the illusion of being so]. It is the ordinary discourse of the everyday, which uses words as tools and is completely oblivious to language's inability to stand for what it names: 'rien de plus étranger à l'arbre que le mot arbre, tel que l'utilise, pourtant, la langue quotidienne' [nothing is more foreign to the tree than the word *tree*, as it is used nonetheless by everyday language].[18] Essential and poetic language, on the other hand, reveals the absence that language necessarily creates, an absence famously symbolized by the flower 'absente de tous bouquets' [absent from every bouquet] from Mallarmé's 'Crise de vers' ('Crisis in Poetry').[19] For Blanchot and Quignard, this essential form of language leads to the recognition of the importance of silence, as the conveyor of such absence. For Quignard, silence, like obscurity, is what literary writing should aim to produce: 'les livres sont du silence à l'état solide' [books are the solid forms taken by silence].[20]

But silence is itself a lure, and being silent is not the same as leaving language. For Blanchot, the illusory nature of this recourse to silence means that literary texts, and art in general, are consumed by a paradoxical relation to language, constantly torn between 'destruction de soi-même, désagrégation infinie' [self-destruction, infinite disintegration] and 'bonheur et éternité' [happiness, eternity].[21] Blanchot and Quignard offer a portrait of the artist as Orpheus, looking to reach an impossible point. Both Blanchot's void and Quignard's *Jadis* aim for this 'point profondément obscur vers lequel l'art, le désir, la mort, la nuit semblent tendre' [profoundly obscure point toward which art and desire, death and night, seem to tend] defined by Blanchot.[22] The image of this unreachable, most obscure point functions as an illusory trick that guides writing through its process of self-destruction. Literature exists only on the condition that it is constantly aware of its own disappearance: 'la littérature s'édifie sur ses propres ruines', as Blanchot writes, 'et ce paradoxe nous est un lieu commun' [literature is built on top of its own ruins: this paradox has become a cliché to us].[23] This familiar paradox leads to three different attitudes, which are detailed throughout the essays regrouped in Blanchot's *La Part du feu*. Firstly, the writer can decide, like Kafka, to condemn his work to actual disappearance by demanding its destruction. Another solution, illustrated by the Surrealist practice, is to transform the inherent destructive and negative nature of literature into a creative force. The title *La Part du feu* is a reference to André Breton's *Nadja*, where the expression 'faire la part du feu' refers to the act of giving something up so that something else can be protected. It relies on the ambiguous and dual nature of fire, which stands both for creation and for destruction. By exposing and exploiting the void that exists within literature, Surrealists were able, according to Blanchot, literally to cut their losses, and to transform destruction into illumination and creation.

A third way to deal with the paradox inherent to literature is again illustrated by Kafka's work, which amounts neither to a real self-annihilation (his texts were never destroyed), nor to the reversal of destruction into a creative force. Kafka's short story 'The Hunter Gracchus' reveals 'cette vérité encore plus dure que la mort n'est pas possible' [this harder truth: death is not possible] by telling the story of a man who has been killed but finds himself unable to die.[24] The work of art exists, or rather survives, by standing between two mirrored illusions, the impossibility of life as creation, affirmation and hope, and the impossibility of death as both void and pure silence. The 'part' thus played by fire in Blanchot's *La Part du feu* is to stand for this in-between state of being, that is neither total destruction nor pure creation, but is constantly pointing towards these two poles.

Quignard relies on the same motif of fire to express the way his work is also positioned in between two unreachable points. This is expressed in *Rhétorique spécu-lative*, which states that 'écrire [...] c'est mourir et survivre' [to write is to die and to survive].[25] The reliance on the figure of fire does not serve a form of transcendence, like the one Blanchot uncovers in Surrealism, but rather adopts the paradoxical *survivance* embodied by Kafka. Fire is deployed in Quignard's texts through the motif of book burning, which the writer simultaneously rejects and embraces. Pierre Skira notes Quignard's 'réticence [...] à l'évocation des livres brûlés' [reticence when burning books are mentioned] and his 'réflexion sur l'horreur que constituent les autodafés et les destructions de livres' [personal reflection on the horrors of history's book burnings and destructions of books].[26] Book burning has long been a recurring symbol of abusive political power, and of the extreme dictatorial and oppressive forms taken by societies. Ray Bradbury's *Fahrenheit 451* and its description of a dystopian society where the destruction of books is systematic, is an obvious example. Historical events such as the destructions of books deemed 'un-German' by the Nazi regime in the 1930s, and the recent destruction of libraries by the self-proclaimed Islamic State in Mosul, symbolize the will of one group to annihilate another, by erasing the knowledge and culture it has produced. As Jonathan Rose writes in the introduction to *The Holocaust and The Book*, 'in literate societies, script and print are the primary means of preserving memory'.[27] To burn them is to erase all traces of a particular culture from collective memory.

The public burning of Meaume's erotic etchings in *Terrasse à Rome* is a symbol of abusive authority: the etchings are burned because a religious and moral institution has condemned them for indecency. Their destruction also points to the practice of auto-da-fé, from the Portuguese for 'act of faith', which refers to the public destruction by fire of both men and books that took place during the Spanish and Portuguese Inquisitions. In *Le Lecteur*, Quignard uses an example of book burning from the Bible, which he borrows from the Acts of the Apostles, the fifth book of the New Testament. In this story of a book burning in Ephesus, the books destroyed belong to pagans and magicians who have been converted to Judaism, and their public burning follows an order given by St Paul. This biblical reference gives way to a larger interrogation and condemnation of such ceremonial destruction: 'selon vous de quelle conversion les lecteurs, [...] soudain voyant dans cette clarté d'une "combustion des livres", donnèrent-ils les preuves [...]?' [what kind of conversion do you think this is? Is it one where readers suddenly 'see the light' produced by the burning of books?].[28] This rhetorical question plays on the conventional association of fire with illumination the better to refute it, and it discards the possibility of a successful conversion and enlightenment through fire.

Quignard's opposition to religious and sacrificial book burnings, where fire is used as the means by which the impure and amoral is destroyed to achieve purification, is further illustrated by the fact that his own work was subjected to a real, but failed, auto-da-fé. In 2007, to mark the publication of his work *La Nuit sexuelle*, the writer was invited to a literary festival at the abbey of Sainte-Marie d'Orbieu in Lagrasse in France. The part of the abbey used for the festival is state-owned, but regular canons live in the grounds of the estate. As the organizers of the event later explained in a press release, the proximity of a religious community to a cultural event devoted to the representation of sex in art quickly gathered interest in the local media, and attracted the attention of numerous religious web forums.[29] This was later suggested as a possible explanation for the incident that newspapers dubbed 'l'autodafé de Lagrasse' [Lagrasse book burning], where more than six thousand books, including copies of Quignard's *La Nuit sexuelle*, were doused in a mixture of lighter fluid and petrol.

Quignard's opposition to autos-da-fé is not rooted in the actual act of book-burning, but rather in the values they are meant to defend. As Lapeyre-Desmaison argues, this stance gives Quignard's work a political dimension. In particular, she examines why *La Nuit sexuelle* 'pose problème et suscite de violentes réactions' [is problematic and why it causes such violent reactions], denouncing 'une forme générale de puritanisme qui rend impossible l'accès à la lecture de Quignard' [a general tendency towards puritanism that forbids access to Quignard's work].[30] Lapeyre-Desmaison also relies on an interview with the writer in which he explains that *La Nuit sexuelle*, defined as a 'recueil d'images indécentes' [collection of indecent images], was conceived for political reasons. Quignard states that he sees his text as an instrument of resistance against the increasing proliferation of puritanism in Europe.[31] Yet while he clearly denounces the puritanism that book burnings seemingly stand for, his work also contains a celebration of the same motif as a voluntary act of self-destruction.

As mentioned in the introduction, as a young man Quignard would destroy his paintings by what he calls 'personal bonfires'. In *Pascal Quignard le solitaire*, he explains how such acts pre-empted the larger enterprise of self-destruction in his body of work: 'à vrai dire je continue pour tous les livres que j'écris' [if truth be told, I have carried on this practice in all my books].[32] Similarly, in *Lycophron et Zétès*, the narrator describes how 'à la campagne, sur le bord de l'Yonne, je brûle tout ce que j'ai écrit et tout ce que j'écris, une fois mêlé aux bois et aux feuilles de lierre' [when I am in the country, on the banks of the river Yonne, I take everything I have written and everything I write, mix it with kindling and ivy leaves, and I burn it].[33] Quignard bases his past and present pyromaniac habits on a historical and religious reference, citing the order received by Clovis during his baptism in Reims by St Remigius in 496: '*Incende quod adorasti*. Cet ordre est si étrange. L'évêque dit au premier roi de France: Brûle ce que tu aimes' [*Incende quod adorasti*. It is such a strange order to give. The bishop tells the first king of France to burn what he loves].[34] Here, Quignard refers to a specific part of the order, which is usually quoted as 'Courbe la tête, fier Sicambre, abaisse humblement ton cou. Adore ce que tu as brûlé et brûle ce que tu as adoré' [Bow thy head, O Sicambrian. Adore what thou hast burned and burn what thou hast adored].[35] The fact that Quignard refers only to the last section, where he uses the present — 'ce que tu aimes' — instead of the past tense, suggests that his borrowing functions as a reversal of the original order. Clovis's baptism marks not only the start of his reign but also the beginning of a French and Catholic royal dynasty. 'Sicambrian' refers to the Sicambri people, a Germanic tribe that lived during the Roman era within the borders of what later became Gaul, and it was a term commonly used for the Salian Franks. To 'adore what thou hast burned and burn what thou hast adored' thus implies to give up one's identity as a Sicamber, and the pagan beliefs associated with it, in order to embrace Roman Catholicism. Quignard reverses the initial logic of the sentence, suggesting that for him, burning does not imply renunciation but rather confirms a sense of fidelity and love for what is being destroyed. This is confirmed in an earlier text, where the writer states that ' "Incende quod adorasti". C'est ma vie' [*Incende quod adorasti:* that is my life] and that, for him, 'incendier et adorer, c'est le même' [to adore and to burn are one and the same].[36]

Quignard's book burnings are in direct opposition to autos-da-fé associated with Christianity and its idealization of purity and transcendence, yet they are close to the form of sacralization through destruction found in Kabbalistic literature, and especially in the work of the eighteenth-century rabbi Nachman of Breslov. Pierre Skira mentions Nachman in his description of the 'Ultima' project,[37] and he also appears in 'Anacrouse' ('Anacrusis'), the fragment Blanchot wrote on Louis-René des Forêts:

> je m'en remets pour l'instant à la parole d'un Maître hassidique (qui a toujours refusé d'être Maître), Rabbi Nahman de Bratslav. 'Il est interdit d'être vieux!' Ce qu'on peut d'abord entendre: interdit de renoncer à se renouveler, de s'en tenir à une réponse qui ne remettrait plus en cause la question — finalement (mais c'est sans fin) n'écrivant que pour effacer l'écrit ou plus exactement l'écrivant par l'effacement même, maintenant ensemble épuisement et inépuisable: la disparition qui ne s'exténue pas.

> [I will give myself over for the moment to the words of a Hassidic Master (who always refused to be Master), Rabbi Nachman of Breslov. / "It is forbidden to be old!"/ Which we can understand first of all as: one is forbidden to reject being renewed, forbidden to confine oneself to an answer that would no longer pose the question — in the end (but there is no end) writing only to erase what has been written, or more precisely writing it by erasure itself, keeping exhaustion and the inexhaustible together: the DISAPPEARANCE that is never worn out.][38]

Nachman was born in the late eighteenth century in North Ukraine, into a family of the Hassidic elite. He quickly asserted himself as an influential *tsaddik*, or spiritual leader, known for his ascetic lifestyle. As Corinna Coulmas explains,

Nachman displayed a strong preference for solitude in the first part of his adult life, before leaving for Israel and then Bratslav, where a disciple, Nathan Sternhartz of Nemirov, joined him and took charge of transcribing his teachings. Yet, as Coulmas notes, Nachman's works are lost to us today. His first book, entitled *Sefer Hanisraf* ('the burned book'), was destroyed on Nachman's orders in 1808, whilst the existence of a second book, *Sefer Haganuz* ('the hidden book'), remains legendary.[39] It is Nachman's *Sefer Hanisraf* that Blanchot uses in 'Anacrouse' to symbolize an inextinguishable form of disappearance. Marc-Alain Ouaknin, in his study of Nachman, defines the rabbi's wish to destroy his own books as rooted in a specific conception of the world. Ouaknin explains how Nachman opposes a Greek view of the world ruled by *logos* and *physis*, and which refuses the possibility of disappearance, to the world as 'Léélem', 'bound to disappear', put forward by the Talmud.[40] He goes on to show how, for Nachman, book burning allows a form of sacralization and the reaching out to a world that embraces disappearance as its horizon: 'le feu transforme le livre en "presque livre"' [fire turns the book into an 'almost-book'].[41]

This image of the 'almost-book' used by Ouaknin could be applied to the texts written and published by Quignard. The body of work he produces does not amount to an oeuvre, a monument that stands tall for all to see, which would turn its internal contradictions and conflicts into the achievement of a presence. Rather, what he writes is a series of almost-works: not failed or missed works, but works that draw their values from the constant exhibition of what they are not and what they can never be. Quignard produces novels as budding *contes*, *contes* on the verge of becoming music, texts on the verge of the visual, and a writing that relentlessly works towards its own disappearance.

Glowing in the Dark

Each of Quignard's texts is part of a burning territory that paradoxically grows larger and larger as it is being consumed. The existence of such a literary landscape raises the question of absence versus presence. Is the body of work ultimately defined by disappearance, deploying what Deguy has called 'une écriture du désastre, en proie au désastre, mesurant l'étendue du désastre' [a writing of disaster, faced with disaster and assessing the extent of disaster]?[42] Or is there a glimmer of hope amongst the surrounding devastation?

One figure occupies a particularly suitable position for the expression of hope and transcendence in Quignard's texts. Both the numerous appearances made by children in the texts and the importance given to childhood have already been noted. Bruno Blanckeman deems the representation of the child 'un para-digme élémentaire [qui] emblématise le mouvement même de l'écriture, qui se fait toujours le support d'une dynamique originaire' [an essential paradigm that stands for the very process of writing, which itself supports a movement towards the origins].[43] Existing studies of childhood in Quignard's texts have often been limited to his novels and to interpretations related to the issue of writing the self. Yet Quignard's child figure is marked by anonymity rather than self-identification: 'l'enfant est *l'inconnu de la naissance*' [the child is *the unknown of birth*].[44] It is also a possible embodiment of the *Jadis*: 'Jadis est un enfant' [Jadis is a child].[45] Not exactly a child, Quignard's 'enfant' is often referred to as an *infans*, 'incapable de parler, bestial' [incapable of speech, animalistic].[46] This equivalence between child and *Jadis* turns the child into a necessarily ambiguous figure. Although Quignard echoes the familiar literary trope of a suffering and unhappy childhood, his children are also violent and murderous. Moreover, if childhood is idealized, it is not as a 'golden age'. Descriptions of children as glowing, radiant figures both conceal and reveal their ultimately fleeing and vanishing nature. They are mirages rather than saviours, optical illusions produced by the surrounding devastation.

Representing the *Jadis* as a child means that childhood is defined by loss. When discussing his conception of childhood, Quignard refers to Perec and praises his 'silence, sa façon [...] de s'adresser au trou vide de son enfance et de ne pas ciller les yeux' [silence, the way he managed to face the void of his childhood without blinking]. Quignard also mentions Marcel Proust, whose work, he thinks, 'ne flotte pas sur le même vide' [doesn't navigate the same void], and who 'croit à la vérité de sa quête' [believes that his quest is true].[47] By opposing Perec and Proust, Quignard suggests that childhood must be treated as a void to be faced rather than as a past that can be located and accessed through writing. By embracing Perec's treatment of childhood, he also gives greater value to its representation not only as a lost state, but also one determined by loss and abandonment. Perec's *W ou le souvenir d'enfance* (*W, Or the Memory of Childhood*) departs from traditional autobiographical childhood accounts by exposing the incapacity of memory to produce truth. Moreover, because it deals with the author's experience of personal losses suffered during the Second World War, the vision of childhood it puts forward is determined by death and disappearance.

In Quignard's texts, the characters embark on a quest for an inaccessible childhood: not paradise lost but 'le perdu tout court' [quite simply the lost].[48] Furthermore, as Blanckeman explains, childhood is simultaneously '[un] âge d'or — non-parole, anti-conscience, adhésion spontanée au monde' [a Golden age away from language and consciousness; a spontaneous adherence to the world] and '[un] âge de fer — temps des séquelles, des orientations irréversibles, des courbes creusées dans la vie adulte' [an Iron age, responsible for the scars, the irreversible tendencies, the bends and curves that mark adulthood].[49] The novel *L'Occupation américaine* deals with this dual representation of childhood. It also offers a representation of the irreparable void created by its loss, through the story of its two main characters, Patrick and Marie-José. Inseparable as children, they start to drift apart as they depart from childhood and begin to experience the sexual awakening of adolescence. From then on, fusion gives way to a growing separation that ends with Marie-José's suicide. Childhood is presented as a place where those who have left it long to return, yet this representation goes hand in hand with its clear portrayal as a period of life marked by abandonment and pain, mostly caused by adults and felt by children. A sentence found at the end of the novel neatly encapsulates this, and provides a summary of the entire plot: 'Une enfant abandonnée avait aimé un enfant unique. Un enfant unique devint un enfant solitaire' [an abandoned child loved an only child. An only child became a solitary child].[50]

L'Occupation américaine takes place immediately after the Second World War in a French town occupied by American troops. Their presence triggers the development of another important theme in the novel: the act of collecting. In contact with the troops, the two protagonists become ardent collectors of all things American: cigarettes, music, English words, items of clothing, and even people are used to fill the gaps left by either absent or disconnected parental figures. The figure of the collector corresponds to a larger trend in Quignard's work, where, as Patrick Wald Lasowski puts it, 'il n'y a pas de véritable antiquité que cette enfance qui serre la gorge des collectionneurs passionnés qui peuplent l'œuvre' [the one real antiquity, the one thing that moves all of the ardent collectors in the work, is childhood].[51] In *Le Salon du Wurtemberg*, Charles Chegogne and Florent Seinecé's friendship is sealed by a shared collector's frenzy, directed towards items that fuel the illusion of a possible return to childhood. During their first encounter, Seinecé hands Chegogne some of the old-fashioned sweets he collects and receives in exchange fragments of childhood lullabies, which Chegogne sings to him. From then on, both characters are implicitly enrolled in the same cult, where the adoration of childhood relics — fetishes in the religious sense — becomes a way to fill and soothe the void it left behind.

Yet it is in the novel *Les Escaliers de Chambord* that the figure of the collector, and the logic of fetishism that accompanies it, is most obviously developed. The novel begins with Edouard Furfooz's discovery of a small hairpin, found discarded in an abandoned junkyard next to a beach in Tarquinia, Italy.[52] The hairpin is kept, and as Furfooz finds himself increasingly but inexplicably attached to this seemingly worthless object, he becomes more and more concerned with finding the specific reason for this attachment. From that point on, the text reads — as Rabaté puts it — like a 'film hollywoodien des années quarante inspiré par la psychanalyse [...] où toute l'histoire est tendue vers la révélation d'un secret qui conditionne l'existence du héros' [a Hollywood film from the 1940s inspired by psychoanalysis [...] where the plot leads to the revelation of a secret that holds the key to the hero's entire existence].[53] The use of fetishism in particular, linked to the relation Quignard's characters have with their lost childhood, reveals this influence of psychoanalysis on the novels.

According to Freud, fetishists obey a logic of 'disavowal',[54] and the fetish object fills two different but simultaneous roles: standing first as a successful substitute for what is actually desired but forever absent, it also points towards the void that it is meant to conceal. As a professional collector of antique toys, Furfooz's life is organized by the fetishization of chosen objects. He makes, to borrow Walter Benjamin's definition of the collector, 'the glorification of things his concern'.[55] The fact that the objects he collects are toys is of course significant. It confirms the idea that the attraction to childhood, of which toys are obvious metonymical embodiments, functions as the sole organizing principle of his existence. Furfooz's toys are fetishes in the first sense of the word: objects to which are attributed magical or religious qualities and values. But they are also fetishes in the Freudian sense, as their possession brings satisfaction and relief. They feed the illusory belief that, through them, the gaping hole left by childhood can be filled, and that to pursue them can give life meaning.

As Freud furthermore explains, fetishism is an abnormal reaction to the castration complex, where the object that has become a fetish functions as a replacement for the absence of a maternal phallus. Whilst the latter 'should normally have been given up, [...] the fetish is precisely designed to preserve it from extinction'. The 'logic of disavowal' that fetishism follows is thus twofold. Firstly, the fetish, as an object of desire, is given the illusory power to stand in place of what has been lost, to fill the lack it is meant to substitute and, as such, it can be enjoyed and become a satisfying source of pleasure, 'a token of triumph over the threat of castration'. This is precisely what is present in the relation that Quignard's collectors have with the collected objects that stand in place of their lost childhood. But, as Freud explains, 'the horror of castration has set up a memorial to itself in the creation of this substitute', and fetishes, precisely because they stand in place of a loss, also signify it; their presence constantly pointing towards and signalling the lack they are meant to disavow.[56] As such, they create suffering, and the attachment to such objects is of a fundamentally repetitious, painful, and morbid nature.

The logic of fetishism developed in the novels shows childhood as both an object of desire and as a void; a domain defined by its unreachable nature. By relating to it through the mediation of fetish objects, Quignard's male protagonists — and female characters such as Ann Hidden, who wears a tooth that belonged to the young Magdalena in a medallion around her neck — [57] idealize childhood all the while realizing its constitution as a lack, and its ultimate inaccessibility. Such characters are not alone in experiencing childhood through this dual logic of fetishism. It extends to Quignard's entire work, where the figure of the child itself — not simply relics from childhood — functions as a fetish at the level of writing. This is best illustrated by a short text entitled 'Les fêtes des chants du Marais' ('The Singing Festivals of the Marais') published as a chapter in *La Barque silencieuse*. If *L'Enfant au visage couleur de la mort* is a parable on reading, 'Les fêtes des chants du Marais' is an allegory of writing. Set in seventeenth-century France, the story starts with a boy named Bernon, who has just won a singing competition performed for an audience that 'appréciait la voix que possèdent les petits garçons avant leur mue' [appreciated the singing of small boys with unbroken voices].[58] Bernon's victory fuels the jealousy of Marcellin, the previous year's winner. The latter, fearing that his voice is about to break, and considering that Bernon, by being allowed to sing two songs instead of one, has won unfairly, decides to take revenge. He does so by killing Bernon, cutting his head off, removing its skin and burying the skull next to the bank of a nearby river.[59] This murderous and savage act has magical consequences. As Marcellin comes back the following year to take part in the same contest, he hears a beautiful song coming from the river. Having lost the competition, and recognizing Bernon's voice, Marcellin unearths the singing skull and decides to use it for gain. He goes on the road, putting on shows in villages, where crowds gather to see and hear the magic skull. Hearing of its success, a local governor promises his weight in gold to whoever will bring him the magic remains. But when Marcellin shows up to claim the prize, the skull stays silent. The text ends with the death of Marcellin, who is killed by one of the governor's men.

'Les fêtes des chants du Marais' centres on the departure from childhood symbolized by the loss of Marcellin's prepubescent voice. The young boy goes from being an object of desire — in the text adults are immersed in a collective admiration of children's voices — to someone who desires what he has lost. By losing his voice and by leaving childhood, he goes from fetish object to fetishist figure. Firstly, the decapitation of Bernon is of a clearly ritualized nature, and as such echoes the sacrificial nature of religious fetishism. The motif of blood pouring is a common element in fetishist rituals and water plays a role in the story too: its erosive force is implicitly responsible for the transformation of the child's severed head into a magic skull. Bernon's sacrifice produces an object endowed with supernatural powers, a fetish in the anthropological and religious meaning of the word. This skull, which Marcellin first hides better to reveal it to the public during his performances, also functions as a fetish in the etymological sense. From the Latin *facticius*, the fetish works an artifice, a prop meant to lure and trick others. As such, its main role is to turn Marcellin back into a fetish, this time in the psychoanalytical sense, allowing him to function as an object of spectacle performing for the pleasure of adults, giving them what they desire and being paid for it. Because Marcellin constantly carries this skull with him, it also shares his own logic of disavowal, offering not only a satisfactory replacement for the loss of his voice and his childhood, but also acting as a constant reminder of their absence.

It is difficult not to see Marcellin as a representation of the writer. After all, Quignard also borrows the voices of others and uses them simultaneously to produce and conceal his own work. Like Marcellin, the writer performs through writing a series of illusions and tricks motivated by the desire to make up for, and denounce, the absence that lies at its core. The figure of the child, as the ultimate fetish object for the writer, follows the dual logic of disavowal. Childhood, through its equivalence with the *Jadis*, is presented as an object of desire in the texts, and children are shown in a positive light. Glorified and glowing, they punctuate the texts with soothing episodes, when the desire for disappearance suddenly gives place to expressions of pleasure and satisfaction. As such they appear like glimmers of hope within the devastated texts, seemingly there to signal that something exists beyond destruction. They are close to the 'figures réfractaires' [refractory figures] des Forêts describes in his *Poèmes de Samuel Wood* (*Poems of Samuel Wood*), which 'rayonnent assez fort pour que s'exerce | Au delà des mots leur hégémonie souveraine' [shine so intensely that they exercise | Words beyond their sovereign dominion]. But this idealization of the child is quickly revealed as a further illusion, as des Forêts also evokes '[une] enfant [...] captive de son image, mais recluse | Dans cette obscurité dévorante' [a child [...] captive of her image, a recluse | In the all consuming dark].[60] If children glow, they do so as creatures belonging to a dark rather than golden age, closer to the bioluminescent life forms found in the ocean abyss than to auratic and angel-like figures.

'Les fêtes des chants du Marais' presents the child not only as a suffering, victimised being, but also as a dark creature, capable of monstrous and murderous acts. This representation of the child as a dark force, also visible in *L'Enfant au visage couleur de la mort*, echoes what Anne Cousseau identifies as a 'tradition, à partir du roman gothique ou fantastique [...] où l'incapacité de l'enfant à mesurer les limites de la cruauté et de l'horreur le conduit à la folie et au crime' [tradition dating back to the Gothic novel and the fantastic genre [...] where children's inability to measure the limits of cruelty and horror leads to madness and crime].[61] By emphasizing the violent nature of the child, Quignard depicts children as situated outside the limits of humanity. Whilst adult violence is clearly denounced, the primitive and non-rational form of violence of children is celebrated. This is visible in the texts through a recurring comparison between children and animals. In *Les Escaliers de Chambord*, Flora — whose name reveals an alignment with the natural rather than the human realm — is metonymically embodied by the hairpin in the form of a frog found by Furfooz. This amphibian figure can be linked to the motif of the sea, which Quignard associates in *Boutès* with 'la vie utérine' [uterine life].[62] In *Boutès,* the origins of mankind are clearly situated in the hybrid combination of two animal species: 'à mi-chemin entre le têtard et les oiseaux' [halfway between birds and tadpoles].[63] Magdalena, in *Villa Amalia*, is described as having 'des jambes aussi maigres que des pattes d'oiseau' [legs as thin as a those of a bird].[64] This analogy runs throughout the novel, symbolizing the fact that Magdalena is still an infant who cannot yet fully master speech. Her physical and vocal presence in the text is interrupted by her sudden disappearance, when, left unsupervised, she chokes on a nut and dies. This tragic event first appears as an implicit condemnation of the carelessness of the adult characters around her. The image of a foreign and ultimately lethal object stuck in the child's throat can also be seen as a variation on the recurring motif of voice breaking. In Quignard's texts, *la mue* [voice breaking] stands for the child's exit from a primitive animal nature — infancy — and its entrance into the linguistic realm. In French, the word *mue* designates both the biological changes to boys and girls at puberty, and animal forms of moulting, such as the renewal of skin in reptiles and of plumage in birds.

This reliance on an image of biological transformation also implies that children possess a specific tongue. The singing children found in 'Les fêtes des chants du Marais' and in *La Leçon de musique* and *Tous les matins du monde*, suggest that this tongue is one that sings rather than speaks. The theme of childhood voice found in Quignard's work is, again, heavily influenced by des Forêts, and in particular by his 1946 text *Le Bavard (The Bavard)*. *Le Bavard* is a monologue dealing with the disgust felt towards speech, in which the unnamed first-person narrator recalls a childhood memory. He tells how, as an altar boy, he suddenly vowed to keep silent after hearing the nearby song of a bird: 'assez! après un tel chant, comment oserais-je encore ouvrir la bouche' ['enough!' After such singing, how could I ever dare open my mouth again?].[65] The celebration of the child figure is based on its inherent opposition to language. At the end of the text, this recollection of a childhood vow of silence once again drives the adult narrator to silence. In des Forêts's text, Quignard's 'Les fêtes des chants du Marais', and *Le Nom sur le bout de la langue*, the child is celebrated for his ability to fight off the hold of language and remain silent. But such representations, where the child is silent not by nature but by will, are in contradiction with the idea of a child as *infans* that Quignard also puts forward: 'celui qui n'a pas encore accédé au langage, n'a pas encore accédé au voile: il voit encore la nudité originaire' [the one who has not yet acquired language — has not yet acquired a veil: he still sees the primal nudity].[66] On the one hand, the child is conceived as being outside of language and to some extent of humanity — a perfect embodiment of the *Jadis*. But on the other, the child is admired for fighting against language, and is thus bound to be a part of it.

Giorgio Agamben, in *Infancy and History*, sees this contradiction as being contained in the very notion of infancy. 'Infancy', he argues, is first 'what in human beings comes before the subject — that is, before language: a "wordless" experience in the literal sense of the term, a human *infancy* [*in-fancy*], whose boundary would be marked by language'. But, it can never truly be as it claims: defined as being outside of language, it is necessarily within it. As Agamben puts it: 'it is not a paradise which, at a certain moment, we leave forever in order to speak; rather it coexists in its origin with language'. Infancy can only be conceived through language, and Agamben locates it 'between pure language and human language' — that is, using Emile Benveniste's terms, between semiotics (sign) and semantics (discourse). Instead of an absence of language, infancy is defined as pointing towards the semiotic, the non-human 'pure pre-babble language of nature'.[67] The child whose voice is idealized in Quignard's texts is therefore an *infant* in the Agambian, rather than in the etymological, sense.

Childhood, or rather infancy, which first appeared as a perfect representation of the *Jadis*, seems more and more distant from it. Just as in *Le Bavard*, where the narrator's first vow of silence follows the sudden awareness that his voice paled in comparison to birdsong, Quignard's children are not equal to animals. They do not belong to the realm of nature, but rather die trying to remain in it, as the fate of Marcellin in 'Les fêtes des chants du Marais' demonstrates. Moreover, if the child figure is explicitly celebrated as an ideal embodiment of the *Jadis*, a satisfactory object of desire for the writer and the characters he creates, such idealization is also denounced as an artificial illusion produced by language.

This simultaneously enchanting and disenchanting attitude can be read as a consequence of the logic of disavowal. The representation of a child-*infans* determined by language rather than by an absence from its realm also points towards the redefinition of fetishism offered by Jacques Lacan, which insists on the symbolic — and therefore linguistic — nature of all desire. In his description of what he names 'le schéma du voile' [the function of the veil],[68] Lacan begins by assessing previous psychoanalytical views on fetishism. Dylan Evans notes how Lacan dismisses Donald Winnicott's object-relations theory as one that 'confuses the object of psychoanalysis with the object of biology and neglects the symbolic dimension of desire'.[69] Whilst Winnicott's position, like Freud's, implies a material existence of the fetish object and of the bodily organ it is meant to replace, Lacan insists that fetishism is ultimately embedded in the symbolic. As such, it is rooted in a linguistic logic that leads to the production of specific images, which are not produced by an actual lack but by the existence of an absence. Through the 'schéma du voile', Lacan goes on to show how fetishism allows the propping-up of a screen on which 'apparaît ce qui devient figuration au manque, le fétiche [...]. C'est sur le voile que le fétiche vient figurer précisément ce qui manque au-delà de l'objet' [appears what becomes the figuration of a lack, the fetish [...]. It is on the veil that the fetish projects the image of the lack that exists beyond the object].[70] This relates to Quignard's work insofar as the child figure appears not only as a voice but also as an image. It is not a material object but a surface onto which is projected the linguistic and imaginary representation of a void that remains forever inaccessible and ultimately absent, and which unveils itself as an illusory trick.

The power of fascination held by the child as image is expressed by its representation as a Medusa figure. In *Le Salon du Wurtemberg*, a young girl named Delphine is described as follows:

> Recroquevillée, les coudes sur les cuisses et le menton dans les paumes, les yeux tournés vers l'un d'entre nous, vers les arbres, un papillon, Mademoiselle Aubier chantant, un ver de terre, un rayon de soleil — c'était une même attention médusée, comme mettant en joue ce qu'elle regardait.

> [Sitting hunched up with her elbows on her knees and her chin in her hands, she would gaze at one of us, the trees, a butterfly, Mademoiselle Aubier singing, a worm, or a sunbeam, with the same amazed intentness, as if taking aim at everything she looked at.][71]

The use of an expression usually reserved for firearms ('mettre en joue') signals a forceful child figure and the mention of her 'attention médusée' implicitly likens Delphine to the mythical Medusa. The ability to petrify onlookers, which she shares with the nameless child in *L'Enfant au visage couleur de la mort*, shows how Quignard moves away from the usual representation of children as objects to be gazed at, portraying them instead as active agents endowed with a specific power. This passage from subordination to defiance takes place poetically through the recurring lexical field of light, which goes through various embodiments, from lightning to fire and flame. Delphine is portrayed as having 'des joues rouges foncées, comme si elle avait eu les joues teintes avec du bois de Pernambouc' [deep red cheeks that looked as if they had been stained and polished].[72] Here, a familiar trope — a child's rosy cheeks — is transformed into a more threatening vision. The mention of the Pernambuco tree in the original French text is a reference to Brazilwood, a type of tree used to produce red dye, which gave its name to the country of Brazil (from the Portuguese *brasil*, 'ember-like'). This comparison implicitly suggests that Delphine is not only a rosy child but also a blazing creature, emitting both fire and light.

This vision of a fiery child appears in a figurative and mostly implicit way in *Le Salon du Wurtemberg*. In *L'Enfant au visage couleur de la mort,* however, it is developed in an explicit manner. The child's metamorphoses can be seen as variations on light as it travels to various positions and takes on different forms. The illuminated manuscripts read by the child contaminate his body with their deadly content, diminishing his physical strength and working to reduce his presence. What follows this initial frailty imposed by reading can be seen as a way for the child to deal with the transformation caused by his contact with books. His gaze emits deadly rays of light, passing on to others the fatal matter that he acquired when reading books. Light travels from the illuminated manuscripts, through the child, to his victims, and back to the child when he is transformed into a book. The last pages of the *conte* tell how the child-turned-book is thrown into an open fire, where 'sous l'effet de la chaleur [se] développe l'image | dans la lumière rouge | puissante | en un bref incendie | de la tête enluminée sur la page du livre' [from the fire's heat an image is developed | in the strong red light | a sudden blaze | that of an illuminated face printed unto one of the book's page].[73] This passage describes how fire produces an image, and by doing so it reminds us that the flames and the red colour of embers are also visual products: the visible and light-emitting parts of fire. The passage borrows terms from photography, implicitly comparing the final apparition of the child to the process of developing a photographic image.

Unlike a photograph, however, this ultimate image is not fixed but temporary. Produced by fire, it will disappear within it. The final fate of the child in *L'Enfant au visage couleur de la mort* provides a telling illustration of children's overall nature in Quignard's work. Neither real nor palpable beings, they are not only reflections of the writer's self — as Lapeyre-Desmaison suggests when she sees in the *conte*'s final transformation 'un autoportrait en miroir de l'auteur' [a mirrored self-portrait of the author].[74] In a passage from *Boutès*, the narrator recalls the windows of his childhood home, where: 'quand le soir tombait je voyais tout se refléter dans la grande-porte fenêtre qui donnait sur le jardin obscur [...] je regardais ces reflets pleins de pénombre, d'éclats, de mouvements d'eau' [as night came I would see it all reflected on the large French windows that opened on the garden, now immersed in darkness [...] I would gaze at reflections filled with obscurity, creating sparkles and aquatic movements].[75] Looking at the window, the narrator remembers seeing what it let through; depicting the writing of childhood as a see-through screen, rather than a look back at the past. The image of the child produced by fire is not a mirror but a screen, and Quignard's child figure functions as a see-through image, a transparent display that does not only project a reflection of the self but also allows the void it replaces to shine through.

Notes to Chapter 5

1. Gilles Anquetil, 'Petits traités par Pascal Quignard', *Le Nouvel Observateur*, 29 November 1990, p.158.
2. Ibid.
3. Roland Barthes, *Le Plaisir du Texte* (Paris: Seuil, 1982), pp. 25–26 (first publ. 1973). *The Pleasure of the Text*, trans. by Richard Miller (New York: Hill and Wang, 1975), p. vi.
4. *LS*, p. 32.
5. Blanchot, *LPF*, p. 19. *LPFe*, p. 11.
6. *LZ*, p. 184.
7. The stylus belongs to the realm of music too: it also refers to gramophone needles, which produce sound upon contact with the record.
8. Roland Barthes, 'Préface à La Bruyère, *Les Caractères*', in *Essais critiques* (Paris: Seuil, 1991), pp. 221–37 (p. 221) (first publ. 1963). 'La Bruyère', in *Critical Essays* (Evanston, IL: Northwestern University Press, 1972), pp. 221–39 (p. 222).
9. Pascal Quignard, *Une gêne technique à l'égard des fragments* (Fontfroide-le-Haut: Fata Morgana, 1986), pp. 7–8.
10. *GTF*, p. 34.
11. This statement could also be read as an ironically veiled self-portrait: Quignard's *Les Tablettes de buis d'Apronenia Avitia* is, literally, a collection of 'forged fragments of Antiquity'.
12. *GTF*, p. 50.
13. *GTF*, p. 53.
14. *GTF*, pp. 62–63.
15. To use the title of one of Maurice Blanchot's works: *La Communauté inavouable* (Paris: Minuit, 1984). *The Unavowable Community*, trans. by Pierre Joris (Barrytown, NY: Station Hill, 2000).
16. Blanchot, *LPF*, p. 31. *LPFe*, p. 23.

17. See Leslie Hill, *Blanchot, Extreme Contemporary* (London: Routledge, 1997), p. 5.
18. Blanchot, 'L'expérience de Mallarmé', in *LEL*, pp. 37–52 (pp. 39–40). 'Mallarmé's Experience', in *LELe*, pp. 38–48 (pp. 39–40).
19. Stéphane Mallarmé, 'Crise de vers', in *Œuvres complètes*, 2 vols (Paris: La Pléiade, 1998–2003), II (2003), pp. 204–13 (p. 213) (first publ. 1895). 'Crisis in Poetry', trans. by Mary Ann Caws, in *Selected Poetry and Prose*, ed. by Mary Ann Caws (New York: New Directions Books, 1982), pp. 75–76 (p. 76).
20. *SLJ*, p. 40.
21. Blanchot, *LPF*, p. 34. *LPFe*, p. 26.
22. Blanchot, 'Le Regard d'Orphée', p. 225. 'Orpheus's Gaze', p. 171.
23. Blanchot, *LPF*, p. 294. *LPFe*, p. 301.
24. Ibid., p. 15. Ibid., p. 7.
25. *RS*, p. 151.
26. Skira, p. 103.
27. Jonathan Rose, *The Holocaust and The Book* (Amherst: University of Massachusetts Press, 2001), p. 1.
28. *LL*, p. 45.
29. 'L'affaire des livres saccagés à Lagrasse, un communiqué de l'association *Le Marque-Page*', *Poezibao* (2007) <http://poezibao.typepad.com/poezibao/2007/08/laffaire-des-li.html> [accessed 4 June 2015] (para. 4, 9 of 23).
30. Chantal Lapeyre-Desmaison, 'L'Ange et la bête, notes sur *La Nuit sexuelle* de Pascal Quignard', *L'Esprit Créateur*, 52 (2012), 107–19 (pp. 107, 115).
31. Jacques Henric and Pascal Quignard, 'La Nuit sexuelle', *Mondesfrancophones.com* (2007) <http://mondesfrancophones.com/espaces/frances/pascal-quignard-la-nuit-sexuelle> [accessed 29 May 2015] (para. 3 of 22).
32. *LS*, p. 32.
33. *LZ*, p. 201.
34. *LS*, p. 32.
35. Gilbert Guislain, Pascal Le Pautremat and Jean-Marie Le Tallec, *500 citations de culture générale* (Paris: Jeunes éditions, 2005), p. 21.
36. Pascal Quignard, 'Ce que Rémi dit à Clovis', in *PT*, VIII, pp. 79–86 (pp. 83, 86).
37. Skira, p. 103.
38. Maurice Blanchot, 'Anacrouse', in *Une voix venue d'ailleurs, sur les poèmes de Louis-René des Forêts* (Plombière-les-Dijon: Ulysse, 1992), pp. 29–40 (p. 36). 'Anacrusis: On the Poems of Louis-René des Forêts', in *A Voice From Elsewhere*, trans. by Charlotte Mandell (Albany: State University of New York Press, 2007), pp. 1–30 (p. 24).
39. Corinna Coulmas, 'Les Contes de Rabbi Nahman de Bratslav', *Actes du colloque 'Aspects de la vie religieuse, l'étude et la prière dans le judaïsme', le 13, 14 et 15 mai 1991 à l'université de Paris-Sorbonne, Paris IV* (n.d.) <http://www.corinna-coulmas.eu/les-contes-de-rabbi-nahman-de-bratslav-l-homme-de-priere.html> [accessed 21 May 2015].
40. Marc-Alain Ouaknin, *Le Livre brûlé* (Paris: Seuil, 1994), p. 399.
41. Ibid., p. 408.
42. Deguy, p. 45.
43. Blanckeman, pp. 177, 182.
44. *LBS*, p. 11. *LBSe*, p. 6.
45. *SO*, p. 72.
46. *LSE*, p. 30. *LSEe*, p. 11.
47. Salgas and Quignard (para. 31 of 45).
48. *LS*, p. 129.
49. Blanckeman, p. 182.
50. Pascal Quignard, *L'Occupation américaine* (Paris, Seuil: 1994), p. 205.
51. Patrick Wald Lasowski, 'Coque Bleue', in *Pascal Quignard, figures d'un lettré*, pp. 35–41 (p. 39).
52. The choice of this location echoes Marguerite Duras's 1953 *Les Petits Chevaux de Tarquinia*, about the figure of a dead child whose remains are collected by his parents in a small box, evoking a similar fetishist relation to a lost childhood.

53. Rabaté, *Pascal Quignard, étude de l'œuvre*, p. 142.

54. Sigmund Freud, 'Fetishism', in *The Standard Edition of the Complete Psychological Works of Sigmund Freud*, XXI, pp. 149–58 (p. 153) (first publ. 1927).

55. Walter Benjamin, 'Paris, Capital of the Nineteenth Century', in *Charles Baudelaire, A Lyric Poet in the Era of High Capitalism*, trans. by Harry Zohn (London: NLB, 1973), pp. 155–76 (p. 168) (first publ. 1935).

56. Freud, 'Fetishism', pp. 152–54.

57. *VA*, p. 296.

58. Pascal Quignard, 'Les fêtes des chants du Marais', in *LBS*, pp. 136–41 (p. 136). 'The Singing Festivals of the Marais', in *LBSe*, pp. 163–71 (p. 163).

59. 'LFCM', p. 137. 'LFCMe', p. 164.

60. Louis-René des Forêts, *Poèmes de Samuel Wood* (Fontfroide-le-Haut: Fata Morgana, 1988), pp. 16, 13, 14. *Poems of Samuel Wood*, trans. by Anthony Barnett (Lewes: Allardyce Book, 2011), pp. 12, 10, 11.

61. Anne Cousseau, 'La Vogue du récit d'enfance dans la seconde moitié du XXᵉ siècle', in *Le Récit d'enfance et ses modèles,* ed. by Anne Chevalier and Carole Dornier (Caen: Université de Caen Basse-Normandie, 2003), pp. 191–200 (p. 197).

62. *BO*, pp. 64, 72.

63. *BO*, p. 33.

64. *VA*, p. 180.

65. Louis-René des Forêts, *Le Bavard* (Paris: Gallimard, 2004), p. 137 (first publ. 1946). 'The Bavard', in *LCEe*, pp. 9–103 (p. 89).

66. *LSE*, p. 134. *LSEe*, p. 72.

67. Giorgio Agamben, *Infancy and History, the Destruction of Experience*, trans. by Liz Heron (London: Verso Books, 1993), pp. 47, 48, 59, 56.

68. Jacques Lacan, *Le Séminaire, livre IV, la relation d'objet, 1956–7*, ed. by Jacques-Alain Miller (Paris: Seuil, 1994), p. 152.

69. Dylan Evans, 'Object-relations theory', in *An Introductory Dictionary of Lacanian Psychoanalysis*, pp. 127–28 (p. 127). See also Jacques Lacan, *Le Séminaire, livre I, les écrits techniques de Freud, 1953–4*, ed. by Jacques-Alain Miller (Paris: Seuil, 1975). *The Seminar of Jacques Lacan: Book 1, Freud's Papers on Technique, 1953–1954*, trans. by John Forrester (New York: Norton, 1991).

70. Lacan, *LSIV*, p. 165.

71. Pascal Quignard, *Le Salon du Wurtemberg* (Paris: Gallimard, 1986), p. 42. *The Salon in Württemberg*, trans. by Barbara Bray (New York: Grove Press, 1986), p. 24.

72. *LSW*, p. 154. *LSWe*, p. 95.

73. *LEVCM*, p. 76.

74. Lapeyre-Desmaison, *Mémoires de l'origine*, p. 275.

75. *BO*, p. 87.

CONCLUSION

❖

In 2002, Pascal Quignard was awarded the Prix Goncourt for *Les Ombres errantes*, the first volume of his *Dernier royaume* series. This event crystallized a debate about his work. Was this prize attributed to a work 'n'ouvr[ant] aucune voie littéraire nouvelle' [a literary dead end], produced by an author 'finalement très parisien, très parisianiste, chic et chiqué' [elegant yet affected, typical of Paris and Parisianism], as Jorge Semprun, a member of the Prix Goncourt jury, argued at the time?[1] Or did it reward a major literary work, establishing and celebrating one of the most prominent French writers of today?

Eight years after the award of the Prix Goncourt, Pascal Quignard's *Tous les matins du monde*, alongside the film version directed by Alain Corneau, were set for the French baccalaureate. Academic research in France has since ceased to debate the significance of Quignard's work, and it recognizes him today as a significant figure in the contemporary canon. Many conferences have been devoted to his work: most recently at the Sorbonne in 2010, in Le Havre in 2013, and twice at the Centre culturel international in Cerisy-la-Salle: first in 2004, and again in 2014, to mark the tenth anniversary of the first conference.[2]

But if Quignard has become, over the past twenty years, an important figure of contemporary French literature, French studies outside France have so far paid little attention to him. In 2013, he was one of the plenary speakers at the 20th and 21st Century French and Francophone Studies International Colloquium' in Atlanta, and in 2012, Pautrot, who teaches at Saint Louis University, devoted a special issue of *L'Esprit Créateur* to Quignard. In his introduction, Pautrot claims that 'Quignard est aussi désormais un "classique" contemporain de ce côté de l'Atlantique' [Quignard is now a contemporary 'classic' on this side of the Atlantic too].[3] Yet this claim remains overstated: to this day, only a handful of articles in English have been written on Quignard's work, only a small number of his books have been translated into English, and his work remains largely absent from the undergraduate French syllabus in American, British, and Irish universities.

Why is this the case? The disparity between his omnipresence in French academia and his relative absence from English-speaking French studies reveals the larger differences that separate them. It can be argued, as Sabine Loucif does in her essay 'French in American Universities: Toward the Reshaping of Frenchness', that the two complement each other by concentrating on distinct corpuses; studies of 'francophone writers, and [...] those whose works can be studied according to feminist and gender studies methodologies' are prominent in the USA, as well as in the UK and Ireland, whilst researchers there, unlike their French counterparts, 'devote little attention to contemporary writers from metropolitan France'.[4] Quignard's work appears at the opposite end of the scope of interests defined by Loucif, on which the anglophone study of contemporary French literature is broadly centred. As a white male writer, in his sixties, who has published more than sixty texts since the end of the 1960s with some of France's leading publishers (Gallimard, Seuil, P.O.L, Grasset) as well as more 'exclusive' small presses (Orange Export Ltd, Fata Morgana, Maeght, Galilée), Quignard encounters a certain resistance on this side of the Channel.

This resistance can also be explained by the first impression given by his texts. His work and life appear to epitomize the 'parisianisme' denounced by Semprun. 'Parisianisme' is a clichéd term used to characterize writers, artists, and intellectuals found within a few Parisian *arrondissements*, and who seem more concerned with lofty ideas than with what goes on in the rest of the world. Quignard's texts seem to brush aside contemporary social and political issues to focus instead on a wide range of erudite references that might easily be labelled as pedantic. The self-consciousness of his work, and the presence of a complex layer of intertextual echoes that are often arcane, mean that Quignard's writing can appear to some as perpetuating the status quo rather than challenging it, and to be addressed to a restricted group of cultured French readers. But books should not be judged by their covers, and in Quignard's case first appearances are misleading. As seen in this study, his writing derives its value from reaching beyond its obvious erudition. Moreover, his readership is not limited to France or the francophone world, and his novels and the *Dernier royaume* volumes are regularly translated and published in Japan, South Korea, China, Russia, and Turkey, for instance. More than thirty of his works have been translated into Spanish, and an international conference on his work was recently held at the University of São Paulo in Brazil. Furthermore, Quignard's conception of writing as a literary 'manière noire' has political implications. The negative reactions that his work provokes, from Semprun's scornful remark to the attempted book burning in Lagrasse in 2007, indirectly confirm the subversion that Quignard sees as inherent in literature.

Another possible reason for the resistance encountered by Quignard's texts is his deeply ambiguous relation to language. The essential realization that Quignard does not trust words implies that critics and readers should not trust his. This study, like the critical corpus in general, makes considerable use of the writer's own statements to explore his work and his writing practice. These statements are numerous and unavoidable: they are made within the body of work but also outside it, in published interviews and at seminars and conferences on Quignard, which he almost always attends. One of the advantages of studying the work of a living author is of course to have access to his intentions as the texts are being produced. But Quignard's active participation in critical discussions about his work also creates its own problems. By denouncing language as faulty, and stating that 'tout est fiction dès que l'on s'exprime' [everything we say or write amounts to fiction],[5] Quignard exploits the power of words against themselves, especially when he adopts the tactics of a rhetorician. Rhetoricians seduce rather than enlighten, and the fascination that Quignard's writing produces in its readers is something that most critics have rightly underlined. Rabaté, for instance, sees fascination as one of the central motifs of a work that is 'sans nul doute difficile, mais qu'il faut savoir accueillir dans sa force de ravissement' [undeniably difficult to access, but which should be embraced in all its rapturous force].[6] Similarly, Jean-Luc Nancy describes a work that 'ne veut pas être lu mais bu' [wants to be imbibed rather than read].[7] To recognize the rhetorical tactics used by the writer is useful insofar as it allows critics to be aware of the struggle they face to exist independently from their object of study. Yet as Gaspard Turin notes, 'l'institution [critique] a rarement osé parler des livres de Quignard selon des modalités que le texte lui-même n'aurait pas prévues' [the critical community rarely dared to discuss Quignard's work outside of modalities predefined by the text].[8] Nancy goes further when he writes that 'il n'est pas possible de commenter les textes ou l'œuvre de Pascal Quignard' [it is simply not possible to analyse Pascal Quignard's texts or work] adding that 'le commentaire ne pourrait rien faire d'autre que de démonter des pièces que [Quignard] remonterait dans un autre ordre' [commentary would be reduced to an endless game of taking apart pieces that the writer would at once reassemble in a different order]. Nancy goes on to conclude: 'il faut lire et fermer le livre [...] Il faut imiter, à la limite' [we should simply read and close the book. Or, if the worst comes to the worst, imitate it].[9]

But what if critics do not wish simply to read texts, or merely oscillate between explanation and pastiche? A possible way of approaching the work critically, whilst at the same time remaining wary of the traps it sets and the fascination it creates, is to consider the statements made by Quignard as inherent parts of his oeuvre, and to acknowledge that they are part of a larger literary enterprise. Not only, as Nancy puts it, to see the texts as unsolvable jigsaw puzzles — although this is an unavoidable pitfall for the critic — but also to bring forth the texts' darkest zones, shed light on the tricks they deploy, and question the contradictions they contain. Quignard actually facilitates this, by including as part of his oeuvre his collaborations with critics, such as *Pascal Quignard le solitaire* or the more recent *La Suite des chats et des ânes*, co-written with Lapeyre-Desmaison and Calle-Gruber respectively. Moreover, his participation in the critical discussion about his oeuvre is often taken a pretext for publishing new works; the *contes* 'La Voix perdue', 'Le Roi au pied mouillé' and *L'Amour conjugal* all appeared in conference proceedings or edited critical volumes. Finally, Quignard often turns his public appearances into artistic performances. He has appeared onstage alongside musicians or dancers, and has staged performances, for instance in Jacques Malaterre's documentary film *À mi-mots*, where he burns one of his manuscripts in front of the camera.[10]

Such attitudes also confirm that Quignard's readers and critics are constantly put in the position of viewers, facing a literary work whose primary aim is to present itself to their gaze. What Quignard's texts produce is first and foremost an image: not the voice of the *infans* as the ideal and lost voice, but the image of the child as a mirage, a comforting and revealing hallucination created by the texts. The final appearance of the child in *L'Enfant au visage couleur de la mort* is eminently visual. In the final passage of the text, the words on the page break away from the prose-form to become a calligram. The line-breaks mimic the curling-up movement of a piece of paper thrown into an open fire, offering readers a visual image of the child's final disappearance.

Coming back to Semprun's dismissive remarks and Quignard's definition, mentioned in the Introduction, of his own work as a literary imposture, it may be said that he is an impostor in the sense that he achieves, through writing, the production of illusions. Through the motif of childhood, and the way it relies on the theme of light and its various embodiments — from the bolt of lightning, to the red light of the photographic shot, to the flames of fire — Quignard works at transforming his texts into illuminated manuscripts, where the visual takes centre stage. What the body of work produces cannot be defined as loss or as something found: as the endless image of disappearance, it shows us that literature, because of the impossibility that characterizes it, is what can best reveal the knowledge that life itself is constantly on the edge, balanced between existence and nothingness.

Notes to the Conclusion

1. Quoted by Pierre Marcelle in 'Quignard et les vieillards', *Libération*, 30 October 2002 <http://www.liberation.fr/tribune/0101429481-quignard-et-les-vieillards> [accessed 1 December 2015] (para.1 of 1).
2. See *Pascal Quignard, ou la littérature démembrée par les muses* for the proceedings of the conference at La Sorbonne-Paris IV in 2010; *Les Lieux de Pascal Quignard*, ed. by Agnès Cousin de Ravel, Chantal Lapeyre-Desmaison, and Dominique Rabaté (Paris: Gallimard, 2013) for the Le Havre colloquium; *Pascal Quignard, figures d'un lettré*, ed. by Philippe Bonnefis and Dolorès Lyotard (Paris: Galilée, 2005) for the conference in Cerisy-la-Salle in 2004; and *Pascal Quignard. Translations et métamorphoses*, ed. by Mireille Calle-Gruber, Jonathan Degenève and Irène Fénoglio (Paris: Hermann, 2015) for the 2014 conference.
3. Pautrot, 'Introduction', *L'Esprit Créateur*, 52 (2012), 1–2 (pp.1–2).
4. Sabine Loucif, 'French in American Universities, Toward the Reshaping of Frenchness', *Yale French Studies*, 115 (2008), 115–31 (p. 130).
5. LS, p. 62.
6. Rabaté, *Étude de l'œuvre*, pp. 7–8.
7. Jean-Luc Nancy, 'Jadis, jamais, bientôt (l'amour)', in *Pascal Quignard, figures d'un lettré*, pp. 383–90 (p. 383).
8. Gaspard Turin, 'Rire en Quignardie, pour une lecture posturale', *L'Esprit Créateur*, 52 (2012), 70–82 (p. 70).
9. Nancy, pp. 385–86.
10. Jacques Malaterre, *À mi-mots* (Mk2 éditions, 2004) [DVD] (first broadcast in 2001).

BIBLIOGRAPHY

❖

Major Publications by Pascal Quignard

L'Être du balbutiement, essai sur Sacher-Masoch (Paris: Mercure de France, 1969)

La Parole de la Délie, essai sur Maurice Scève (Paris: Mercure de France, 1974)

Écho, suivi D'Epistolē Alexandrou' (Paris: le Collet de Buffle, 1975) (republ. as part of Écrits de l'éphémère, 2005)

Michel Deguy (Paris: Seghers, 1975)

Hiems (Malakoff: Orange Export Ltd, 1976) (republ. as part of Écrits de l'éphémère, 2005)

Le Lecteur (Paris: Gallimard, 1976)

Sang (Malakoff: Orange Export Ltd, 1976) (republ. as part of Écrits de l'éphémère, 2005)

——and GÉRARD TITUS-CARMEL, Sarx (Paris: Maeght, 1977) (republ. as part of Écrits de l'éphémère, 2005)

Sarx, trans. by Keith Waldrop (Providence, RI: Burning Deck, 1997)

——and LOUIS CORDESSE, Les Mots de la terre, de la peur et du sol (Paris: Clivages, 1978) (republ. as part of Écrits de l'Éphémère in 2005)

Carus (Paris: Gallimard, 1979) (final ed. 2000)

Inter ærias fagos (Malakoff: Orange Export Ltd, 1979) (republ. in 2005 with illustrations by Valerio Adami)

——and LOUIS CORDESSE, Sur le défaut de terre (Paris: Clivages, 1979) (republ. as part of Écrits de l'éphémère in 2005)

——and JEAN GARONNAIRE, Le Secret du domaine (Paris: Éditions de l'Amitié, 1980) (republ. as L'Enfant au visage couleur de la mort, 2006)

Blasons anatomiques du corps féminin, ed. by Pascal Quignard and Pascal Laîné (Paris: Gallimard, 1982)

Les Tablettes de buis d'Apronenia Avitia (Paris: Gallimard, 1984)

On Wooden Tablets: Apronenia Avitia, trans. by Bruce X (Providence, RI: Burning Deck, 2001)

Le Vœu de silence, essai sur Louis-René des Forêts (Fontfroide-le-Haut: Fata Morgana, 1985)

Une gêne technique à l'égard des fragments (Fontfroide-le-Haut: Fata Morgana, 1986)

Le Salon du Wurtemberg (Paris: Gallimard, 1986)

The Salon in Württemberg, trans. by Barbara Bray (New York: Grove Press, 1986)

La Leçon de musique (Paris: Hachette, 1987)

Les Escaliers de Chambord (Paris: Gallimard, 1989)

Albucius (Paris: P.O.L, 1990)

Albucius, trans. by Bruce Boone (Venice, CA: The Lapis Press, 1992)

Petits traités, 8 vols (Paris: Maeght, 1990)

La Raison (Paris: le Promeneur, 1990)

Georges de La Tour et Pascal Quignard (Paris: Flohic, 1991) (final ed., 2005)

Georges de La Tour and Pascal Quignard, trans. by Barbara Wright (Paris: Flohic, 1991)

Tous les matins du monde (Paris: Gallimard, 1991)

All the World's Mornings, trans. by James Kirkup (St. Paul, MN: Graywolf, 1993)

La Frontière (Paris: Chandeigne, 1992)

'Préface' to *Notes de Li Yi-Chan*, trans. by Georges Bonmarchand (Paris: le Promeneur, 1992), pp. 12–19.

'Préface' to *'Sentences, divisions et couleurs, des orateurs et des rhéteurs' de Sénèque le Père*, trans. by Henri Bornecque (Paris: Aubier, 1992), pp. 7–21

Le Nom sur le bout de la langue (Paris: P.O.L, 1993)

'Préface' to *'Le Démon de Socrate' d'Apulée*, trans. by Colette Lazam (Paris: Payot, 1993), pp. 7–40

L'Occupation américaine (Paris: Seuil, 1994)

——and PIERRE SKIRA, *Les Septante* (Paris: Patrice Trigano, 1994)

Le Sexe et l'effroi (Paris: Gallimard, 1994)

Sex and Terror, trans. by Chris Turner (Calcutta: Seagull Books, 2011)

——and PIERRE SKIRA, *L'Amour conjugal* (Paris: Patrice Trigano, 1995)

La Nuit et le silence, Georges de La Tour (Paris: Flohic, 1995)

Rhétorique spéculative (Paris: Calmann-Lévy, 1995)

La Haine de la musique (Paris: Calmann-Lévy, 1996)

The Hatred of Music, trans. by Matthew Amos and Fredrik Rönnbäck (New Haven, CT: Yale University Press, 2016)

'Traité sur Esprit', in Jacques Esprit, *La Fausseté des vertus humaines* (Paris: Aubier, 1996), pp. 9–66

Vie secrète (*Dernier royaume VIII*) (Paris: Gallimard, 1998)

'1640', *Scherzo*, 9 (1999), 7–18

Terrasse à Rome (Paris: Gallimard, 2000)

'La Voix perdue', in *Pascal Quignard, la mise au silence*, ed. by Adriano Marchetti (Seyssel: Champ-Vallon, 2000), pp. 7–34

——and CHANTAL LAPEYRE-DESMAISON, *Pascal Quignard le solitaire* (Paris: Flohic, 2001)

——and OTHERS, *Kuroda* (Paris: Maeght, 2002) (with texts by Pascal Quignard and Marguerite Duras)

Les Ombres errantes (*Dernier royaume I*) (Paris: Grasset 2002)

The Roving Shadows, trans. by Chris Turner (Calcutta: Seagull Books, 2011)

Sur le Jadis (*Dernier royaume II*) (Paris: Grasset, 2002)

Abîmes (*Dernier royaume III*) (Paris: Grasset, 2002)

——AND PIERRE SKIRA, *Tondo* (Paris: Flammarion, 2002)

——AND OTHERS, *Picasso érotique* (Paris: Réunion des Musées Nationaux, 2002)

'La Métayère de Rodez', *Études Françaises*, 'Pascal Quignard ou le noyau incommunicable', 40 (2004), 9–11

Les Paradisiaques (*Dernier royaume IV*) (Paris: Grasset, 2004)

Écrits de l'éphémère (Paris: Galilée, 2005)

'Portraits crachés', in *Histoires d'amour du temps jadis*, ed. and trans. by Dominique Lavigne-Kurihara (Arles: Philippe Picquier, 2005), pp. 9–38

Pour trouver les enfers (Paris: Galilée, 2005)

Sordidissimes (*Dernier royaume V*) (Paris: Grasset 2005)

Cécile Reims grave Hans Bellmer (Paris: Éditions du Cercle d'art, 2006)

L'Enfant au visage couleur de la mort (Paris: Galilée, 2006)

Ethelrude et Wolframm (Paris: Galilée, 2006)

Le Petit Cupidon (Paris: Galilée, 2006)

Requiem (Paris: Galilée, 2006)

Triomphe du temps (Paris: Galilée, 2006)

——AND OTHERS, *Valerio Adami* (Paris: Galilée, 2006) (with texts by Pascal Quignard, Philippe Bonnefis and Michel Deguy)

Villa Amalia (Paris: Gallimard, 2006)

La Nuit sexuelle (Paris: Flammarion, 2007)

The Sexual Night, trans. by Chris Turner (Calcutta: Seagull Books, 2014)

Boutès (Paris: Galilée, 2008)

La Barque silencieuse (Dernier royaume VI) (Paris: Seuil, 2009)

The Silent Crossing, trans. by Chris Turner (Calcutta: Seagull Books, 2013)

——, PIERRE BOURGEADE, and DANIEL MARCHESSEAU, *Marie Morel, peintures* (Donnemarie-Dontilly: Éditions Chalut-mots, 2009)

Lycophron et Zétès (Paris: Gallimard, 2010)

Pierre Skira, Marie Morel & Valerio Adami (Paris: Éditions des cendres, 2010)

Les Solidarités mystérieuses (Paris: Gallimard, 2011)

——and IRÈNE FENOGLIO, *Sur le désir de se jeter à l'eau* (Paris: Presses Sorbonne nouvelle, 2011)

Médéa, précédé de 'Danse perdue' (Bordeaux: Association Ritournelles, 2011)

Les Désarçonnés (Dernier royaume VII) (Paris: Grasset, 2012)

——and MIREILLE CALLE-GRUBER, *La Suite des chats et des ânes* (Paris: Presses Sorbonne nouvelle, 2013)

Leçons de solfège et de piano (Paris: Arléa, 2013)

Mourir de penser (Dernier royaume IX) (Paris: Grasset, 2014)

Sur l'image qui manque à nos jours (Paris: Arléa, 2014)

Critique du jugement (Paris: Galilée, 2015)

Sur l'idée d'une communauté de solitaires (Paris: Arléa, 2015)

Princesse vieille reine (Paris: Galilée, 2015)

Collaborations on Films, Musical and Other Live Performances by Pascal Quignard

Screenplay for *Tous les matins du monde*, dir by Alain Corneau (Bac Films, 1991) [on DVD]

Screenplay for *Le Nouveau monde*, dir. by Alain Corneau (Bac Films, 1995), based on *L'Occupation américaine*

Screenplay for *L'Amour conjugal*, dir. by Benoît Barbier (AFMD, 1995)

Text for *L'Anoure*, dir. by Angelin Preljoca (Paris: Daniel Cande, 1995)

Text for *Le Nom sur le bout de la langue*, music by Michèle Reverdy (Mionnay: Notissimo, 2004) (first performed in 1993)

Text for *Medea*, with Carlotta Ikeda and Alain Mahé (first performed in 2010)

Works on Pascal Quignard

'L'énigme Agustina Izquierdo. Est-ce Quignard qui narre ?', *Le Nouvel Observateur*, 15 April 1993, p. 96.

'Rencontre avec Pascal Quignard, à l'occasion de la parution de *Le Sexe et l'effroi* (1994)' <http://www.gallimard.fr/catalog/entretiens/01025213.htm>

ANQUETIL, GILLES, '*Petits traités* par Pascal Quignard', *Le Nouvel Observateur*, 29 November 1990, pp. 157–58

ARGAND, CATHERINE, and PASCAL QUIGNARD, 'Entretien', *Lire*, 1 October 2002 <http://www.lexpress.fr/culture/livre/pascal-quignard-goncourt 2002_806807.html>

BLANCKEMAN, BRUNO, *Les Récits indécidables, Jean Echenoz, Hervé Guibert, Pascal Quignard* (Villeneuve d'Ascq: Presses Universitaires du Septentrion, 2000)

BOGOYA, CAMILO, '*Les Tablettes de buis d'Apronenia Avitia*, à la recherche du manuscrit perdu', *L'Esprit Créateur*, 52 (2012), 12–21

BONNEFIS, PHILIPPE, and DOLORÈS LYOTARD, eds, *Pascal Quignard, figures d'un lettré* (Paris: Galilée, 2005)

CALLE-GRUBER, MIREILLE, GILLES DECLERCQ, and STELLA SPRIET, eds, *Pascal Quignard, ou la littérature démembrée par les muses* (Paris: Presses Sorbonne nouvelle, 2011)

——and JONATHAN DEGENÈVE, IRÈNE FÉNOGLIO, *Pascal Quignard. Translations et métamorphoses* (Paris: Hermann, 2015)

CLAUDE, CHRYSTELLE, 'Les Stèles du recueillement, un dialogue avec Pascal Quignard', *L'Esprit Créateur*, 52 (2012), 3–11

COUSIN DE RAVEL, AGNÈS, 'La Peinture, pré-texte à l'écriture chez Pascal Quignard', *L'Esprit Créateur*, 52 (2012), 48–58

——, CHANTAL LAPEYRE-DESMAISON, and DOMINIQUE RABATÉ, eds, *Les Lieux de Pascal Quignard* (Paris: Gallimard, 2014)

CROS, JEAN-LOUIS, *Pascal Quignard, 'Tous les matins du monde'*, dir. by (Futuroscope/SCEREN-CNDP, 2011) [on DVD], in *Pascal Quignard, ou la littérature démembrée par les muses*, ed. by Mireille Calle-Gruber, Gilles Declercq and Stella Spriet (Paris: Presses Sorbonne nouvelle, 2011)

DAMBRE, MARC, and BRUNO BLANCKEMAN, 'Écrire la modernité', in *Séminaire 'Proses narratives en France, 2001–2010'* (set up by the CERACC at the Université Paris 3-Sorbonne Nouvelle in 2010)

DEGUY, MICHEL, 'L'Écriture sidérante', in *Pascal Quignard, la mise au silence*, ed. by Adriano Marchetti (Seyssel: Champ Vallon, 2000), pp. 45–64

FARGE, ARLETTE, 'Brisures du temps', in *Pascal Quignard, ou la littérature démembrée par les muses*, ed. by Mireille Calle-Gruber, Gilles Declercq and Stella Spriet (Paris: Presses Sorbonne nouvelle, 2011), pp. 241–47

GARCIN, JÉRÔME, and PASCAL QUIGNARD, 'Les Pensées de Pascal (Quignard)', *Le Nouvel Observateur*, 28 September 2011 <http://bibliobs.nouvelobs.com/romans/20110928.OBS1315/les-pensees-de-pascal-quignard.html>

GORILLOT, BÉNÉDICTE, '*Inter ærias fagos*, le salut d'une écriture latine', in *Pascal Quignard, ou la littérature démembrée par les muses*, ed. by Mireille Calle-Gruber, Gilles Declercq, and Stella Spriet (Paris: Presses Sorbonne nouvelle, 2011), pp. 85–97

HENRIC, JACQUES, and PASCAL QUIGNARD, 'La Nuit sexuelle', *Mondesfrancophones.com* (2007) <http://mondesfrancophones.com/espaces/frances/pascal-quignard-la-nuit-sexuelle>

JOURDAIN, LOÏC, and BENOÎT CANU, dirs, *Histoires d'écrivains, Pascal Quignard* (La Cinquième MK2 TV, 2000) [DVD]

KANTCHEFF, CHRISTOPHE, and PASCAL QUIGNARD, 'La littérature est le langage qui ignore sa puissance', *Le Matricule des anges*, 10 (1994–95), <http://www.lelibraire.com/dossiers/AR1003.html>

KEMP, SIMON, *French Fiction into the Twenty-First Century, The Return to the Story* (Cardiff: University of Wales Press, 2010)

KOLB, KATHERINE, 'Music and the Feminine in Pascal Quignard', *L'Esprit Créateur*, 47 (2007), 101–14

LAPEYRE-DESMAISON, CHANTAL, *Mémoires de l'origine* (Paris: Flohic, 2001)

——'Pascal Quignard, une poétique de l'agalma', *Études Françaises*, 'Pascal Quignard ou le noyau incommunicable', 40 (2004), 39–53

——'Genèses de l'écriture', in *Pascal Quignard, figures d'un lettré*, ed. by Philippe Bonnefis et Dolorès Lyotard (Paris: Galilée, 2005), pp. 327–39

—— 'L'Ange et la bête, notes sur *La Nuit sexuelle* de Pascal Quignard', ed. by Jean-Louis Pautrot, *L'Esprit Créateur*, 1, 52 (2012), 107–19

LASOWSKI, PATRICK WALD, 'Coque Bleue', in *Pascal Quignard, figures d'un lettré*, ed. by Philippe Bonnefis and Dolorès Lyotard (Paris: Galilée, 2005), pp. 35–41

MALATERRE, JACQUES, dir, *À mi-mots* (Mk2 éditions, 2004) [DVD] (first broadcast in 2001)

MARCHETTI, ADRIANO, ed., *Pascal Quignard, la mise au silence* (Seyssel: Champ Vallon, 2000)

NANCY, JEAN-LUC, 'Jadis, jamais, bientôt (l'amour)', in *Pascal Quignard, figures d'un lettré*, ed. by Philippe Bonnefis and Dolorès Lyotard (Paris: Galilée, 2005), pp. 383–90

NORA, PIERRE and MARCEL GAUCHET, 'La Déprogrammation de la littérature', in *Écrits de l'Éphémère* (Paris: Galilée, 2005), pp. 233–49 (first publ. in *Débat*, 1989)

NOVARINA, VALÈRE, 'De l'espace', in *Pascal Quignard, ou la littérature démembrée par les muses*, ed. by Mireille Calle-Gruber, Gilles Declercq, and Stella Spriet (Paris: Presses Sorbonne nouvelle, 2011), pp. 213–19

OGAWA, MIDORI, '*La Frontière*, un roman selon Pascal Quignard', *Gallia*, 42 (2002), 57–64

PAUTROT, JEAN-LOUIS, 'Pascal Quignard et la pensée mythique', *The French Review*, 76 (2003), 752–64

——and DOMINIQUE ALLÈGRE, eds, *Études Françaises*, 'Pascal Quignard ou le noyau incommunicable', 40 (2004)

——'Dix questions à Pascal Quignard', *Études Françaises*, 'Pascal Quignard ou le noyau incommunicable', 40 (2004), 87–92

——*Pascal Quignard ou le fonds du monde* (Amsterdam: Rodopi, 2007)

——ed., *L'Esprit Créateur*, 'Numéro spécial sur Pascal Quignard', 52 (2012)

——'Introduction', *L'Esprit Créateur* 'Numéro spécial sur Pascal Quignard', 52 (2012), 1–2

MARCELLE, PIERRE, 'Quignard et les vieillards', *Libération*, 30 October 2002 <http://www.liberation.fr/tribune/0101429481-quignard-et-les-vieillards>

RABATÉ, DOMINIQUE, 'Vérités et affirmations chez Pascal Quignard', *Études Françaises*, 'Pascal Quignard ou le noyau incommunicable', 40 (2004), 77–85

——*Pascal Quignard, étude de l'œuvre* (Paris: Bordas, 2008)

——'Figures de la disparition dans le roman contemporain', in *Un Retour des normes romanesques dans la littérature française contemporaine*, ed. by Marc Dambre and Wolfgang Asholt (Paris: Presses Sorbonne nouvelle, 2011), pp. 67–75

RICHARD, JEAN-PIERRE, 'Sensation, dépression, écriture', in *L'État des choses, études sur huit écrivains d'aujourd'hui* (Paris: Gallimard, 1990), pp. 39–66. First published in *Poétique*, 71 (1987), 357–74

SALGAS, JEAN-PIERRE, 'Écrire n'est pas un choix mais un symptôme', *La Quinzaine littéraire*, 565 (1990) <http://www.quinzaine-litteraire.presse.fr/articles/entretiens/pascal-quignard-ecrire-n-est-pas-un-choix-mais-un-symptome.php>

SKIRA, PIERRE, 'De l'amitié', in *Pascal Quignard, ou la littérature démembrée par les muses*, ed. by Mireille Calle-Gruber, Gilles Declercq, and Stella Spriet (Paris: Presses Sorbonne nouvelle, 2011), pp. 101–03

TURIN, GASPARD, 'Rire en Quignardie, pour une lecture posturale Gaspard Turin', *L'Esprit Créateur*, 52 (2012), 70–82

VEINSTEIN, ALAIN, 'Tout autre, purs pluriels et dehors', in *Pascal Quignard, ou la littérature démembrée par les muses*, ed. by Mireille Calle-Gruber, Gilles Declercq, and Stella Spriet (Paris: Presses Sorbonne nouvelle, 2011), pp. 257–66

ZAJDERMANN, PAULE, and PASCAL QUIGNARD, 'Pascal Quignard, le latin', in *Vie et mort des langues*, dir. by Paule Zajdermann (Bibliothèque Publique d'information, 2007) [DVD]

Other Works Cited

'L'affaire des livres saccagés à Lagrasse, un communiqué de l'association *Le Marque-Page*', *Poezibao* (2007) <http://poezibao.typepad.com/poezibao/2007/08/laffaire-des-li.html>

AGAMBEN, GIORGIO, *Infancy and History, the Destruction of Experience*, trans. by Liz Heron (London: Verso, 1993)

ATTURO, VALENTINA and ALICE BOURKE, 'Contemplating Wonder: "ad-miratio" in Richard of St. Victor and Dante', *Dante Studies*, 129 (2011), 99–124

BADIOU, ALAIN, *L'Antiphilosophie de Wittgenstein* (Caen: Nous, 2009)

——*Wittgenstein's Antiphilosophy*, trans. by Bruno Bosteels (London: Verso Books, 2011)

BAKHTIN, MIKHAIL, *Rabelais and His World* (Bloomington: Indiana University Press, 1984).

BARNES, JULIAN, 'World Within Words', *The Guardian*, 28 June 2003 <www.guardian. co.uk/books/2003/jun/28/classics.julianbarnes>

BARTH, JOHN, 'The Literature of Exhaustion', *Atlantic Monthly*, 220 (1967), 29–34

—— 'The Literature of Replenishment, Postmodernist Fiction', *Atlantic Monthly*, 245 (1980), 65–71

BARTHES, ROLAND, *Le Plaisir du Texte* (Paris: Seuil, 1982) (first publ. 1973)

The Pleasure of the Text, trans. by Richard Miller (New York: Hill and Wang, 1975)

—— 'La mort de l'auteur', in *Le Bruissement de la langue* (Paris: Seuil, 1984), pp. 63–69

'The Death of the Author', in *The Rustle of Language*, trans. by Richard Howard (Oakland: University of California Press, 1989), pp. 49–55

—— 'Préface à La Bruyère, *Les Caractères*', in *Essais critiques*, (Paris: Seuil, 1991), pp. 221–37 (first publ. 1963)

'La Bruyère', in *Critical Essays* (Evanston, IL: Northwestern University Press, 1972), pp. 221–39

BATAILLE, GEORGES, 'Lascaux, ou la naissance de l'art', in *Œuvres complètes*, 12 vols (Paris: Gallimard, 1970–88), IX (1979) (first publ. 1955)

Lascaux or the Birth of Art, trans. by Austryn Wainhouse (Lausanne: Skira, 1955)

BENJAMIN, WALTER, 'The Storyteller', trans. by Harry Zohn, in *Illuminations*, ed. by Hannah Arendt (London: Jonathan Cape, 1970), pp. 83–109 (first publ. 1936)

—— 'Paris, Capital of the Nineteenth Century', in *Charles Baudelaire, A Lyric Poet in the Era of High Capitalism*, trans. by Harry Zohn (London: NLB, 1973), pp. 155–76 (first publ. 1935)

—— 'Central Park', trans. by Lloyd Spencer, *New German Critique*, 34 (1985), 32–58

BETTELHEIM, BRUNO, *The Uses of Enchantment, the Meaning and Importance of Fairy Tales* (London: Thames and Hudson, 1976)

BLANCHOT, MAURICE, *La Part du feu* (Paris: Gallimard, 1949)

The Work of Fire, trans. by Charlotte Mandell (Stanford, CA: Stanford University Press, 1995)

—— *L'Espace littéraire* (Paris: Gallimard, 1955)

The Space of Literature, trans. by Ann Smock (Lincoln: University of Nebraska Press, 1982)

—— 'La Parole vaine' in *L'Amitié* (Paris: Gallimard, 1971), pp. 137–49

'Idle Speech', in *Friendship*, trans. by Elizabeth Rottenberg (Stanford, CA: Stanford University Press, 1997), pp. 117–28

—— *La Communauté inavouable* (Paris: Minuit, 1984)

The Unavowable Community, trans. by Pierre Joris (Barrytown, NY: Station Hill, 2000)

—— 'Une voix venue d'ailleurs, sur les poèmes de Louis-René des Forêts* (Plombière-lès-Dijon: Ulysse, 1992)

A Voice From Elsewhere, trans. by Charlotte Mandell (Albany: State University of New York Press, 2007)

BRADBURY, RAY, *Fahrenheit 451* (New York: Ballantine Books, 1953)

CLOSSON, MARIANNE, *L'Imaginaire démoniaque en France (1550–1650)* (Geneva: Droz, 2000)

COULMAS, CORINNA, 'Les Contes de Rabbi Nahman de Bratslav', in *Actes du colloque 'Aspects de la vie religieuse, l'étude et la prière dans le judaïsme', le 13, 14 et 15 mai 1991 à l'université de Paris-Sorbonne, Paris IV* (n.d.) <http://www.corinna-coulmas.eu/les-contes-de-rabbi-nahman-de-bratslav-l-homme-de-priere.html>

COUSSEAU, ANNE, 'La Vogue du récit d'enfance dans la seconde moitié du XXᵉ siècle', in *Le Récit d'enfance et ses modèles*, ed. by Anne Chevalier and Carole Dornier (Caen: Université de Caen Basse-Normandie, 2003), pp. 191–200

CROWLEY, SHARON, 'On Gorgias and Grammatology', *College Composition and Communication*, 30 (1979), 279–84

DEGUY, MICHEL, trans.,'l'*Eloge d'Hélène* de Gorgias', *Revue de Poésie*, 90 (1964), 36–49

DES FORÊTS, LOUIS-RENÉ, *Les Mendiants* (Paris: Gallimard, 1943)

—— *The Beggars*, trans. by Helen Beauclerk (London: Dennis Dobson, 1948)

—— *La Chambre des enfants* (Paris: Gallimard, 1960)

—— *The Children's Room*, trans. by Jean Stewart (London: John Calder, 1963)

—— *Poèmes de Samuel Wood* (Fontfroide-le-Haut: Fata Morgana, 1988)

—— *Poems of Samuel Wood*, trans. by Anthony Barnett (Lewes: Allardyce Books, 2011)

—— *Le Bavard* (Paris: Gallimard, 2004) (first publ. 1946)

—— 'The Bavard', in *The Children's Room*, trans. by Jean Stewart (London: John Calder, 1963), pp. 9–103

—— *Lettre sur 'Les Mendiants'* (Paris: La Bibliothèque Littéraire, 1991) (first publ. 1943)

DURAS, MARGUERITE, *Les Petits Chevaux de Tarquinia* (Paris: Gallimard, 1953)

—— *Moderato Cantabile* (Paris: Éditions de Minuit, 1958)

DYER, THOMAS HENRY, *Pompeii, Its History, Buildings and Antiquities* (London: Bell & Daldy, 1867)

EVANS, DYLAN, *An Introductory Dictionary of Lacanian Psychoanalysis* (London: Routledge, 1996)

FOUCAULT, MICHEL, *Histoire de la sexualité*, 3 vols (Paris: Gallimard, 1976–84)

FOURNIER, EDOUARD, *Variétés historiques et littéraires*, 10 vols (Paris: P. Jannet, 1855)

FRALEIGH, SONDRA, *Butoh: Metamorphic Dance and Global Alchemy* (Champaign: University of Illinois Press, 2010)

FREUD, SIGMUND, 'The Ego and the Id', in *The Standard Edition of the Complete Psychological Works of Sigmund Freud*, 24 vols (London: Vintage, 2001), XIX, pp. 3–68 (first publ. 1923)

—— 'Fetishism', in *The Standard Edition of the Complete Psychological Works of Sigmund Freud*, 24 vols (London: Vintage, 2001), XXI, pp. 149–58 (first publ. 1927)

GAUNT, SIMON, *Retelling the Tale, an Introduction to Medieval French Literature* (London: Duckworth, 2001)

GOUGAUD, HENRI, 'Nukar', in *Le Livre des amours* (Paris: Seuil, 1996), pp. 238–39

GRIMM, JACOB, and WILHELM GRIMM, 'The Frog Prince', in *Grimm's Household Stories*, trans. by Lucy Crane (London: Macmillan, 1882), pp. 32–36

GROSFILLIER, JEAN, 'Quelques considérations sur l'influence du *De contemplatione* de Richard de Saint-Victor', *Sacris Erudiri*, 52 (2013), 235–74

GUISLAIN, GILBERT, PASCAL LE PAUTREMAT, and JEAN-MARIE LE TALLEC, *500 citations de culture générale* (Paris: Jeunes éditions, 2005)

HILL, LESLIE, *Blanchot, Extreme Contemporary* (London: Routledge, 1997)

HOLLOWAY, R. ROSS, 'The Tomb of the Diver', *American Journal of Archaeology*, 110 (2006), 365–88

IZQUIERDO, AGUSTINA, *Un Souvenir indécent* ((Paris: P.O.L, 1992)

—— *L'Amour pur* (Paris: P.O.L, 1993)

KRISTEVA, JULIA, *Le Langage, cet inconnu* (Paris: Seuil, 1981) (first publ. 1970)

Language: the Unknown, trans. by Anne M. Menke (New York: Columbia University Press, 1989)

—— *La Révolution du langage poétique* (Paris: Seuil, 1985)

Revolution in Poetic Language, trans. by Margaret Waller (New York: Columbia University Press, 1984)

LA BRUYÈRE, JEAN DE, *Les Caractères* (Paris: Gallimard, 1951) (first publ. 1688)

LACAN, JACQUES, *Écrits* (Paris: Seuil, 1966)

Écrits: The First Complete Edition in English, trans. by Bruce Fink (New York: Norton, 2006)

—— *Le Séminaire, livre I, les écrits techniques de Freud, 1953–4*, ed. by Jacques-Alain Miller (Paris: Seuil, 1975)

The Seminar of Jacques Lacan: Book 1, Freud's Papers on Technique, 1953–1954, trans. by John Forrester (New York: Norton, 1991)

——*Le Séminaire, livre IV, la relation d'objet, 1956–7*, ed. by Jacques-Alain Miller (Paris: Seuil, 1994)

——*Le Séminaire, livre VII, l'éthique de la psychanalyse la relation d'objet, 1959–60*, ed. by Jacques-Alain Miller (Paris: Seuil, 1986)

The Ethics of Psychoanalysis (1959–1960). The Seminar of Jacques Lacan edited by Jacques-Alain Miller, Book VII, trans. by Dennis Porter (London: Routledge, 1992)

LAERTIUS, DIOGENES, *The Lives and Opinions of Eminent Philosophers*, trans. by C. D. Yonge (London: Henry G. Bohn, 1853)

LANGLOIS, CHARLES-VICTOR and CHARLES SEIGNOBOS, *Introduction aux études historiques* (Paris: Hachette, 1898)

LEVI, PRIMO, *If This is a Man*, trans. by Stuart Woolf (London: Abacus, 1987) (first publ. 1958)

LÉVI-STRAUSS, CLAUDE, *Le Cru et le Cuit* (Paris: Plon, 1964)

The Raw and the Cooked, trans. by John and Doreen Weightman (Harmondsworth: Penguin, 1986)

LONG, KONG-SOUEN (Gongsun Lung), *Sur le doigt qui montre cela*, trans. and ed. by Pascal Quignard (Paris: Michel Chandeigne, 1990)

LOUCIF, SABINE, 'French in American Universities, Toward the Reshaping of Frenchness', *Yale French Studies*, 115 (2008), 115–31

LYCOPHRON, *Alexandra*, ed. and trans. by Pascal Quignard (Paris: Mercure de France, 1971)

LYOTARD, JEAN-FRANÇOIS, *La Condition postmoderne, rapport sur le savoir* (Paris: Minuit, 1979)

The Postmodern Condition: A Report on Knowledge, trans. by Geoff Bennington and Brian Massumi (Manchester: Manchester University Press, 1984)

——'La peinture, anamnèse du visible', in *Misère de la philosophie* (Paris: Galilée, 2000), pp. 97–115

'Anamnesis of the Visible 2', trans. by John Ronan, *Qui Parle*, 11 (1999), 21–36

MALLARMÉ, STÉPHANE, *Œuvres complètes*, 2 vols (Paris: Gallimard, Bibliothèque de la Pléiade, 1998–2003), II (2003), pp. 204–13 (first publ. 1895)

Selected Poetry and Prose, ed. by Mary Ann Caws (New York: New Directions Books, 1982)

MEAUME, EDOUARD, *Recherches sur la vie et les ouvrages de Jacques Callot*, 2 vols (Paris: Renouard, 1860)

NIETZSCHE, FRIEDRICH, *Thus Spoke Zarathustra*, trans. by Reginald John Hollingdale (London: Penguin, 1969) (first publ. 1885)

OUAKNIN, MARC-ALAIN, *Le Livre brûlé* (Paris: Seuil, 1994)

OVID, *The Metamorphoses*, trans. by Allen Mandelbaum (London: Harcourt Brace, 1995)

PEREC, GEORGES, *La Disparition* (Paris: Denoël, 1969)

——*W ou le souvenir d'enfance* (Paris: Gallimard, 1993) (first publ. 1975)

PERRAULT, CHARLES *Contes*, ed. by Marc Soriano (Paris: Flammarion, 1989)

The Complete Fairy Tales in Verse and Prose, trans. and ed. by Stanley Appelbaum (Mineola, NY: Dover, 2002)

PETTERSON, JAMES, *Postwar Figures of L'Éphémère* (Lewisburg, PA: Bucknell University Press, 2000)

PLATO, *Gorgias*, trans. by Terence Irwin (Oxford: Clarendon Press, 1979)

RABATÉ, DOMINIQUE, *Vers une littérature de l'épuisement* (Paris: José Corti, 1991)

——'Figures de la disparition dans le roman contemporain', in *Un retour des normes roman-esques dans la littératures française contemporaine*, ed. by Marc Dambre and Wolfgang Asholt (Paris: Presses Sorbonne nouvelle, 2011)

ROSE, JONATHAN, *The Holocaust and The Book* (Amherst: University of Massachusetts Press, 2001)

ROUDINESCO, ELISABETH, 'The Mirror Stage, an Obliterated Archive', trans. by Barbara Bray, in *The Cambridge Companion to Lacan*, ed. by Jean-Michel Rabaté (Cambridge: CUP, 2003), pp. 25–34

SANDERS, VICKI, 'Dancing and the Dark Soul of Japan: an Aesthetic Analysis of "Butō"',
  Asian Theatre Journal, 5 (1988), 148–63

SCÈVE, MAURICE, *Œuvres complètes*, ed. by Pascal Quignard (Paris: Mercure de France, 1974)

SPRAGUE, ROSAMUND, *The Older Sophists* (Columbia: South Carolina Press, 1972)

STENDHAL, *Le Rouge et le Noir* (Paris: Livre de Poche, 1997) (first publ. 1830)

The Red and the Black, trans. by Roger Gard (New York: Penguin, 2002)

TISSOT, SAMUEL AUGUSTE, *De la santé des gens de lettres* (Liège: Bassompierre, 1768)

TODOROV, TZVETAN, *The Fantastic: A Structural Approach to a Literary Genre*, trans. by Richard
  Howard (Cleveland, OH: Case Western Reserve University Press, 1973)

TONDEUR, CLAIRE-LISE and ANNIE ERNAUX, 'Entretien avec Annie Ernaux', *French Review*,
  69 (1995), 37–44

ZIPES, JACK, 'Introduction, Towards a Definition of the Literary Fairy Tale', in *The Oxford
  Companion to Fairy Tales*, ed. by Jack Zipes (Oxford: OUP, 2000), pp. xv–xxxii

INDEX

❖

Acts of the Apostles, *see* Bible 82
Adami, Valerio 15
Agamben, Giorgio 91
Alighieri, Dante 48
Ancenis, France 4
animality 7, 28, 32–33, 36, 61–62, 68, 70–75, 78, 86, 90–91
Anquetil, Gilles 77
antiphilosophy, *see* Badiou, Alain 69
Apuleius 6
archaeology 63–68
   see also Foucault, Michel 62, 64–66
   and Paestum 1–2, 7
   and Pompeii 64–67
Ars Poetica 55
auto-da-fé, *see* book burning 78–85, 98

Badiou, Alain 69
Bakhtin, Mikhail 58
Barth, John 2, 8
Barthes, Roland 2, 13, 77, 79–80
Bataille, Georges 53, 71–73, 80
Baudelaire, Charles 64
Baudrillard, Jean 63
Bellmer, Hans 52
Benjamin, Walter 27–29, 63–64, 87
Benveniste, Emile 91
Bettelheim, Bruno 28
Bible 82
Bion, Wilfred 9
black manner, *see* manière noire 52–59, 61, 98
Blanchot, Maurice 3–5, 7, 38, 54, 78, 79–85
Blanckeman, Bruno 85, 86
Bonnefoy, Yves 1
book burning 78–85, 98
   see also fire 7, 30, 62, 78, 80–85, 92–93, 99–100
Bosch, Hieronymus 58
Bosse, Abraham 55
Bradbury, Ray 82
Breton, André 81
   see also Surrealism 82
Brittany, France 17, 20, 21
Bruges, Belgium 55, 57
Bruneau, Anne 3, 22
Bruneau, Jean 3, 22
Bruneau, Marie 15
Burgundy, France, *see* Sens 1, 12, 46
Butoh (*butô, Butō*) 40–41

Calle-Gruber, Mireille 20, 99
Callot, Jacques 58
Caravaggio 65
Carrère, Emmanuel 2
Celan, Paul 1
Cerisy-la-Salle, France 97
childhood 4, 7, 17, 18, 20, 33–34, 40, 85–93, 100
   see also infancy 19, 33, 86, 90–91, 99
   and *l'enfant* 29–30, 33–34, 37, 47–52
Clovis 83–84
collaboration 1, 6, 10, 14–16, 38–40, 45–46, 52, 77, 99
Le Concert des Nations 4
contes 6, 11, 27–42, 49–52, 54–55, 85, 92–93, 99
Cordesse, Louis 52
Corneau, Alain 75, 97
Coulmas, Corinna 84, 85
Cousin de Ravel, Agnès 50
Cousseau, Anne 89
Crowley, Sharon 70
cuculliform 12

Dachau, *see* Bruneau, Jean 3, 22
Dali, Salvador 58
dance 1, 6, 16, 33, 38, 40–41, 52–53, 99
Deguy, Michel 9, 37, 67, 85
Duras, Marguerite 17, 24, 94
Dyer, Thomas Henry 66

é-érudition 62–63, 73–74
Echenoz, Jean 2–3
Eckhart (Meister) 48
ekphrasis 56–58
l'enfant 29–30, 33–34, 37, 47–52
   see also childhood 4, 7, 17, 18, 20, 33–34, 40, 85–93, 100
   and infancy 19, 33, 86, 90–91, 99
Ephesus, *see* Bible 82
Ernaux, Annie 3, 4
von Eschenbach, Wolfram 35
Evans, Dylan 91

fairy tale, *see contes* 6, 11, 27–42, 49–52, 54–55, 85, 92–93, 99
Farge, Arlette 64
Fenoglio, Irène 45–46
Fiorelli, Giuseppe 66
fire 7, 30, 62, 78, 80–85, 92–93, 99–100
   see also book burning 78–85, 98

folktale, see *contes* 11, 27–42, 49–52, 54–55, 85, 92–93, 99
des Forêts, Louis-René 1, 3, 10, 21, 34, 38, 80, 81, 84, 89, 90
Foucault, Michel 62, 64–66
  see also archaeology 63–68
Fournier, Edouard 32
fragmentation 7, 78–82
Fraleigh, Sondra 41
Freud, Sigmund 18–19, 30, 50, 53, 87–88, 91
  death drive 18, 30, 49–50, 52
  fetishism, logic of 87–92
  primal scene 50, 53, 56, 61
Fronteira Palace, see Lisbon 53

Gallimard 1, 4, 47, 98
Garonnaire, Jean 49
Gellée, Claude (Le Lorrain) 55
Gorgias 37, 69–70, 74, 77
Gorillot, Bénédicte 74
Gougaud, Henri 31
Goya, Francisco 54
Grimm Brothers 30, 37–38

Hijikata, Tatsumi 40
  see also Butoh (*butô*, *Butō*) 40–41
Hildebrand 56, 57
Hill, Leslie 80
Hiroshima, Japan 40
history 61–68, 70, 75
Hocquard, Emmanuel 4
Holloway, R. Ross 1
Homer 10, 30, 38
Houellebecq, Michel 3, 9

Ikeda, Carlotta 16, 40–41
  see also Butoh (*butô*, *Butō*) 40–41
infancy 19, 33, 86, 90–91, 99
  see also childhood 4, 7, 17, 18, 20, 33–34, 40, 35–93, 100
  and *l'enfant* 29–30, 33–34, 37, 47–52
Izquierdo, Agustina 11
the *Jadis* 3, 7, 59, 61–75, 81, 86, 89, 91

Jankélévitch, Vladimir 38–39

Kafka, Franz 78, 80–82
Kierkegaard, Søren 69
Kolb, Katherine 39
Kristeva, Julia 36, 39–40, 70–72

de La Bruyère, Jean 79–80
de La Tour, Georges 14, 16, 52–53
Lacan, Jacques 7, 10, 49–50, 61, 66, 69, 91
  the Law of the father 49
  the real 7, 61
  schéma du voile 91
  symbolic death 49–50

Laertius, Diogenes 51
Lagrasse, France 83
Lapeyre-Desmaison, Chantal 9, 20, 47, 49, 67, 83, 93, 99
Lascaux cave paintings 53–55, 71–72
Latin language 12, 48, 74–75
Latro, Marcus Porcius 68
Le Havre, France 4, 40, 97
Léélem, see Nachman of Breslov 84–85
Leiris, Michel 1
Leskov, Nikolai 27
Lévi-Strauss, Claude 29
Levi, Primo 39
Lévinas, Emmanuel 80–81
Lisbon, Portugal 53
logos 68–69, 74, 85
Long, Gongsun 14
Loucif, Sabine 97, 98
Lully, Jean-Baptiste 4
Lycophron 11, 14
Lyotard, Jean-François 58, 63

Mahé, Alain 40
Mallarmé, Stéphane 2, 79–81
manière noire 52–59, 61, 98
Marais, Marin 14, 38
Marie de France 35
Meaume, Edouard 55
metamorphosis 4, 7, 13, 21–22, 29–32, 38, 41, 51. 64, 71, 74
  see also Ovid 6, 21–23, 28, 38
mezzotint, see manière noire 52–59, 61, 98
Modiano, Patrick 2, 3, 9
Morel, Marie 15, 16, 52
mue, see voice breaking 39, 88, 90, 99
music 4, 5, 6, 7, 11, 16, 19, 23, 33, 38–40, 52, 69, 77, 85, 87, 93
myth 3, 6, 12, 14, 19, 21–23, 28–30, 36, 38, 51, 54–57, 61–63, 66–67, 73, 92
  Antigone 49–50
  Baubo 58
  Butes 19, 30, 40
  Helen of Troy 37
  Medea 40–41
  Medusa 12, 29, 33, 51, 65–66, 92
  Narcissus and Echo 21–23, 28, 65
  Odysseus 10, 19, 30
  Oedipus 56–57
  Orpheus, see Orphic quest 13–14, 29, 40, 54. 61, 66, 68, 81
  Penelope 36
  Perseus 11–12, 65
  Polyphemus 10
  Underworld 13, 61

Nachman of Breslov 84–85
Nancy, Jean-Luc 99

Naples, Italy 1, 17
Napoli, Mario 1
Nietzsche, Friedrich 64, 69

Ogawa, Midori 53
Orphic quest 13–14, 29, 40, 54, 61, 66, 68, 81
Ouaknin, Marc-Alain 85
Ovid 6, 21–23, 28, 38

Paestum, Italy 1, 2, 7
Paris 1, 3, 9, 14, 97
Parisianism 97–98
Paul (*Saint*) 82
Pautrot, Jean-Louis 10, 13, 14, 29, 63, 73, 97
Perec, Georges 47, 52, 86
Perrault, Charles 37, 41, 42
philosophy 1, 5, 63, 64, 68–70
Plato 36–37, 62, 68, 69, 70
Pompeii, Italy 65–67
Port-Royal des Champs 9
Poseidonia, *see* Paestum 1, 2, 7
Preljocaj, Angelin 16, 38
Prix Goncourt 2, 97
Proust, Marcel 86

Quignard, Jacques 3
Quignard, Marthe 4
Quignard, Pascal:
  Albucius 14, 63
  Boutès 19, 28, 38, 40, 45, 90, 93
  Carus 16, 19
  Dernier royaume 1, 2, 27, 72, 98
  Ethelrude et Wolframm 27, 35–36, 40
  Inter ærias fagos 74
  L'Amour conjugal 27, 99
  L'Enfant au visage couleur de la mort 27–30, 33, 37,
    47–52, 78, 88–93, 99
    see also l'enfant 29–30, 33–34, 37, 47–52
  L'Être du balbutiement, essai sur Sacher-Masoch 10
  L'Occupation américaine 67, 86–87
  La Barque silencieuse (Dernier royaume VI) 5, 12, 19,
    31–33, 88–91
      'Les fêtes des chants du Marais' 88–91
    de Hornoc, Countess 31–33, 36, 41
  La Frontière 52–53, 62
  La Haine de la musique 38–39
  La Leçon de musique 38, 90
  'La Métayère de Rodez' 34, 37
  La Nuit sexuelle 53–55, 62, 83
  La Parole de la Délie, essai sur Maurice Scève 6, 69
  La Raison 68–69
  La Suite des chats et des ânes 20, 99
  'La Voix perdue' 27, 30–31, 36, 38, 40, 73, 99
  Le Lecteur 1, 10, 12, 13, 19, 29, 47–52, 53, 82–83
  'Le Manuscrit sur l'air' 59
  Le Nom sur le bout de la langue 33, 38, 40, 90
    'Petit traité sur la Méduse' 33, 34

'Le Roi au pied mouillé' 99
Le Salon du Wurtemberg 17, 29, 87, 92
  Charles Chegogne 17, 19, 21, 22, 87
Le Secret du domaine 29, 47, 48, 49, 52
Le Sexe et l'effroi 21, 53, 58, 62, 64–67, 74
Le Vœu de silence, essai sur Louis-René des Forêts
  34–35, 38
Les Escaliers de Chambord 29, 73, 87, 90
  Edouard Furfooz 73, 87
Les Ombres errantes (Dernier royaume I) 97
Les Solidarités mystérieuses 16, 19–22, 27, 28
  Claire 19–22
Les Tablettes de buis d'Apronenia Avitia 11, 14, 15, 56,
  67, 78
    Avitia, Apronenia 11, 15, 76, 78–79
Lycophron et Zétès 12, 13, 14, 19, 29, 83
Medea 40, 41
Mourir de penser (Dernier royaume IX) 2, 34, 40
Pascal Quignard le solitaire 9, 45, 55, 73, 83, 99
  see also Lapeyre-Desmaison, Chantal 9, 20, 47, 49,
    67, 83, 93, 99
Petits traités 50
Pierre Skira, Marie Morel & Valerio Adami 15
Rhétorique spéculative 69–72
Sarx 33
Sur l'idée d'une communauté de solitaires 9, 16, 40
  'Les Ruines de Port-Royal' 16
  and 'Compléments aux ruines' 16
Sur le désir de se jeter à l'eau 45–46, 59
Sur le doigt qui montre cela 14
Terrasse à Rome 11, 29, 55–59, 62, 67, 82
  Geoffroy Meaume 55–59, 67, 82
Tous les matins du monde 12, 14, 23, 29, 38, 90, 97
  de Sainte-Colombe, M. 14, 16, 23
Triomphe du temps 27
Une gêne technique à l'égard des fragments 79–80
Vie secrète (Dernier royaume VIII) 2, 5, 16, 27, 31–33, 53
  Nukar 31–33, 41
Villa Amalia 16–22, 27–28, 40, 90
  Hidden, Ann 16–22, 27–28, 39, 40, 88

Rabaté, Dominique 2–3, 5, 8, 19, 29, 36, 72, 87, 99
Racine, Jean 9
Remigius (*Saint*) 84
Reverdy, Michèle 16, 38, 40
Richard, Jean-Pierre 19
Rose, Jonathan 82
Roudinesco, Elisabeth 19

Saint Victor, Hugh of 48
Saint Victor, Richard of 48, 51, 52
Sainte-Marie d'Orbieu, *see* Lagrasse, France 83
Salgas, Jean-Pierre 13
Sanders, Vicki 40
Savall, Jordi 16
Scève, Maurice 6, 38, 69
Second World War 3, 4, 39, 40, 67, 86, 87

Semprun, Jorge 97, 98, 100
Sens, France 1, 12, 46
Sèvres, France 3, 4
shunga 54
Skira, Pierre 15, 16, 52, 82, 84
   'Ultima' 15, 84
Socrates 36–37, 62, 68–70
   see also Plato 36–37, 62, 68, 69, 70
Sophocles 49
Stendhal 50, 64
Surrealism 82

Talmud 85
Tarquinia, Italy 87, 94
Tatsumi, Hijikata 40
   see also butô 40–41

Tissot, Samuel Auguste 50–51
Tomb of the Diver 1, 2, 7
   see also Paestum, Italy 1, 2, 7
Turin, Gaspar 99

Veinstein, Alain 4, 5
visual art 46, 49, 52–59, 61–62, 66, 77, 85, 93, 99
voice breaking 39, 88, 90, 99

Wald Lasowski, Patrick 87
Winnicott, Donald 91
Wittgenstein, Ludwig 69

Yonne (river), *see* Sens 1, 12, 46

Zipes, Jack 37

www.ingramcontent.com/pod-product-compliance
Lightning Source LLC
LaVergne TN
LVHW061327060426
835511LV00012B/1906